AF518669

ANIMAL BEHAVIOUR

THIRD ENLARGED EDITION

Dr. M. M. Ranga
P. G. Department of Zoology
Government P. G. College, Ajmer

AGROBIOS

Published by:
AGROBIOS (INDIA)
Behind Nasrani Cinema
Chopasani Road, Jodhpur 342003
Phone: 91-0291-2643993
E. mail: agrobiosindia@gmial.com
Website: agrobiosonline.com

© All Rights Reserved, 2026

All rights reserved. No part of the book or part thereof, including the title of the book, be reprinted in any form or language without the written permission of the author and the publishers. The copyists shall be rosecuted.

ISBN (13): 978-81-77541-50-2

Published by: Updesh Purohit for Agrobios (Inida)
Lasertypeset at: Yashee Computers, Jodhpur
Cover Design by: Reena
Printed at: Agrobios Digitals, Jodhpur

Preface

The behaviour is the action, which changes the relationship between the animal and its environment, as no animal lives alone in the biosphere. Each comes in contact with other animals during its lifetime. Even those animals whose reproductive needs can be satisfied in solitude do not live alone. The behaviour is the action, which changes the relationship between the animal and its environment, as no animal lives alone in the biosphere. Each comes in contact with other animals during its lifetime. Even those animals whose reproductive needs can be satisfied in solitude do not live alone.

The second edition of the book has been prepared for the students taking their first course in Animal Behaviour and will provide an introductory treatment of entire domain of the subject. The book will prove as a learning tool for students in understanding the depth of the subject.

I am thankful to M/s Agrobios (India) for publishing the book in record time.

Author

Contents

CHAPTER 1

The Behaviour

INTRODUCTION

The behaviour is the action, which changes the relationship between the animal and its environment, as no animal lives alone in the biosphere. Each comes in contact with other animals during its lifetime. Even those animals whose reproductive needs can be satisfied in solitude do not live alone. They have contact with other animals for food. Therefore, animals depend on other animals for their survival. The survival also depends on the maintenance of suitable relations with nonliving environment. The sparrow fluffs its feathers when it is cold, the locust orients its body towards the sun when it is hot and the bat hibernates during winter. These are some examples of their adaptive relation with their surrounding environment.

All organisms maintain relation with their surrounding nonliving or living environment. This implies that an organism changes in response to the change in its environment. These changes are directed-action, which is known as behaviour. The survival depends on the maintenance of relations with the environment, hence, this adaptive relation between animal and its environment is also referred to as behaviour. Behaviour is what an individual does. It is the response of an individual to wards the stimuli.

The behaviour may occur as a result of an external stimulus. Receptors are necessary to detect the stimulus. The nerves are needed to coordinate the response and the effectors carry out the action. Behaviour may also occur as a result of an internal stimulus. A hungry animal searches for food. A thirsty animal behaves in a way, which will lead to satisfynig its thirst. Therefore, the behaviour of an animal results from the combination of both external and internal stimuli. The internal stimuli, such as thirst and hunger, give motivation for the action.

A behaviour pattern is typically triggered in response to some variation in the environment or animals may make behavioural response changes in their biotic environment. Specific behaviour pattern may be triggered by the presence of certain other organisms. Changes in an animal's internal environment may also initiate specific behaviour patterns. When a cat has not eaten for some time, the concentration of glucose in its blood decreases. In response to these and other stimuli, the animal becomes restless, moves about and looks for food. When it has eaten its, internal conditions are changed. This is an example of behaviour.

Behavioural responses are adaptive either for the survival of the individual or for the survival of species. Each animal's behaviour patterns must enable it to live long enough to reproduce. It must avoid deleterious environments, predators, parasites and competition from members of its own species. It must obtain an adequate supply of raw materials for its biosynthentic processes and an adequate supply of energy for its metabolic machinery. At the appropriate time it may need to locate and mate with another of its kind.

Behaviour types are determined by the capabilities of the organism's receptor, effector and nervous system. When there is change in the environmental variable. The stimulus depends on how the receptor, effector and nervous systems are interconnected and integrated. Their organization may be direct, so that the stimulus triggers a simple set of muscle action that proceeds automatically once started. As muscular action proceeds, it may be constantly monitored by other stimuli that it has generated in the body, which therefore, steer and guide it. The stimulus may trigger a complex response that is completely programmed genetically in the central nervous system. The response mechanism in other behavioural system may involve both (muscular and nervous system) and genetically programmed components.

Ethologists are concerned with the biological significance of behaviour pattern and how these patterns have evolved. Many of the biologically important behaviour patterns studied by ethologists appeared to be primarily the product of genetic expression and less result of learning. Ethologists recognize the behaviour that an animal shows at any moment is the result of past selective forces. These determine a particular morphologic, biochemical and neuronal structure in an animal. The functional characteristics of this structure are continually altered by experience, hormones and other physiologic changes. The sum of these factors results in the maintenance of animal in its proper condition, and stimuli from the biotic and the abiotic environment can then elicit particular behaviour.

IRRITABILITY

The response to stimuli is called irritability and it is an essential property of living matter. Responses that do not harm the survival are preserved in the course of time, others are lost. The suitability of changes that took place in each cell tissue or organ began to be measured in terms of the survival requirements of the whole individual and not in terms of individual units. The cell that responded unsuitably was eliminated. Therefore, the evolution of responsiveness has been shaped by the requirement of the organism.

No animal can free itself from its heredity, therefore, its behaviour is essentially connected to its evolutionary history. In the multicellular animals there is a need for coordination of information within the organism. For this, certain animal cells specialized in developing their irritability and the rapid conduction of irritability changes. With further specialization, these cells then become nervous system, which is the matrix of behaviour. Thus the behaviour of an individual is the expression of the capabilities of its nervous system.

The behaviour includes all processes by which an individual senses the external world and the internal state of its body, and responds to change which it perceives. The expressions depend on stimulus and response.

Ethology is the comparative study of animal behaviour. In 1930s and 1940s two European scientists, Konrad Lorenz and Niko

Tinbergen, developed the ethological strategy of combining observation of animals in their natural habitat with evolutionary analysis of the observed behaviour pattern.

THE EVOLUTION OF BEHAVIOUR: HISTORICAL PATHWAYS

There is a proximate basis for the ability of some male mantises to copulate even after their heads have been removed. Male neural wiring is such that elimination of the brain frees other regions of the nervous system form inhibitory control, activating the movements that enable males to copulate even as their mating partners are making them headless and thereby brainless. The existence of this proximate neural mechanism and the behaviour it controls raises evolutionary questions about the history behind the "head off, try to copulate anyway" trait: How did the behaviour originate? Has it been subsequently modified over evolutionary time?

Evolutionary questions about the origin of a trait and the changes it has been through differ from evolutionary questions about the possible adaptive value of the attribute, such as, when the trait first appeared, did it confer a reproductive advantage on the males that possessed it? Is the trait currently adaptive for its existing owners? Questions of this sort are intertwined with, but distinct from, questions about historical sequence.

How might we gain information about the *origin* of the male mantis's ability to copulate without a brain? The nervous systems of insects do not fossilize well, needless to say, and therefore tracing the history of this mechanisms and the behaviour it commands cannot be done by examination of the fossil record (although fossils can sometimes tell us a surprising amount about the history of behaviour.) But what we can do is survey the brain mechanisms of living insects, and our survey will reveal that most insects have an inhibition-providing brain that regulates command units elsewhere in the central nervous system, which activate complete behaviour patterns once freed form higher inhibition.

Because this form of neural organization is widespread among insects, we can conclude that is arose very early in the history of the group and has been maintained as new species arose form ancient ones over time. Traits that occur in many related species are usually assumed to have been present in the distant ancestor that gave rise to them all. This explanation for the current distribution of a trait strikes most researchers as more reasonable than the alternative hypothesis, which requires that many mutant genes with similar effects arose by chance in many different species, resulting in the repeated independent evolution of the same kind of trait in a host of species.

If we accept the logic of the argument that traits widely distributed in a lineage of animals are ancient traits, then we can offer a hypothesis for the origin of the headless male mantis's ability to mate, namely, that it is founded on a standard insect system of neuronal organization inherited from a distant ancestor. This system made mating attempts by males a direct consequence of head removal, so that when in the distant past, the first female mantis happened to grab a male and began working her way through his head, the cannibalized male had in place an inherited proximate mechanism that produced a mating attempt.

This historical scenario for the origin of the behaviour it testable, as the following predictions illustrate:

1. Male mantises belonging to species whose females do not engage in sexual cannibalism should also exhibit the mating attempt behaviour upon removal of their heads by an experimenter.
2. Female mantises whose heads are removed should also exhibit certain complete behavioural responses, even if they are not naturally subjected to cannibalism.

These predictions remain to be tested in a formal sense, although I have learned that when females of some species of mantises lose their heads their bodies begin building an egg case of sorts.

The improved design caused by natural selection following the origin of the trait should be detectable if it has occurred. We would predict, for example, that if there was variation among species of mantises in the extent of female sexual cannibalism, males of those species especially subject to cannibalism should be especially adept at copulating minus their heads. This in another prediction that has yet to be tested, but the point is that there are ways to examine historical scenarios.

ETHOLOGY: HISTORICAL BACKGROUND

What causes an animal to behave in a particular way was first realized by Aristotle. The scientific study of Ethology was done by Gilbert White (1720-1793) and Charles Leroy (1723-1789). However, Charles Darwin (1809-1882) is regarded as the father of scientific study of Ethology.

Charles Darwin

At this time the word Ethology was not proposed. Darwin influenced the development of Ethology in the following three ways:

1. He proposed the theory of natural selection, which is an important aspect of animal behaviour;
2. He expressed the views on the instinct, and explained various behaviour patterns;
3. His observations on the behaviour in natural habitat.

In his book The Expression of the Emotions in Man and Animals (1872), he explained the bristling of hairs under the influence of terror, and the uncovering of the teeth under that of furious rage. In his another book The Descent of Man and Selection in Relation to Sex (1871), he mentioned about various emotions and faculties such as love, memory, attention and imitation in man. He explained that these are also developed in lower animals. George Romanes continued the work of Darwin on animal behaviour and published a book titled-Animal Intelligence in 1882. It was the first book, which deals systematically with this subject. He credited animals with mental abilities such as reasoning and with feelings, such as jealously.

Conway Lloyd in his book *Introduction to Comparative Psychology* (1894) mentioned that in no case we interpret an action as the outcome of the exercise of a higher psychical faculty, if it can be interpreted as the outcome of one which stands lower in the psychological scale. This attitude resulted in a vast improvement in the control of experiments and the assessment of evidence. H.S. Jenning (1906) made extensive studies regarding response of Protozoans towards stimuli. The Protozoans were kept in a single drop of water under a microscope and he observed the behavioural activities. He published the book entitled The Behaviour of Lower Organisms. This book is a standard reference and a model of clear exposition.

C.S. Sherrington's book The *Integrative Action of the Neurons System* was published in 1906. In his book he considered the way in which reflexes operate and how the central nervous system integrates them into adaptive behaviour, combining information gathered from different sources. The concept of reflex was the out come of his work.

The European ethologists Konrad Lorenz and Niko Tinbergen gave the emphasis on the studies of behaviour in the natural condition. In 1930 they coined the term Ethology for the study of animal behaviour. Lorenz emphasized the accurate observations and Tinbergen emphasized that the experiments should be carried out under natural conditions. Konrad Lorenz (1930) investigated the phenomena of imprinting in birds as a unique learning process. W.B. Cannon (1929) explained physiological causes of behaviour in mammals and particularly in human beings in his publication Bodily changes in pain, hunger, fear and rage. Ray Carpenter (1931) studied the social behaviour of howler monkeys. In 1927, I.P. Pavlov gave the concept of conditioned reflexes. He explained the neurological explanation of learning F.F. Darling (1937) in his book A herd of red deer explained the technique of studying large mammals under field conditions. B. F. Skinner (1938) explained operant conditioning in The Behaviour of Organisms.

The modern approach to ethology gives emphasis on the explanation of behaviour in terms of the activity of the nervous system.

Ethologists and their Work

Konrad Lorenz

Konrad Lorenz born in Austria (1903). He was a lecturer in Comparative Anatomy and Animal Psychology. He also studied animal behaviour. In 1973 Konrad Lorenz and Niko Tinbergen were awarded the Nobel Prize for medicine. They emphasized the importance of straightforward observations of animal behaviour under natural conditions. Lorenz studies are mainly based on the development of social relationship, specially the phenomena of imprinting.

Korard Lorenz

Niko Tinbergen

Niko Tinbergen born in Hague (The Netherlands) and studied biology at Leiden University. In 1949 he became lecturer in Zoology at Oxford University and founded the Animal Behaviour Group. In 1951 he published The Study of Instinct, which is an authoritative book on the comparative study of animal behaviour patterns and their evolution. In 1963 in his paper On Aims and Methods in Ethology he pointed out many questions and thoughts which are necessary to present a full

Niko Tinbergen

account at any aspect of behaviour. According to him, an ethologist should answer the questions of the causation, development, survival value and evolution of any behaviour patterns under study.

Karlvon Frisch

He was the Professor of Zoology at Rostock University in 1921. He discovered that fishes are capable of colour vision and of discriminating under water sound waves. His great contribution was his work on honey bee communication. He demonstrated that bees are responsive to colour when foraging for food. His observations led to the discovery of bee language system. He shared Nobel Prize with Niko Tinbergen in 1973.

Karl von Frisch

I. P. Pavlov

He was a Russian Physiologist, who gave the term Conditioned Reflex. Pavlov's classical experiments with dogs involved the salivary reflex. He gave neurological explanations of learning. Pavlov and Sherrington worked together, but their aims were different. Sherrington studied the organization of reflexes in the isolated spinal cord of cats, deliberately cut off influences from the higher centres. Pavlov worked with intact animals and considered that a simple reflexis a property of the spinal cord. Therefore, conditioned reflexes are the property of higher centres of brain.

I. P. Pavlov

B. F. Skinner

B.F. Skinner (1938) published the book "*The Behaviour of Organism*" in which he mentioned his original work on operant conditioning. He also designed a box, called Skinner box, by which one can study the different patterns of behaviour.

B. F. Skinner

ANIMAL BEHAVIOUR: AN EVOLUTIONARY APPROACH

Questions about Behaviour

The ultraviolet rays produced by the device attracted hundreds of months on a good night, and many stayed and clinging to the sheet until morning. This attractive moth, a member of the genus *Automeris*, held its forewings so that they covered its abdomen and hindwings. In the chilly dawn, the sluggish moth will not struggle if one pick up them carefully, but if one jostled it suddenly, or poked it sharply on its thorax, the moth abruptly lifts its forewings and held them up to expose its previously concealed hindwings. The hindwings are marvelously decorated, with large circular patches of blue, black, and white scales set on a deep yellow background. The patches looked like tow eyes, which seemed to stare back to the person who picked up them.

Anyone seeing *Automeris* abruptly expose its hindwing eyes for the first time, he will wonder *what is going on*. The questions about Automeris wing-flipping grew into a substantial list. There are two important questions about their action: (1) Proximate causes of the behaviour, (2) Ultimate causes of the behaviour.

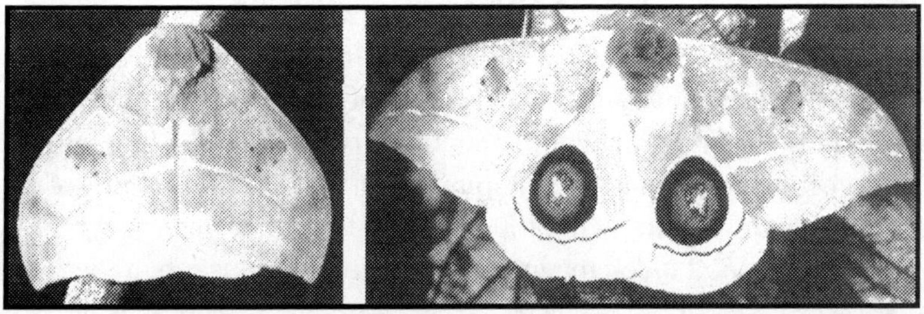

FIG. 1.1: Automeris moth from Costa Rica. **Left:** Moth in the resting position with the forewings held over the hindwings. **Right:** After being jabbed in the thorax.

The basic questions about their behaviour are:

1. How an individual manages to carry out an activity?
2. What is the mechanism(s) within an animal operate, enabling the creature to behave in a certain way?
3. Why the animal has evolved the proximate mechanisms that cause it to perform an activity.

The two kinds of questions are complementary, not antagonistic, because they deal with fundamentally different level of analysis.

There are series of questions about the wing-flipping reaction of an *Automeris* moth to a sharp poke;

1. What is the causal relationship between the animal's genes and its behaviour ?
2. Is the trait to some extent inherited form the moth's parents?
3. How has the development of the moth from a single cell to a multimillion-celled adult affected it behaviour?
4. What stimuli trigger the response and how are these stimuli detected?
5. How are the animal's nervous and muscular systems integrated to enable it to react to a poke in the side?

Diversity

What these five questions have in common, despite their diversity, is an interest in the operation of mechanisms within the moth that cause it to pull its forewings forward, revealing its amazing hindwings. The diversity of proximate questions is great enough, however, that we can subdivide them into tow complementary groups, one dealing with the effects of heredity and development on the construction of the mechanisms underlying wing-flipping, and the other dealing with how the fully developed mechanisms actually work to cause the reaction.

Influence of Heredity on Development

With respect to the influence of heredity on development, one can ask how the special touch receptors, brain cells, and muscle controllers used in the wing-flipping reaction arise in an individual. The adult moth began life as a fertilized egg, a single cell that contained genetic instructions donated by its father and mother. There instructions affected the development of the moth, channeling the proliferation and specialization of cells along certain pathways that produced a nervous system with special features in the adult insect. This is a complex process and still poorly understood for any organism.

Though we know about the development of the response, but still we unable explore how the fully developed neural mechanisms within the adult moth detect certain kinds of stimulation and how messages are then relayed to activate a muscular response. Yet neurophysiological foundation of the behaviour of the *Automeris* moth has not been examined.

The genetic-developmental and sensory-motor causes of the wing-flipping behaviour of *Automeris* moths has been examined but there are several questions about their behaviour:

1. What is the purpose, the function, of the behaviour?
2. How does the behaviour assist the individual in overcoming obstacles to survival and reproduction?
3. How has the behaviour evolved and how has it changed over evolutionary time?
4. What was the original step in the historical process that led to the existence of the current behaviour?

5. Why an animal does something.
6. Why does the moth suddenly lift its forewings and expose its eye spots when it is molested?

The British scientist David Blest suggested that the action became common because it protects the moth form predators, startling and frightening away moth eating birds that mistake the eye spots for the eyes of their enemy, predatory owls.

Wing-flipping behaviour can save the lives of moths in the past, then the evolutionary process is partly responsible for the behaviour of individuals today also. The genes that exist in contemporary moths are a tiny subset of all the genes that have ever existed. Those that have managed to persist to the present are genes that have in some way contributed to their own survival. If a gene influenced the appearance or behaviour of a moth in ways that helped the moth frighten away predatory birds, that gene would presumably have a better chance of being passed on to descendants of that moth. *Automeris* moths have inherited genetic mechanisms that promote the development of wing-flipping behaviour. *The developmental plan, and therefore the behavioural abilities, of each member of the species alive today has been defined by differences in gene survival that occurred during the history of the species.*

The example of *Automeris* moth's behaviour gives us an insight into the ultimate or evolutionary causes of behaviour, however, there is another component to the evolutionary analysis of behaviour, and that has to do with how the trait came into being and then was (perhaps) modified over time until it reached its current state.

In the study of behaviour there are two fundamental levels of analysis, *proximate* and *ultimate.* One should now be able to discriminate between mechanistic and evolutionary explanations. If someone were to make the claim that *Automeris* moths expose their hindwings when pecked because their nervous system controls the wing-flipping response, this is a proximate explanation-as are all hypotheses based on genetic, developmental, neural, or hormonal mechanisms found within the body of an individual.

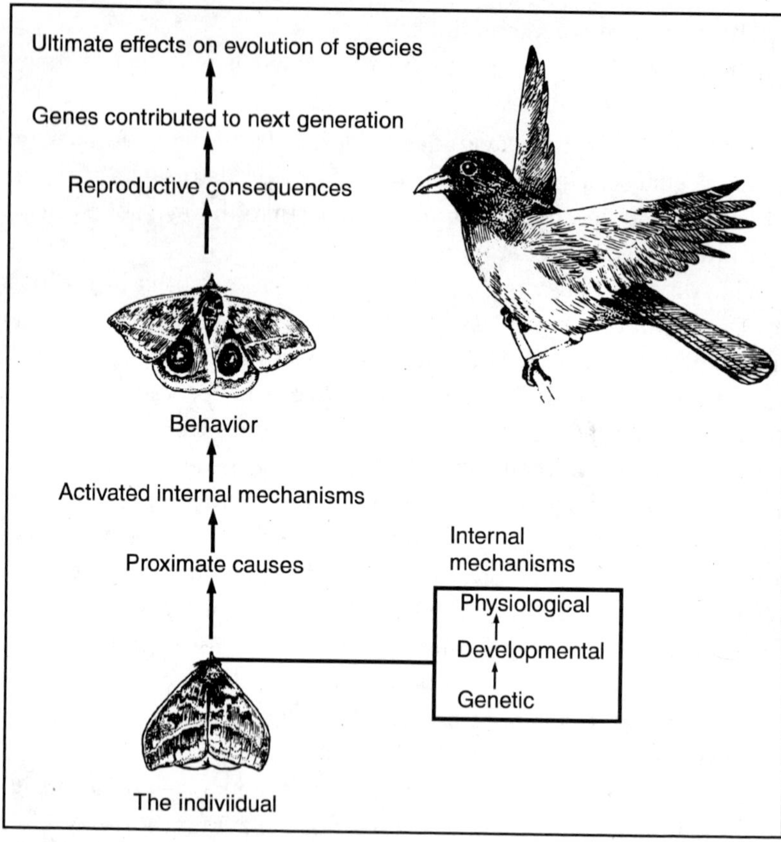

FIG. 1.2: Proximate and ultimate causes of the behaviour as illustrated by *Automeris* moth wing-flipping. At the proximate level, various mechanisms internal to an individual moth enable it to execute the behaviour. At ultimate level, the moth's response to potential predators affects its reproductive success as measured by the number of copies of its genes that are passed on to the next generation.

Table 1.1: Levels of analysis in the study of animal behaviour

PROXIMATE CAUSES
1. Genetic-developmental mechanisms a) Effects of heredity on behaviour b) Genetic-environmental interactions during development that produce sensory-motor mechanisms

2. Sensory-motor mechanisms
    a) Detection of environmental stimuli: Operation of nervous systems
    b) Adjustment of internal responsiveness: Operation of hormonal system
    c) Carrying our responses: Operation of skeletal-muscular system

ULTIMATE CAUSES

1. Historical pathways leading to a behaviour
    a) Origin of the behaviour and its alteration over time
2. Past effects of natural selection in shaping a current behaviour
    a) Past and current utility of the behaviour in reproductive terms

The above example of wing-flipping by *Automeris* moths shows that behaviour involves in various diverse phenomena:

1. The action of genes,
2. the structure of an animal's brain,
3. the relation of an individual to is predator, and
4. evolutionary events occurring over millions of years.

Evolutionary Theory and Behaviour

The Darwinian theory of evolution can explain about behaviour which has had an enormous impact on the way researchers have explored ultimate questions about living things. Darwinian Theory came to us in 1859, courtesy of Charles Darwin, who wrote On *the Origin of Species*, with its explanation of how natural selection causes evolution to occur. The theory of evolution by natural selection was immediately recognized by many as an extraordinarily important idea because of its simplicity, its predictive power, and its vast scope of application to biological matters. Darwin's idea rests on observed features of many species:

1. **Variation:** Members of a species may differ in their characteristic.
2. **Heredity:** Parents can sometimes pass on their distinctive characteristics to their offspring.
3. **Differential reproduction:** Because of their special inherited characteristics, some individuals leave more offspring than others. When certain individuals reproduce more than others, and when their offspring have inherited the trait that enabled their parents to

reproduce so successfully, then they too will spread the reproduction-enhancing trait.

If some individuals leave fewer offspring than others because of their inherited characteristics, their offspring will inherit their parents' disadvantage and leave few progeny themselves. As a consequence, traits that compromise reproduction will become progressively rare over evolutionary time.

Darwin called this process **natural selection.** He saw the elimination of unfavorable traits and the spread of beneficial ones as the natural consequence of differences among individuals in *reproductive success*, or *direct fitness.* Direct fitness is measured by the number of reproduction offspring left by an individual. This logic leads to the expectation that animals will evolve traits that promote individual reproductive success. Darwin developed the theory of natural selection before critical discoveries about the nature of heredity.

Genes and Behaviour

Genes are now known to be nucleic acids that faithfully code the information needed for the synthesis of proteins, the building blocks of all living things. One can apply Darwinian logic at the genetic level in much the same way that Darwin applied it to individuals. This helps to understand the modern evolutionary approach to animal behaviour.

Genetic variation: Genes can occur in tow or more alternative forms, or alleles, within a species. Different alleles lead to the production of slightly different forms of the same protein.

Heredity: Alleles can be transmitted form parent to offspring.

Differential reproduction: Certain alleles produce effects that usually cause their bearers to replicate the alleles more often than other individuals with different alleles of the gene in question.

If these three conditions apply, then reproductively *successful* alleles will be more common in any population. Their competitors could be completely replaced if the relationship between genetic differences and reproductive success remains constant long enough.

The selection of individuals will favor alleles that help build bodies and will promote the survival and propagation of those alleles.

This explains the view, that individuals have *survival machines* which built by natural selection to promote the survival of the alleles within animals/plants. Individuals do not actually reproduce themselves, instead they reproduce (some of) their genetic material, which they transmit to their offspring.

Darwinian Logic and the Study of Behaviour

Darwinian logic and the study of behaviour was the blockbuster of an idea, and this was apparent to many people. Darwinian Theory offers a worldview of animal behaviour. The academic field of animal behaviour can be said to have originated in 1937 when the first journal of animal behaviour appeared (in Germany). But it was not until the 1950s that the discipline was widely accepted as a serious scientific endeavor.

Karl von Frisch, Niko Tinbergen, and Konrad Lorenz, played a primary role in the development of the modern approach to animal behaviour. These were the founders of ethology and received the Nobel Prize in Physiology or Medicine in 1973 for their pioneering studies.

Importance of their work was, the early ethologists often assumed that natural selection would produce animals that sacrificed personal reproductive success for the general benefit of their species. This way of thinking is based on group selection theory.

There are certain objections with the proposed theory, let us examine it in more detail.

The Problem with Group Selection

V.C. Wynne-Edwards in 1967 wrote a book entitled: *Animal Dispersion in Relation to Social Behaviour* in which he proposed that almost all aspects of animal behaviour helped species keep their populations down to avoid destroying the food base on which their survival depended. Wynne-Edwards's key argument was that only those species that possessed population-regulating mechanisms had survived to the present; others that lacked these mechanisms had surely become extinct through overexploitation of the critical resources on which the species depended. He forced biologists to examine the theoretical basis for the evolution of social behaviour.

G.C. Williams's in his publication - *Adaptation and Natural Selection* (1966) recognized the critical flaw in Wynne-Edwards's argument. Wynne-Edwards proposed that selection took place primarily on the basis of differences among groups, with populations competing unconsciously to survive; those groups whose members sacrificed potential reproductive output for the benefit of their population would be most likely to survive. Williams explained that the theory of group selection was entirely different form the Darwinian Theory of natural selection. Darwinian natural selection takes place as a result of differences among individuals, and selection at this level is far more likely to cause evolutionary change than selection at the level of the group.

The general point that Williams made in that selection acting on differences among variant individuals will usually have a stronger effect than selection acting on differences among groups in shaping the genetic makeup of subsequent generations. As a result, most persons interested in the adaptive function of a trait invoke selection operating at the level of alleles or individuals, not groups, when developing their hypotheses.

Almost all behavioural biologists have accepted the arguments of Williams. For the moment, the Darwinian theory of natural selection is the most widely used foundation for the development of working hypotheses about the ultimate, reproductive function of biological characteristics. There is plenty of room of disagreement, exploration, and invention within its framework.

The Science of Testing Hypotheses

Theory shapes our hypotheses. Persons who use Darwinian (individual selection) theory develop different kinds of ultimate hypotheses than those who rely on the theory of evolution by group selection. For example, the theory that the development of an organism occurs because of an interplay between the individual's genetic inheritance and its environment has had great influence in the debate over the causes of instinctive and learned behaviour.

But once a scientist has dreamed up a possible explanation, proximate or ultimate, then what? For example, someone might wish to explain how the nervous system of an *Automeris* moth enables it to perform the wing-flipping behaviour. Such a person might propose that there is a special nerve cell responsible for eliciting the muscle contractions that produce the response. Similar cells exist in other creatures. If this hypothesis is true, then one can able to find the *one critical nerve cell* that, when stimulated, causes the wing-flipping behaviour to occur in a living but restrained moth (the prediction).

Someone interested in the reproductive value of wing-flipping follows fundamentally the same steps. He might hypothesize that exposing the eye spots deters predators, increasing the survival and reproductive chances for wing-flipping individuals, which is why the behaviour had been naturally selected in this species. If true, then it logically follows that *Automeris* moths with their eye spots experimentally covered with yellow paint should be eaten by predators at a higher rate than those with intact eye spots. Finding that this prediction was not true would make us skeptical of the predator-deterrence hypothesis for eye spots.

Alternative Hypotheses

Hanuman langurs live in bands. They consist of one large, reproductively active male and a group of smaller adult females and their offspring. From time to time, the resident male is pushed out of the group by a newcomer, usually after a series of violent clashes. After such a takeover, infant death rates often rise sharply. It shows that the new male is responsible for the death of the infants, even though females tried to protect their babies. Hrdy devised hypotheses about the effects of a takeover on male testosterone levels and aggressive behaviour, or she might have considered the effects of early social experiences on males that later became infanticidal. But Hrdy was interested in the ultimate significance of male infanticide. She proposed that killer males increased their reproductive success by eliminating nursing offspring sired by a rival male.

Lactating females do not ovulate and so are not available to produce offspring with a new male. But females that lose their dependent young cease lactating and resume sexual cycling, producing an egg that can be fertilized by the new male. According to

Hrdy, an infanticidal male might increase the number of descendants he produced by making females sexually receptive to him sooner than otherwise.

The Sexual Competition Hypothesis

According to this hypothesis infanticidal males get to reproduce sooner and more often by disposing of infants whose presence would prevent mother *langurs* from coming into heat for a long time. One of many predictions taken from this hypothesis is that new resident males should stop killing infants by the time the first of their own offspring are born to the resident females. If males did destroy their own progeny, their actions would reduce, not increase, their reproductive success.

Testing Hypotheses on Infanticide

The prediction of "selective" infanticide is supported by observations of *langur* bands. This does constitute a test of the sexual competitions hypothesis if males routinely killed their own progeny. But there may be alternatives to the sexual competitions argument, each one of which deserves to be tested in its own right. A second alternative is that infanticide is not adaptive at all but instead is a social pathology induced by abnormal conditions for which *langurs* have no evolved response. There is no guarantee that every characteristic of a species actually raises the reproductive success of individuals.

The Social Pathology Hypothesis

This hypothesis predicts that male infanticide will be absent in low-density population of the *langurs* or those that do not receive food supplements. Dispute continues on this point, but infanticide by male *langurs* occurs in at least two locations where they are not fed by humans. If these *langurs* are not abnormally crowded, their practice of infanticide is damaging to the social pathology hypothesis.

The hypothesis also predicts that infanticide in animals other than *langurs* should also be restricted to cases in which human intervention and interference has dramatically altered the social environment of a species.

Sexual Competition

Sexual competition alternative gives an additional support from some experimental studies of birds, including one involving jacanas. In these water birds, the typical sex roles are reversed, with females defending *harems* of males that care for their offspring.

Aggression Hypothesis

This was proposed by Davis and Downes. According to them infanticide in *langurs* is a nonadaptive incidental effect of an adaptive trait, namely, the ability of potential usurper males to become highly aggressive during and shortly after a takeover. The hypothesis suggests that the adaptive capacity for extreme aggression helps previously subordinate outsider males to defeat the dominant male(s) in the band and to overcome resistance to their presence form others as well. But in the course of being aggressive during the takeover and during the unsettled weeks or months that follow, newcomer males may sometimes attack young band members and even kill them as an incidental effect to their heightened aggressiveness.

CHAPTER 2

Ethological Concepts

INTRODUCTION

To understand behaviour one must learn about following concepts of ethology. These are: (1) Stimulus - responses concept, (2) Releaser or sign stimuli-Mimetic releaser, Supernormal releaser Importance of releaser, (3) Reflexes, (4) Innate releasing mechanism, (5) Fixed action pattern, (6) Relation among releaser I R M and fixed action pattern, (7) Stimulus filtering.

These concepts are the result of extensive study of several animal species. Ethologists have observed and analyzed the behaviour of hundreds of different animal species among these are stickleback fish, the greylag goose, a digger wasp and herring gull. Ethologists developed the following ethological concepts

STIMULUS-RESPONSE CONCEPT

This is a very simple idea; that the behaviour, which is called a response, always has some kind of cause, which precedes it. It may be written as S-R. The cause or stimulus may be internal or external. The following are some considerations of the S-R theory.

Stimulus is Always a Change

In Protozoa it is easy to study. H.S. Jenning in 1900s, studied the behaviour of Protozoa and published in his book The Behaviour of Lower organisms. He found that any sort of environmental changes will produce a response. *Englena*, if placed in strong sunlight, swims away but if the light is weak, it swims towards the source. If the light is cut off the Euglena stops swimming in a circle and then starts out in the general direction of any light, which may be left. The same phenomena can be seen in higher animals. The principle that a stimulus is a change has many practical applications in animal behaviour.

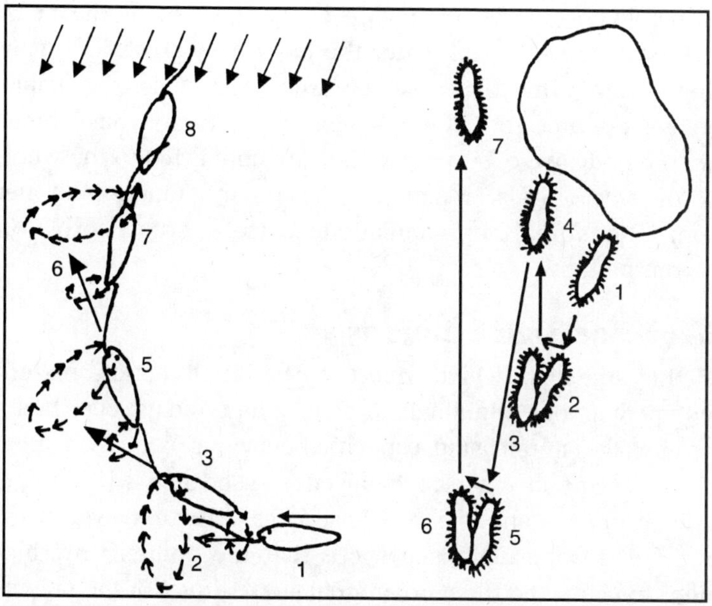

FIG. 2.1: Stimulus response concept. **Left:** *Euglina* responses to a change in direction to weak light. **Right:** Avoiding response in *Paramecium.*

The Response is an Attempt to Adapt to a Change

In the presence of light, *Euglelna* is able to manufacture its own food and most of its behaviour is related to this fact. In fresh water its continual reaction to changing light conditions keep it moving towards moderate sunlight which permits photosynthesis but is still not strong enough to kill the animal. Thus its behaviour is adaptive to changing light condition. All adaptations are not successful. When we put a Paramecium in a weak salt solution, it responds by moving rapidly in all directions. Such response is an attempt to adaptation.

The Nature of Adaptation

Adaptation is a basic biological principle, which may be stated as animals tends to react in ways which are favourable to their existence.

The Study of Stimulation

The phenomena of stimulation leads to a study of the causes of behaviour External stimuli enter the body through sense organs and we immediately find that animals differ in their sensory capacities. When we attempt to follow the pathways of nervous stimulation within the body, we observe that they are connected to the whole network of physiological reactions. This is the function of nervous system. Therefore, the stimulation plays a primary role in the behaviour patterns.

Releaser or Sign Stimulus

It is the stimulus, which releases the fixed action patterns or stereotyped actions in animals. It acts as an effective cue (hint about how to behave) in releasing a specific behaviour patterns. Animals are sensitive to certain environmental cues associated with biologically significant objects and events. These cues, when received trigger an appropriate response. It is to note that the context in which the stimulus appears and the motivational state (drive) of the receiver are important in determining what effect it will have. The term releaser was given by Konrad Loren in 1935. He used this term for those charateristics expressed by an individual of a given animal speices which activate releasing mechanisms in co-species and elicit certain instinctive behaviour patterns.

F. Goethe, a German ornithologist, discovered that newly hathched herring gull chicks would peck at the red dot at the tip of the beak of a dead herring gull's head. If the red dot is covered with yellow paint, then the babybirds will give lesser pecks. After these observation Niko Tinbergen studied the stimuli that elicit the begging response of the herring gull chicks. He described how the chick of herring gull is fed by a parent. When the parent arrives at the nest after foraging, it will call the chicks. The chicks approach to the parent and pecks at the red spot at the tip of parent's beak. This stimulates the parent to regurgitate food, which it then picks up from the ground and holds at the tip of its bill. The responsiveness of chicks was measured in terms of then umber of pecks.

The motivational state of the perceiver plays an important role in response. For example the reaction of mature female herring gulls to a herring gull egg. The stimuli that are associated with an egg will release feeding behaviour, if the female is not breeding and not incubating eggs. The same egg will release incubation behaviour, if it is in her nest with other egg. The same egg may release retrieval behaviour in which it will take back egg into her nest, if it lies just outside its own nest.

Mimetic Releaser

There are variety of animals which have mechanism that exploit the relationship between a cue (hint about how to behave) and a response by another species. An excellent example of natural mimetic releaser is seen in parrot fish. The cleaner fish removes the parasite and fungi from the body of parrot fish. The true cleaner fish approaches the parrot fish with an undulating dance. This behaviour induces the parrot fish to adopt the tilted cleaning position. The false cleaner fish also resembles the true cleaner fish, it mimics its behaviour. The mimic attacks the parrot fish and departs with a piece of its flesh. The hawkmoth caterpiller (Leucorampha) mimics the snake (both rops schlagelli). When the caterpiller is disturbed it raises its head and inflates it. The head bears false eyes and resembles as that of a snake.

Supernormal Releaser

It is possible to exaggerate the special cues that release a response by a animal and thus to exaggerate that response. For example the infant gulls pecks more often at the unrealistic supernormal bill than at the three dimensional model of the gull head. Similarly an oystercatcher incubate giant egg in preference to its own egg.

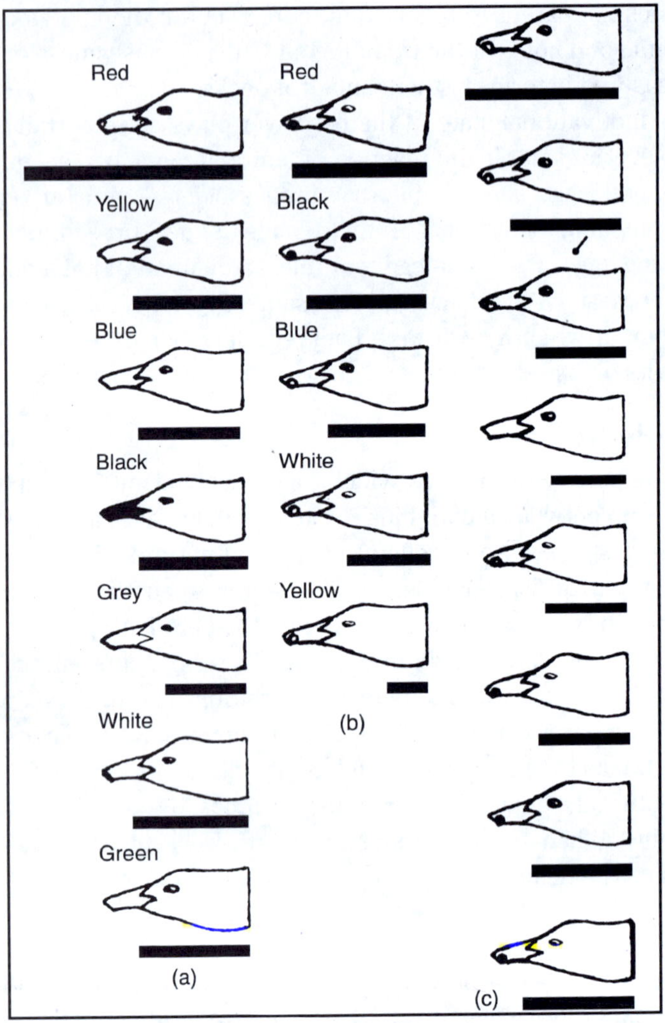

FIG. 2.2: Models used to study food begging behaviour of herring gull chicks. The length of the bar indicates number of peck delivered to the model. **(a)** Model having different bill colour. **(b)** Models differing in colour of the spot on a yellow bill. **(c)** Models with grey bills and spots differing contrast (Tinbergen and Perdeck),

FIG. 2.3: Egg retrival in herring gull.

Importance of Releaser

The releaser or sign stimuli are necessary for fixed action patterns. Supernormal releasers are very interesting. Their existence suggests that natural selection has no opportunity in some cases to favor individuals with limits on what is an acceptable releaser.

REFLEXES

Reflexes are very rapid and unlearned response to a stimulus. They are ordinarily not subject to voluntary control. They are the out come of inherited neural mechanisms. Reflexes, like flexion of a leg in response to painful stimuli or the constriction of a pupil to intense light are simple examples. They may involve all or most of the body, but, typically there are responses of parts of the body. Reflexes are adaptive. It is not possible to draw a clear line between reflexes and complex behaviour. Complex behaviour includes many reflexes. For example, swallowing reflex is the climax of complex food seeking behaviour Similarly reflexes controlling balance and walking are involved in all complex behaviour, therefore, the patterns of behaviour are complex arrays of reflexes. There are two types of reflexes:

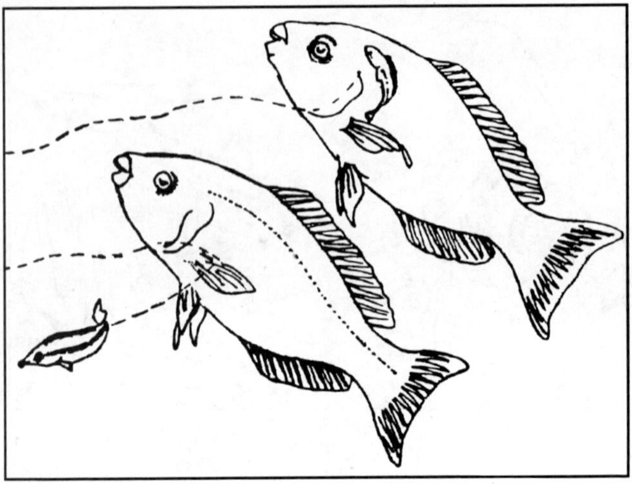

FIG. 2.4: Mimetic releaser in parrot fish.

Tonic Reflexes

They are slow, long lasting adjustments that maintain muscular posture and equilibrium.

Phasic Reflexes

They are rapid and short-lived adjustments. Example flexion response.

Innate Releasing Mechanisms

Lorenz emphasized that animals sometimes respond to specific stimuli, such stimuli are sign stimuli; and are the parts of a stimulus configuration. For example, a male three spined stickleback has a red belly during breeding conditions. This is a sign stimulus elicits aggression in other territorial males. The models of male stickleback with red belly provide a sign stimulus to elicit attack. The selective responses to stimuli indicate that there must be some built-mechanism by, which such sign stimuli were recognized. This mechanism is called innate releasing mechanism. (IRM).

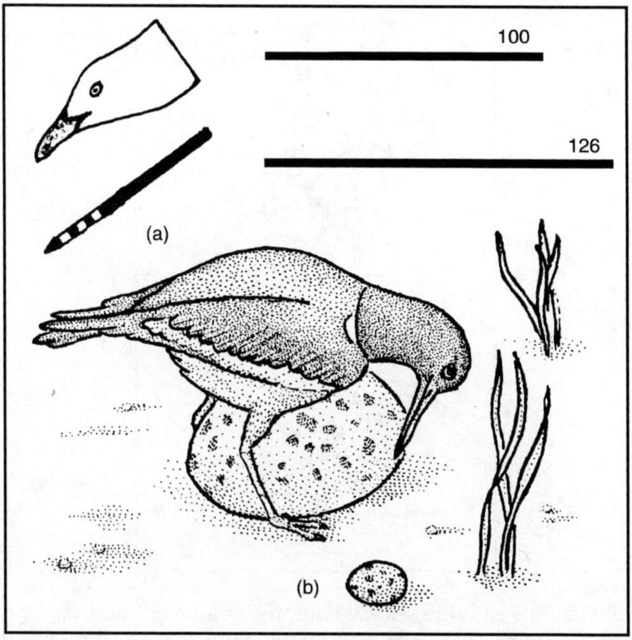

FIG. 2.5: Super normal releaser. **(a)** Infant gulls pecks more often at supernormal bill, that at three dimensional model at gull head. **(b)** An oystercatcher attempt to incubate a giant egg.

Fixed Action Pattern

It is the complex organization of hereditary responses and triggered by sign stimuli. The central nervous systems of many organisms are capable of filtering out environmental stimuli. If an animal were to process all the sensory information it could receive, its central nervous system would be swamped. Certain segments of the retina of the frog's eye are specialized to react to small, dark, circular moving objects near them than to larger, more diffuse or distant objects. Such sign stimuli often serve as triggers for fixed action patterns of behaviour. When quick action is essential, as in escaping from a predator, a danger sign is more useful. Alarm signs may be sight or sounds. Small birds show an immediate flight reaction to animal with large eyes.

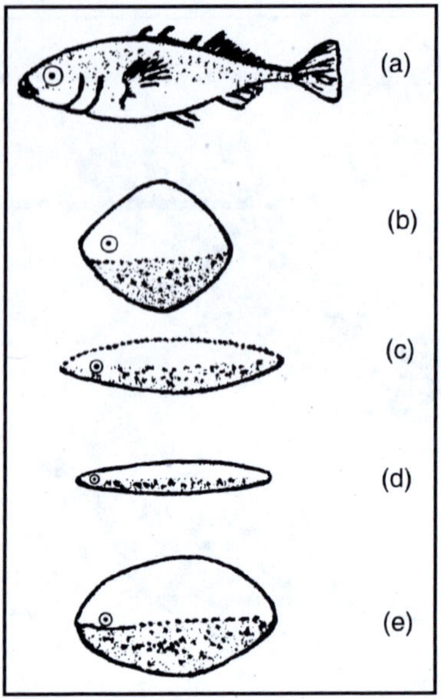

FIG. 2.6: Models of male stickle-back that initiates attack by territorial males. **(a)** Dead male lacking innuptial colours, **(b)**, **(c)** and **(d)**: Their red underside provides signs stimulus to elicit attack.

Some birds show flight reaction with large eyes. Small birds flee any staring eye, and many moths, the prey of birds, have evolved eye-shaped spots on their hind wings. These eyes are concealed by the forewings when the moth is at rest but spring into view when the moth is disturbed and extends its forewings.

Sounds are major determinants of behaviour among the vertebrates. Certain species of frogs have distinctive mating calls; the female of each species will respond only to those mating calls from the males of its species and will ignore those of others. Similarly, the songs of birds provide determinants for many behaviour sound acts as means of communication. The sensory capacties of animals throughout the Animal Kingdom are different.

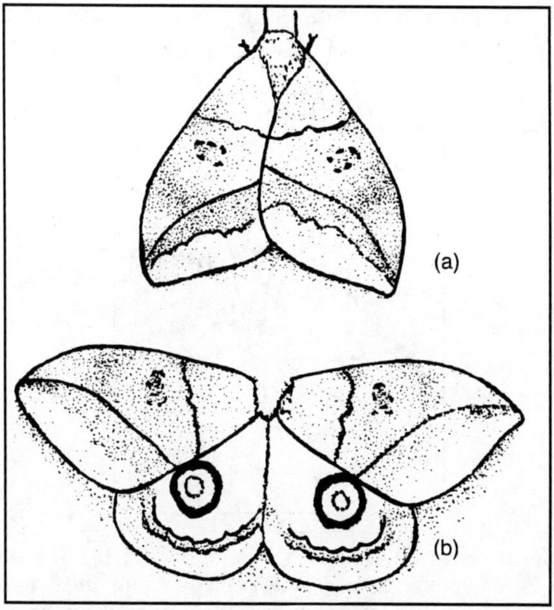

FIG. 2.7: *Automeris corosus* (moth) **(a)**: at rest, **(b)** Displayed the vivid eye spot on its hind wings in response to touch.

The bat emits sound with frequencies far beyond the range of the human ear. These sounds bounce off any insect flying in the vicinity and by echoloction the bat is able to home in on the insect and catch it. Porpoises utilize sonar for underwater navigation by echolocation. And spiders can interpret the vibrations produced on their webs by ensnared insects. A rattlesnake can sense heat enough to strike.

Relationship among Releaser

IRM and Fixed Action Pattern

The relationship among these concepts can be explained by the responses between a newborn gull and its mother. The hungry newborn gull is sensitive to visual stimuli received by it. The presence of newborn gull, also acts as visual stimuli, to the adult gull. The messages generated by releaser stimuli move via optic nerve to a system within the brain, that responds to specific messages. The IMR orders certain muscle to perform contractions and relaxation. The result of these motor commands is the pecks directed at the red spot on the adult gull's beak. It is the fixed action pattern.

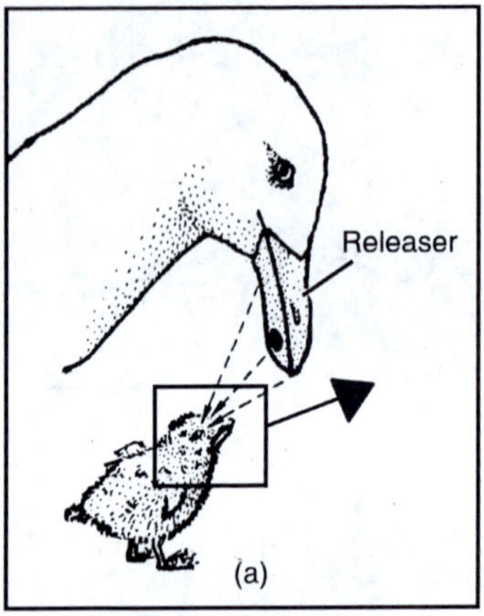

FIG. 2.8: Relation among releaser, IRM and FAP. (a) The hungry new born gull is sensitive to key cues present in the visual stimuli bornbarding it. (b) The visual messages initiated by visual stimuli reaches the brain. The IRM orders specific muscles to connect and relax, (c) The result of the motor commands is the FAP. Series at competent pecks directs at the red spot on adult gull's beak.

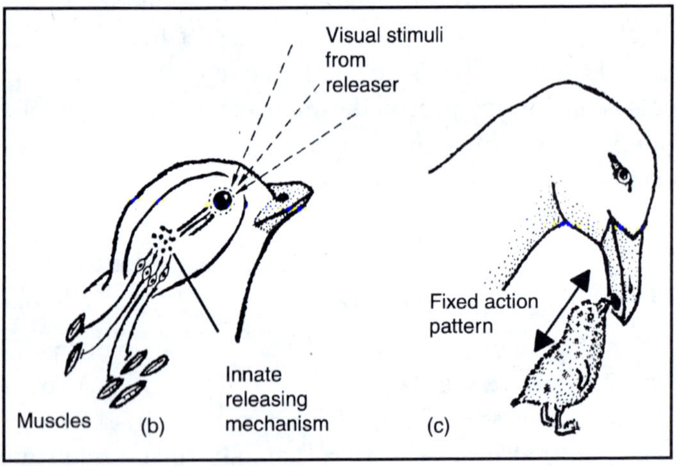

Stimulus Filtering

The basic property of perceptual system is stimulus filtering. The receptors, sensory interneurons and decoders screen out some of the stimulation. Therefore, the discriminating behaviour is the function of discriminating nerve cells. The stimulus filtering by component of nervous system is as follows:

Selective Sensory Reciptors

1. Response to limited class of stimuli.
2. Adaptation to continuing stimuli.

Sensory Interneurons

1. Failure to react to low level and constant stimulation.
2. Consolidation of inputs into a single message

Selective Decoder Neurons

1. Failure to respond to one or two sensory signals.
2. Selective analysis of innate releasing mechanism.

The stimulus filtering provides the mechanism for rejecting, ignoring and selecting some potential information.

MOTIVATION OR DRIVE

It is the state within a person or an animal that drives behaviour towards some specific some goal. It has there following aspects:

- A driving state within the animal.
- The behaviour aroused and directed by this state.
- The goal towards which the behaviour is directed.

The short-term changes in responsiveness are motivation. For example, an animal that is deprived of food is thought to change its behaviour because of a change in motivation. It's searching behaviour and attention to food stimuli are said to result from a hunger drive similarly each category of behaviour, each biological goal, can be said to be governed by a drive or tendency, a mating drive, a nest-building tendency, an incubation drive. A hungry dog will respond differently from one that has just been fed, when both are presented with a dish of food. Physiologic research has revealed further types of interaction between external stimuli and motivation. Each stimulus may evoke a response within the brain by its specific sensory pathways. In addition, it may elicit many less specific responses. In the vertebrate, incoming sensory pathways have side branches, or collaterals, extending to a diffuse series of fibre tracts, the reticular formation, (RS) which is connected to the brain's higher centers. Impulses from the reticular formation arouse the brain's higher centers into action. Thus, any stimulus may not only evoke a specific response pertaining to itself but also change the animal's state of arousal and responsiveness to other stimuli. A given stimulus applied to the same animal at different times does not always evoke the same response. The relationship between stimulus and response may be altered by maturation, and learning. Some examples of motivated behaviour are feeding, drinking, courting, nest-building, territorial defence and care of the young. Perhaps the most striking feature of motivational behaviour is that it is highly specific to a particular state and to a particular stimuli. In general, a hungry animal will not court and an animal in a highly receptive sexual state will not feed.

The specific motivation causes the person or an animal to orient its behaviour towards some specific goal. The pattern begins with a searching phase, usually called appetitive behaviour. It simply means that there is a phase of undirected behaviour, which, in the normal course of events will lead to a particular source of further stimulation. A hungry fox simply gets up and eats; ordinarily it must hunt, and the behaviour patterns used in hunting may be many and diverse. It is impossible to identify the nature of appetitive behaviour until the actual goal can be observed. An animal searching for food, water or a mate may behave quite similarly. But with each, the stimuli required to bring the search to an end are highly specific. When a fox hunting for food, encounters prey, it switches to an orient type of behaviour; when the food is seized, eating ensues. At this time the various searching patterns give way to a series of responses directed to the goal.

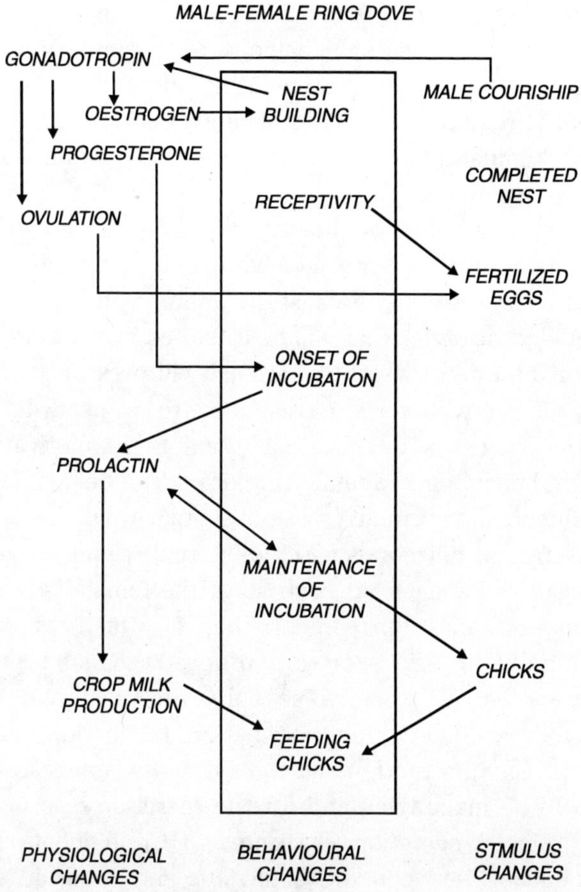

FIG. 2.9: Motivation and reproductive behaviour of ring doves.

These responses, called consummatory acts, are stereotyped, and are called fixed action patterns. Consummatory acts are normally followed by a period of quiescence or rest during which the animal is no longer responsive to any stimuli. Thus a well-fed animal shows no further appetitive behaviour even though the appropriate stimuli may be present. Quiescence relates only to one type of behaviour; the animal may be actively pursuing some other sort of goal. Responsiveness gradually increases again after some time.

The hypothalamus which is the ventral division of diencrphalon, influences feeding and drinking behaviour, sexual behaviour, sleep, and maternal behaviour. It is considered to be the control center for motivated behaviour. Feeding behaviour, for example is controlled by feeding and satiety centers. Stimulating the satiety center in the ventral medial region of the hypothalamus decreases the amount of food eaten. Stimulating the feeding centers in the lateral hypothlamus causes the animal to eat.

Motivation can only be measured indirectly. For example to determine the motivation towards feeding behaviour one can measure the amount of food eaten, how fast the animal will run towards food, the level of electric shock that will be tolerated by the animal to get to the food, or the rate at which the animal will press a bar to obtain a food reward. Motivation is a response to a need to restore a homeostatic balance. The classical example of motivation is the reproductive behaviour of female ring dove. The behaviour of female dove is influenced by a number of physiological factors, including at least four different hormones and by external stimuli from her mate, the nest, eggs and squabs. At each stage the female is stimulated to secrete the hormones that prepare her for the next stage. Male courtship stimulates the secretion of oestrogen and progesteron, which causes her to become sexually receptive and which are necessary for nest building and incubation. Incubation in both sexes stimulates prolactin secretion and this hormone is necessary both for incubation to be maintained and for the secretion of crop milk. The fact that prolactin secretion is stimulated by in-cubation indicates positive feedback between the behaviour and a casual factor that underlies it. This mechanism ensures not only that incubation is maintained but also that when it ends and the eggs hatch, the birds are secreting crop milk and are thus ready to feed the young immediately.

It is clear that animals show enormous diversity in the motivational mechanisms that they possess and is only through the synthesis and integration of a variety of approaches that we are ever likely to understand those mechanisms.

CHAPTER 3

Patterns of Behaviour

INTRODUCTION

The patterns of behaviour occur spontaneously because of external and internal stimuli. These stimuli serve to release a certainly patterned complex neural programme. The marine lugworm, *Arenicola*, lives in an L-shaped burrow in the mud and keeps the burrow open by rhythmic movements. These arise not in response to environmental stimuli but are initiated by a series of spontaneously active clocks in the various ganglia of the worm. The behaviour programs are built into the central nervous systems and need only be triggered or released by specific stimuli. Wind blowing on special receptors on the head of the locust initiates impulses from the brain to the thoracic ganglion; these in turn send impulses to the motor nerves innervating the wing muscles, and result in flight. The pattern of impulse from the thoracic ganglion determines the sequence to flight muscles. Even when all the muscles have been removed, therefore, there is no feedback from proprioceptors in the wings. Normal neural patterns are delivered by the thoracic ganglion.

The graylag goose nest on the ground, retrieve any egg that happens to roll out of the nest by placing their bill on the far side of the egg and rolling the egg back into the nest with side-to-side movements of the bill, that prevent the egg from slipping away. When the egg is replaced with a cylinder that does not wobble, the side-to-side compensatory movement ceases. Alternatively, if the egg or the cylinder is removed once the retrieving movement has started, the bill is still drawn back to the breast. This is a behaviour pattern that, once elicited by the stimulus continues independently. Following are the patterns of behaviour:

PATTERNS OF BEHAVIOUR

Feeding Behaviour

Generally all animals show characteristic behaviour patterns in finding and consuming food. Even the oyster and other sessile filter feeders that do not hunt their food, utilize sense organs. Filtering mechanisms and coordinated muscle contractions are performed to obtain particles of food of the correct size.

FIG. 3.1: Feeding behaviour in black bird.

Most animals search actively for specific kinds of food when their sense organs get stimulus. Young birds initially peck at any small round object that contrasts with the background. By trial and error, their pecking movements become more accurate and discriminating, and they learn not to peck at objects, such as pebbles or any other undesirable objects.

Predatory Behaviour

In which one animal kills another for food, there is interaction between the attack patterns of the predator and the defense pattern of the prey. Lions and leopards show a complex set of movements as they move along downwind of a herd of antelope; they creep toward one animal and run it down with a short burst of speed. Some birds are attracted to the visual patterns presented by insects. Insects have eyespot patterns that are suddenly exposed when the insect is disturbed, creating a non-insect pattern. Other insects resemble their environment closely and become immobile when disturbed. Predators are usually attracted by movements, some prays have excellent defense devices. In a number of arthropods and some vertebrates behaviour patterns involving chemical warning and defence devices have evolved as a means of protection against predators. The predator-pray interaction, is called protean behaviour, it occurs when the prey goes through a sequence of possible escape patterns and the predator can not predict the exact path of the prey's movements. A stickleback fish being chased by a duck follows an erratic path that is very difficult to follow and can not be predicted.

Agonistic Behaviour

Competition for food shelter, mating partners and nesting space, may result in aggressive behaviour patterns, primarily between members of the same species. When an animal is approached too closely by another its first response is often defensive posture. Many arthropods and vertebrates have an individual distance, the minimum distance required to separate two animal without a fight ensuing. This space is distinct from an animal's territory. In its territory, an animal obtains the food, shelter, nest materials and space needed for the rearing of its young. Since only the members of the same species are likely to utilize the same portion of the environment, territorial defense is shown only towards members of the same species, and aggressive interactions are at territorial boundaries. Such *boundary encounters* are more complex than fights occurring within an individual's territory. One animal will retreat from the other when the meeting occurs within the second one's territory. At the boundary between the territories neither animal retreats, nor complex patterns of behaviour may be exchanged. The animals may show ambivalent behaviour patterns as they are simultaneously motivated to attack and retreat. This is a confusing state. Herring gulls, after a series of aggressive postures at a territorial boundary, may either pull grass from the ground, an activity associated with nest building, or go through motions similar to grass pulling.

Intraspecific fighting rarely results in any physical damage to the combatants. When one individual wins an encounter the loser frequently assumes a submissive posture that inhibits further attack by the winner. Fighting, in some species, continue until severe damage is done

Moyler (1968) has classified aggressive behaviour into following types:

- **Predatory aggression:** Elicited by a narrow range of stimuli. It is slightly influenced by either the presence or absence of gonadal hormones. The hypothalamus is involved in predation.
- **Inter-male aggression:** Elicited by a strange male of the same species and is inhibited by the particular submissive behaviour of that male. It is particularly dependent on male hormone for its development.
- **Fear induced aggression:** Occurs only in cases where escape has been attempted but is not possible. It is increased by stimulation of the hypothalamus anterior or to the ventromedial nucleus.
- **Irritable aggression:** May be increased frustration, deprivation and pain. A wide range of stimuli will elicit aggression. The ventromedial hypothalamus is involved in it. It is increased by the stimulation or ablation of this area. It is reduced by amygdalectomy.
- **Territorial aggression:** Maternal aggression appears to be specific to the situation involved. Nothing is known about the neural basis of these kinds of aggression.
- **Intragroup aggression:** A phenomena which is found in present day anoymous civilized society in contrast to intragroup aggression.
- **Intergroup aggression:** Fighting between various groups, populations within the same species.

The term agonistic behaviour may preferably be used as a general term when the specific kind of aggression involved is not known.

FIG. 3.2: Aggressive bared teeth display in carnivores.

Dominance Hierarchies

In many animal species the social interactions of the members of a local group are well organized and help to decrease aggressive activity among the members of the group. In the simplest form of such a social hierarchy which is peck order one individual α is dominant over all others, a second β is dominant over all except α. Dominance is expressed by winning in aggressive inter-action, by having first chance at the available food and mating partners and by having first choice of nesting locations. The other subordinate animals assume submissive posture than that of more dominant animal.

Reproductive Behaviour

Bisexual animals possess mechanisms for getting egg and sperm together to continue the existence of the species. In some species the presence and movements of individuals of the opposite sex initiate the physiologic changes. Mutual exchanges of early courtship movements initiate and synchronize physiological changes so that the sexes are ready to mate at the same time.

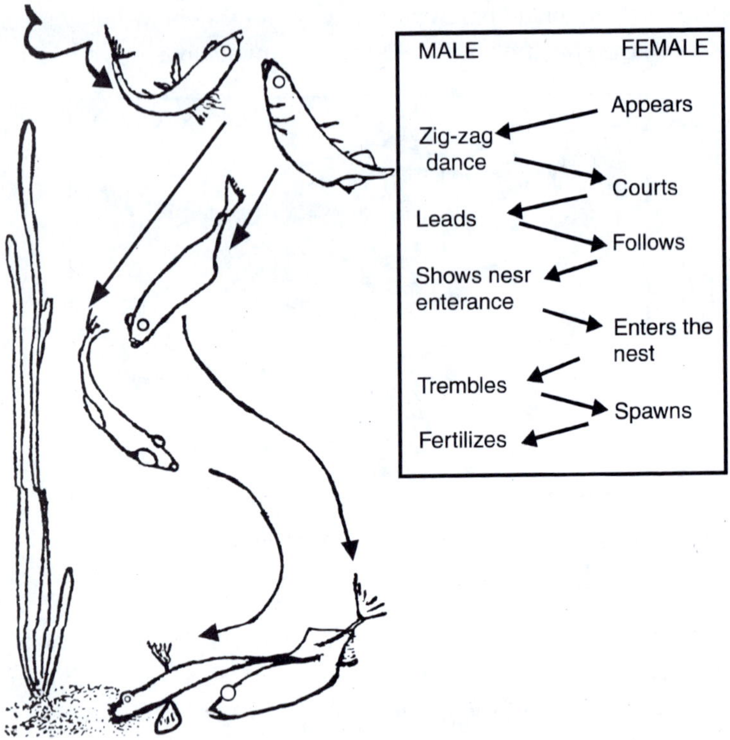

FIG. 3.3: Reproductive behaviour in three-spined stickle back. The territory holder male performed zig-zag dance when saw the female in breeding conditions. Female follows the male who leads her to the enterance at nest he has built.

The precopulatory behaviour pattern serves two following important functions:

- It decreases aggressiveness, and
- It establishes species and sexual identification.

The first function is needed, two animals are to avoid fighting long enough to mate. The pattern of reproductive behaviour of the stickleback has been studied intensively. After the male has migrated and staked out his territory, he builds a nest and courts any egg-laden female who enters his territory. In courting, he performs a special zigzag dance. The female follows the male and he leads her to the nest, at which point he directs his head towards the entrance. The pointing stimulates the female to enter the nest and she in turn stimulates the male to tremble. The trembling stimulates the female to spawn and the male fertilizes the eggs. The presence of the eggs stimulates his sexual behaviour. The tendency towards sex and aggression can be measured by presenting to a male on his home terrrtory either another male or a female fish, confined in a glass tube. If the fish presented to him is a receptive female with a swollen belly, male performs the *zigzag* dance. A count of the number of bites or zigzags per unit time is a measure of the respective strengths of the male's sexual and aggressive tendencies.

Epimeletic Behaviour

Care-giving behaviour or epimeletic behaviour between one generation and the next is well developed in the social insects, birds and mammals. Many young birds respond to tactile, acoustic and visual stimuli given by the adult by gaping-stretching upward, towards the parent with open mouth. The parent responds to this by feeding the young and because this act is a sign stimuli to the parents. The prolonged exchanges between mother and the young in primates often have long-term effects on the behavioural development of the young. Rhesus monkeys deprived of their normal social and sexual relationship with mothers or siblings develop normal social and sexual relationship. Monkeys reared by artificial mothers do not interact normally with other members of the species nor are they able to mate when mature. The mother-young association is important from psychological point of view.

The maternal-infant relationship was studied by Dr. Harry Harlow using surrogate mothers of cloth wire. He observed that both bodily contact and visual stimuli are important to this relationship. Young monkeys have strong emotional attachment to cloth mothers, run to them when frightended by a mechanical teddy bear beating a drum and would explore strange objects in the room only as long as the mothers was present as psychologic refuge. Monkeys without appropriate surrogate mother fled to a corner of the room.

In the primate societies there is close affinity between the young are and the mother. The young of many primates receive attention from several of the adult females of the troop, which is the social unit consisting of several adult males. Initially, the mother will not allow any one to hold the infant, but soon it is held and carried by other females, each of which touches, smells and licks it. If the infant begins to struggle, another female comes over and takes it. The touch and color of the fur and the movements of the mother elicit a clinging response in the infant; the infant's color pattern elicits the interest and movements of the female, who then facilitates clinging. These mutual responses of mother and newborn are very important in the development of the social behaviour

Allelopmimetic Behaviour

When the young birds leave the nest they show a tendency to fly together in flocksd with wonderfully intigrated movement. The long axis of the flock is at right angles to the direction of movement so that the flock itself is roughly shaped like a great bird. As each bird flicks along, it does the same thing as those on either side. The old and young show this behaviour. In this the visual stimuli from the leader determines the direction of the movement.

FIG. 3.4: Allelomimetic behaviour.

Social Behaviour

The interaction between two or more individual constitutes social behaviour. Social relationship implies interaction among members of the same species. But the mere presence of more than one individual does not constitute social behaviour. The physical environmental factors bring animals together in aggregation. In many animals a long-term relationship between male, female and young is a natural consequence of sexual relation. The basis of family relationship is the provision of shelter and food for the young.

There are following adaptive advantages of social behaviour:

- A group is more alert to danger than a single individual,
- A group offers protection against attack,
- The group has an effective communication system,
- The group is capable of communal attack and defence, and
- They have the territorial range or home range so the entruder be prevented.

Learning Introduction

According to Thorpe, learning is a long lasting adaptive change in the behaviour resulting from experience. This is the process by which life experiences leave their mark on the animal and the one that permits an individual to develop new adaptation in the light of past experience. Thorpe classified learning into following types:

(i) Habituation, (ii) Classical conditioning or conditioned reflex (CR) type-I, (iii) Trial and error and CR-type II, (iv) Latent learning. (v) Imprinting, and (vi) Insight learning.

Habituation

This is the simple form of learning. When repeated stimuli is given to the animal its response gradually decreases.

Classical Conditioning

It was discovered by I.P. Pavlov. He restrained a dog in a harness and repeatedly blew meat powder into its mouth and recorded the amount of saliva. Then he associated the sound of a bell with the meat powder, and repeated this for many times. The bell did not at first cause salivation but after repeated synchronisation with the meat, it came to do so. Pavlov called the salivation to the bell as conditioned reflex (CR), the bell as conditioned stimulus (CS), the salivation to the meat as unconditioned reflex (UCR) and the meat as unconditioned stimulus (UCS). Conditioned reflexes of this type have been observed in many different animals from arthropods to primates but the degree at conditioning is different.

Imprinting

Konrad Lorenz investigated this phenomena in the 1930's. He described imprinting as a unique learning process whereby the young of precocial birds (those who are able to walk just after hatching) form an attachment with the mother. If we expose them to mother figure or to any moving object they will follow hatching.

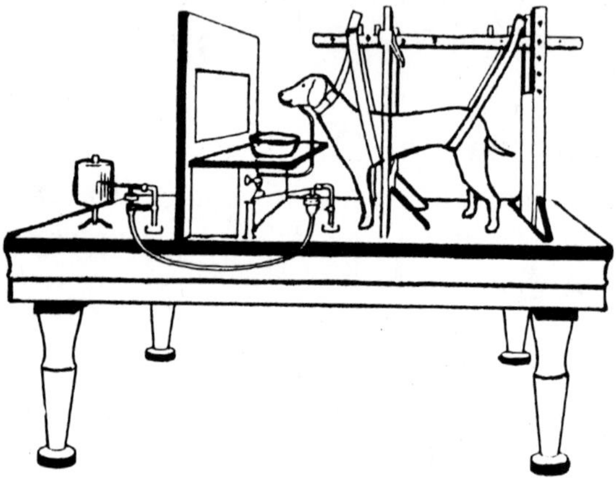

FIG. 3.5: Pavlov's experimental arrangement for salivary conditioning.

This response has adaptive value in keeping the young bird close behind its parent and well within the protective range of the parent. Lorenz found that the young birds choice of a mother figure during this critical period also affected its choice of a sexual partner on maturation. Young birds reared by a foster mother cease to follow her when they become independent. When they become mature they court and attempt to mate with birds the of foster mother's species. This imprinting is also present in sheep, deer and other animals.

Rhythmic Behaviour and Biological Clocks

Many animals express behaviour that recur with a regular periodicity, each year each lunar month, each day or with the tides. Some behaviour are regulated by a complex intraction of several types of periods. These cycles are regulated by some type of intrinsic mechanisms, which are called biological clocks. These endogenous biological clocks coordinate with rhythmic aspects of environment. The organisms in the temperate zones of the world show marked seasonal activity. Most fishes, birds and mammals have a single breeding season in the spring. Certain animals migrate at specific times to higher altitude or latitudes. Some animals show decrease in activity and metabolism during the winter and is called hibernation.

FIG. 3.6: Gosling following Konard Loernz representing Imprinting phenomena.

In tropics, there is no sharp change in temperature from one month to the next, a period of heavy rainfall alternates with the period of little or no rain. The cycles of animals in such regions are geared to these changes in the physical environment. Other cycles of animal activity reflect the phases of the moon. The swarming of the Palolo worm at a particular time of the year is governed by a combination of annual, lunar and tidal rhythms. The grunion, a pelagic fish of the Pacific coast of U.S.A., swarms from April through June on those three or four nights, when the spring tide, occurs. At high point of tide the fish squirm on to the beach, deposit eggs and sperm in the sand and return to the sea in the next wave. By the time the next spring tide reaches that position of the beach 15 days later, the young fish have hatched and are ready to enter the sea. The menstrual cycles of humans and apes also follow lunar periods.

Many which organisms show repeated sequences of events occur at about 24 hours intervals in the lives of these organisms. These are called circadian rhythms.

Some animals are diurnal showing greatest activity during the day whereas others are nocturnal and are most active during the hours of darkness. Other animals are crepuscular, having greatest activity during twilight hours. Our physiological processes exhibit circadidan rhythms. Our body temperature is highest at 4 or 5 p.m. and lowest at 4 or 5 p.m. Similarly secretions of a number of hormones the heart rate and blood pressure, rate of excretion of sodium and potassium show circadian peaks. All are associated with the behaviour patterns.

Animals have evolved biological clocks by means of which their activities are adapted to the regularly recurring changes in the physical environment. These biological clocks, with the signals from the external environment, inform the animal about the time of day most suitable for some activity or physiological processes. Birds and bees have highly developed timing devices and can be used in navigation or migration.

CHAPTER 4

The Behaviour Diversity

An ultimate analysis of the different kinds of behaviour suggests that no one category of behaviour is intrinsically superior to another in terms of its contribution to individual reproductive success. Simple rules of behaviour can be more adaptive than complex learning abilities when, for example, making a mistake in dealing with a key stimulus is fatal. Under other conditions, individuals gain by modifying their behaviour in response to factors that could not be predicted accurately prior to the birth of an individual. Thus, for example, many animals that travel widely learn the spatial features of their environment. An evolutionary hypothesis is that the diversity of proximate mechanisms regulating animal behaviour is a response to the diversity of ecological problems confronting animal species.

INSTINCTS

Instinct is the behaviour that appears in fully functional form. It is typically performed and triggered mechanically by a simple cue of some sort.

The Galah, (*Cacatua roseicapilla*, small in size), and the pink cockatoo (*Cacatua leadbeateri*, large in size) are large parrots and are found in the same eucalyptus woodlands in some parts of Australia. Both species use holes in trees as nest sites, and very occasionally the same tree hole attracts a nesting pair of galahs and a nesting pair of pink cockatoos. The two pairs may share the same nest for a time without interacting because the birds do not begin steady incubation of their eggs until the entire clutch is laid, a task that takes 3 or 4 days.

In due course of time conflict arises when both cockatoo and galah try to incubate simultaneously. The larger pink cockatoo drives the smaller galah away; the victor then unwittingly incubates both its own eggs and those of the evicted galah. That pink cockatoos will sometimes rear young galahs provides a fascinating natural experiment on the effect of experience on the development of behaviour.

Australian ornithologists, Ian Rowley and Greame Chapman took advantage of this experiment and discussed - *How will the crossfostered galahs behave-like galahs or link pink cockatoos*? The answer depends on the following behaviour.

- The cockatto-reared galah chicks give galah begging calls when they want to be fed by their foster parents.
- The pink cockatoos oblige, even though these calls are decidedly different form those used by their genetic offspring.
- Long after they left the nest.
- The cross-fostered galahas give galah alarm calls when surprised by something frightening.
- When it comes to the contact calls that parrots use to maintain contact with other members of their flock, the fostered galahs sound exactly link pink cockatoos.
- The galahs usually fly with the slow sweeping wingbeats of pink cockatoos, not the rapid, shallow wingbeats of galahs.
- Finally, the galahs feed on foods that pink cockatoos consume, foods that are normally avoided by galahs.
- The above observations enabled Rowley and Chapman to classified the behaviour of the adopted galahs as follows:
- The begging call was innate, the contact call learned.
- The alarm call was also innate, but the flight pattern and feeding preferences were learned.

The development of the begging and alarm calls was not altered by the novel experiences provided by pink cockatoo foster parents, but the contact calls, food habits, and flight pattern were modified by these particular experiences.

Ethology and Instincts

The early ethologists studied many behavioural cases, *e.g.*, above alarm calls of the galah. The behaviour is not easily altered by specific environmental influences that might be expected to affect their development.

FIG. 4.1: Instinctive behaviour. **(A)** A gull chick pecks at a long, thin stick with a striped tip, amore effective releaser of begging behaviour than a realistic model of a parent gull-when the chick is very young. **(B)** A red-winged blackbird "copulates" with a model that consists of a bunch of feathers with a female's tail raised in the precopulatory display position. **(C)** A greylag goose in the midst of rolling an egg back into the nest. The goose will complete the retrieval behaviour even if the egg is taken away midway through the process.

Niko Tinbergen observed that newly hatched herring gulls somehow *know* how to get fed. They peck at a red dot on the bills of their parents, and the adults respond by regurgitating a half-digested fish or other tasty morsel.

Instinctive response may be a **fixed action pattern** (FAP). It is a response that plays itself out of completion, once activated by a simple sensory cue. Ethologists called the key component of the object that triggers the FAP a **sign stimulus** (or *releaser*, if the sign stimulus was a signal from one individual to another).

Code Breakers

The simple relationship between cue and FAP is highlighted by code breakers, members of one species that exploit the FAPs of another species. A premier code breaker is the rove beetle *Atemeles pubicollis*, which lays its eggs in the nest of the ant *Formica polyctena*. The resulting larvae produce an attractant scent, or pheromone, that causes ant workers to carry the parasitic beetle grubs into their brood chambers, where the beetles feast on ant eggs and ant larvae.

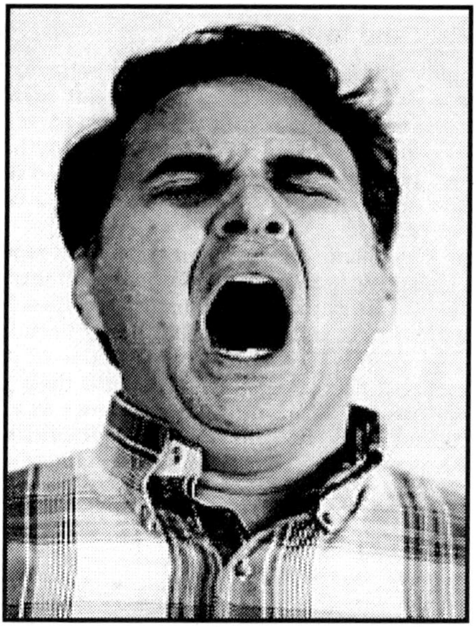

FIG. 4.2: A yan, a releaser of yawing in other humans.

Not content with this larder, the parasites also mimic the food-begging behaviour of ant larvae by tapping a worker ant's mandibles with their own mouthparts. This action is a releaser that triggers regurgitation (an FAP) of liquid food by the ant. The larvae eventually metamorphose into adult beetles, which also mimic the releasers that cause adult worker ants to feed them.

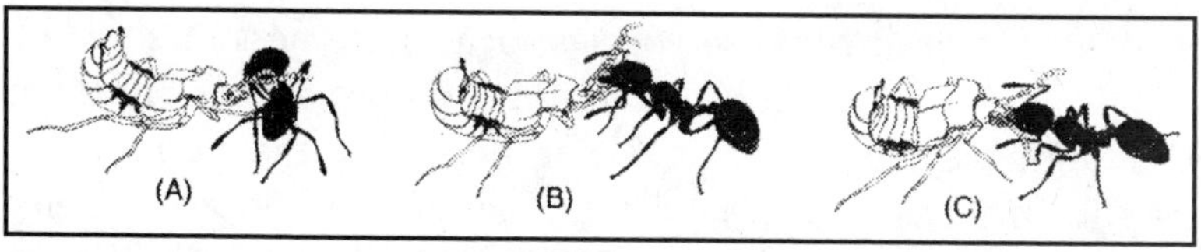

FIG. 4.3: Code-breaking rove beetle, whose behaviour mimics releasers of feeling behaviour in its ant host. **(A-C)** The beetle first taps a worker ant with its antennae, then touches the ant's mouth parts with its forelegs, and then consumes the food regurgitated by the ant.

FIG. 4.4: Egg ejection behaviour. A very young cuckoo instincitivity pushes an egg out of its host's nest.

Code-breaking species may even provide an exaggerated sign stimulus or supernormal stimulus that is more effective than that of the biologically correct object. Several bird species, among them the European cuckoo and the North American cowbird, are brood parasites. A female of these species locates the nest of some other bird, generally one smaller than herself. When the owner of the nest leaves during a pause in egg laying or incubation, the lurking parasite slips into the nest, quickly lays an egg, and disappears. When the owner returns, it often accepts the addition to its clutch, incubates the egg, and hatches the parasite.

The hatchling cowbird or cuckoo may instinctively eject some of the other eggs in the nest, the better to monopolize the food brought to the nest by its foster parents. The parasite grows rapidly and soon becomes larger and more active than its hosts' offspring would be. The stimulation of food-giving behaviour in most songbird parents depends on how high a nestling reaches, how noisy its begging calls are, and how energetically it bobs its head and body. Host parents confronted by a large voracious nestling cowbird or cuckoo are subjected to a supernormal begging stimulus, and they react by working overtime to satisfy the parasite's large demands.

Learning

Ethologist gives emphasis on instinctive behaviour. A person interested in instincts have discovered many examples of blindly mechanical behaviour, while a psychologist made the analysis of learned behaviour and can point to an equally large number of cases of learning- the durable modification of behaviour in response to information acquired form specific experiences.

For example, consider the kinds of learned changes in behaviour that occur as animals form an association between environmental events and their own responses.

One kind of associative learning is classical conditioning. It was first studied by Ivan Pavlov (a Russian physiologist). He demonstrated that if one consistently made a particular sound or showed a light just as he placed meat powder in a dog's mouth soon the dog would begin to salivate whenever it heard the tone or saw the light, even without the meat powder stimulus. **Salivation** is an automatic or unconditioned response to exposure to a food stimulus, an *unconditioned stimulus*. But dogs can learn through experience that a particular sound is associated with access to food, and in so doing form an association that leads to salivation when the sound is heard. Salivation is then a conditioned response to the sound, a conditioned stimulus that initially did not trigger the response.

FIG. 4.5: A supernormal stimulus. The fledgling cuckoo provides exaggerated key cues that trigger parental feeding by the host more effectively than the host's own offspring do.

FIG. 4.6: Trial-and-error learning. After one experience with a foultasting millipede, the toad will reject this prey on sight.

Classical Conditioning

It occurs in a great variety of animals, from roundworms to humans. Roundworm (*Caenorhabditis elegans*) is about 1 millimeter long and its entire nervous system contains just 302 nerve cells. Despite of its modest neural equipment, this worm can learn to associate food (the bacterium *E. coli*) with sodium or chloride ions in the food solution. After just one trial of feeding on the bacterium in the presence of one or the other of the ions, the worms subsequently tend to *wiggle* towards foodless solutions containing only the sodium (or chloride) ions that had been present when they were fed.

Operant Conditioning

It is another form of associative learning. In this case the animal learns to associate a voluntary activity with the consequences that follow. It is also called *trial-and-error* learning. It occurs outside psychology laboratories but it has been studied extensively in **Skinner boxes** (named after the famous psychologist B.F. Skinner).

In a laboratory when rat is introduced into a Skinner box, it may accidentally push a bar on the wall of cage perhaps as it reaches up to look for a way. When the bar is pressed down, a rat chow pellet pops into a food hopper and sometimes passes before the rat happens upon the pellet. After eating it, the rat may continue to explore its rather limited surroundings for a while before again happening to press the bar. Out comes another food pellet. The rat may find it quickly this time and then turn back to the bar and press it repeatedly. It has learned to associate a particular activity with food. It is now operantly conditioned to press the bar.

Skinnerian techniques have been used with success to guide the learning of responses far more complex than pressing a bar. These techniques have also been used to condition humans and other animals to regulate internal activities, such as heart rate or brain electrical activity, which were at one time thought to be entirely unconsciously controlled.

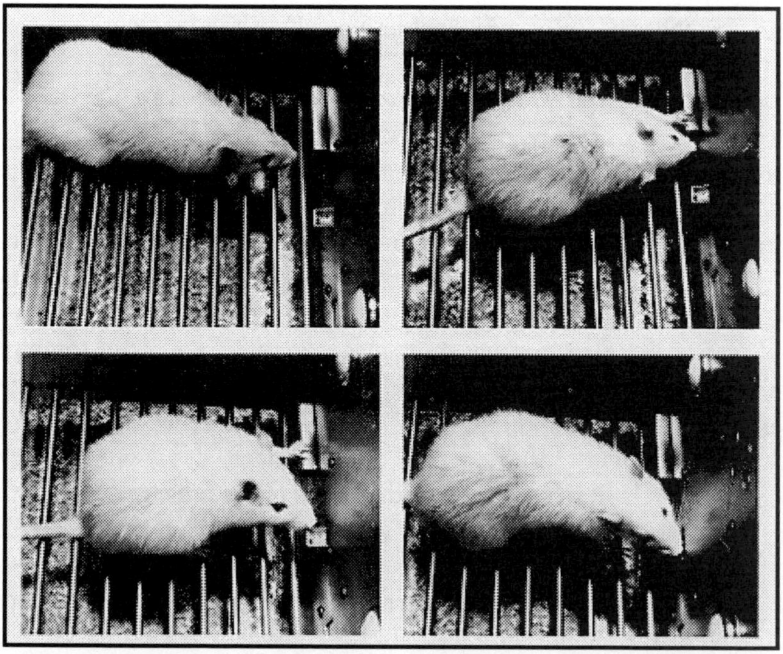

FIG. 4.7: Rat in a Skinner box. The operantly conditioned rat approaches the bar **(tap left)** and then presses it **(top right).** The animal awaits the arrival of a pellet of rat chow **(bottom left),** which it consumes **(bottom right),** and so is reinforced for pressing the bar.

Spatial Learning

Spatial learning occurs without the overt reinforcement, typical of operant conditioning. These behaviours defy classification as innate or learned because they seem to be fully functional upon first performance, but do require specific experience. Spatial learning has been studied in digger wasp females. When a digger wasp has dug her burrow in the ground, she then leaves to collect pray to feed her offspring. As she leaves her nest for the first hunting trip, she circles the area for a few seconds and than darts off. Studied of Niko Tinbergen showed long ago that if you displace objects around the nest entrance after the wasp has performed the initial orientation flight and left on a hunting trip, when she comes back she will search for her nest entrance by the displaced landmarks. Her behaviour indicates that she has learned something about the landmarks around her small, concealed nest entrance.

Birds

They store food have excellent spatial memory. A black-capped chickadee may hide several hundred seeds or small insects in bark crevices or patches of moss in a single day. In nature, the bird stores only one food item in each hiding spot and never uses the same location twice. For example the birds were given a chance to store food in holes drilled in small trees places in an aviary. After the birds had placed a sunflower seed in 4 or 5 of 72 possible storage sites, they were shooed into a holding cage of 24 hours. The seed were removed in the interim and closed each of the 72 storage sites with a Velcro cover. When the birds were permitted back in the aviary to search for the food, they spent much more time inspecting and pulling at the covers at their hoard sites than at spots where they had not store food 24 hours previously. Since the storage holes were empty and covered, there were no olfactory or visual cues provided by stored food to guide the birds in their search; they could only rely on their *memory* of where they had hidden food previously.

Misconceptions about Instincts and Learning

There is a great diversity in behaviour and it makes difficult to claim that all behavioural traits can be neatly assigned either to the learning or the instincts category.

Instincts are not purely genetically determined.

Learning is not purely environmentally determined. Learned behaviours are independent of genetic influence and instead require only the environment, the experience, of the animal.

Innate behaviours are somehow encoded in a gene of genes.

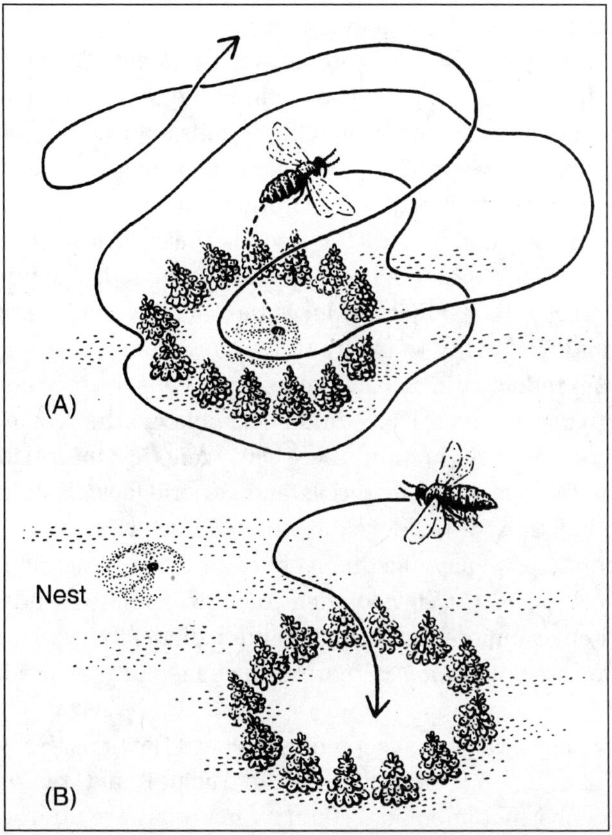

FIG. 4.8: Spatial learning by a wasp. **(A)** Female digger wasps learn the landmarks around their nest burrow's entrance in a matter of seconds, as shown experimentally by the response of a returning female to displacement of local landmarks **(B)** After Tinbergen [928].

Galah Chick

Innate (begging call) and learned (contact call) behaviour were studied in an adult foster-reared galah chick. Both calls were produced by the vocal apparatus of the bird. These were under the control of their brain. These structures are not simply encoded in the genes of the bird, nor do they arise spontaneously from the environment. Both genes and environment contribute to brain development. The galah's brain is so structured that a nestling tends to give a begging call when it is hungry and in the presence of an adult.

This signal is much the same for all galah chicks, no matter what sound are present in their prehatching environment. The signal is also resistant to change, even if galah chicks hear only pink cockatoo communication signals rather than the sounds made by parent galahs.

The brain of a young galah has also been studied. It has components that apparently store information about the contact calls. It hears from the members of the flock its joins. If it stays with pink cockatoos, it hears pink cockatoo contact calls and, when motivated to give contact calls itself, it produces the sounds it has heard from its companions. The ability to incorporate information about the contact calls it hears reflects the capacity of its brain cells to store information about particular sounds. These brain cells, like all the rest, developed because of an interaction between genetic information and environmentally supplied materials and experiences. Thus there is a genetic foundation for the development of all behaviours.

The ability of behave instinctively or to learn something depends or nerve cells, and the development of those cells depends on both genes and environment. Instincts is more genetically determined than learning, whereas learning is more environmentally determined than instincts?

This concept was not accepted by Richard Dawkins. He was of the opinion that genetic information (the recipe) and the molecules needed to construct an animal (the raw material) are utterly different entities. The two things play complementary roles in the development of a nervous system that permits its owner to do some things innately and to do others through learning.

Instincts can be modified by Experience

It is inappropriate to talk about purely genetic (or purely environmentally) behaviours or even mostly genetic (or mostly environmental) behaviours. Instincts are modified by experience, whereas most learned behaviours are far from completely flexible responses to the environment.

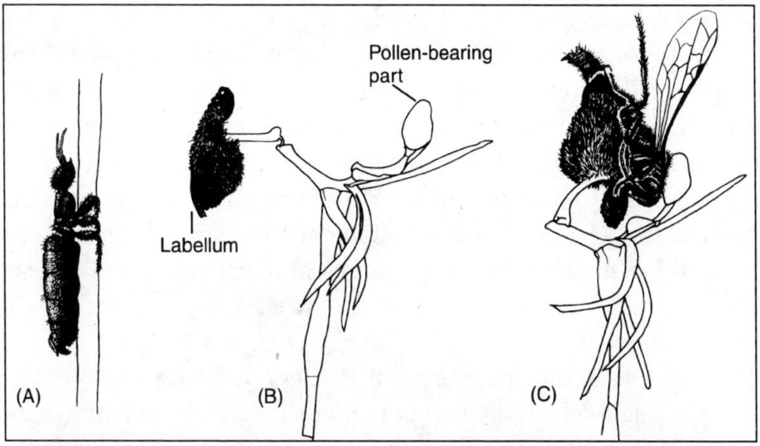

FIG. 4.9: Orchid deception. **(A)** A wingless female thynnine wasp on her perch, where she releases a sex pheramone that will attract males of her species. **(B)** An Australian orchid with a highly modified petal, the labellum, that vaguely resembles and smell like a wingless, pheromone-releasing female wasp. **(C)** A male wasp drawn to the orchid may attempt to grasp the lebellum and fly off with it. If so, he will catapulted into the pollen-bearing part of the flower.

The flowers of wasp-pollinated orchids are code-breakers. They take advantage of wasp mating systems by producing a mimetic sex pheromone that smells like the scent of a particular species of wasp. Male wasps track this odor to an orchid, which has a special flower petal that (vaguely) resembles the body of a wingless female wasp. The male pounces upon and tries (unsuccessfully) to pick up the petal. In the course of the attempt, the male's body comes into contact with the pollinia, or pollen-bearing sacs, of the flower. The sticky pollinia adhere to the male, and when he finally gives up the futile task of trying to carry the "female" away, the pollinia go with him. Should he be drawn to another individual of the orchid species that deceived him, he will transfer pollen to the plant, fertilizing it rather than a female of his species.

Superficially, the wasp's behaviour appears to be that of an automation, with its tracking and copulatory responses (FAPs) mechanically triggered by simple sign stimuli in its environment-so simple that an orchid can successfully imitate the key cues and deceive the male wasp into behaving in ways that waste the wasp's time and energy. But the fact that one almost never sees wasps visiting orchids growing naturally on the forest floor suggests that the wasps are not quite as thick-headed as they seem. Males searching in an area apparently become familiar with the local orchids and eventually come to avoid them. But these same wasps are highly attuned to the scent of sex pheromone coming form different places, and it is the sensitivity to novel sources of novel sources of the scent that botanists can exploit to find out what wasp pollinates which orchid species.

The fact that the number of males coming to a sample of cut specimens declines rapidly within minutes is further evidence that the males learn, probably form the unrewarding consequences of grappling with orchid flowers, not to respond to odors coming from certain locations. Thus, the local male wasps habituate to some stimuli, learning not to react to cues that originally triggered copulatory attempts.

Niko Tinbergen established that newborn herring gulls prefer to peck at:

- Long, pointed objects more than short, stubby ones.
- Red objects more than all other colored objects.
- High-contrast dots more than low-contrast dots.
- Moving objects more than stationery ones.

A three-dimensional model or stuffed head of a herring gulls is no more effective in stimulating begging pecks by newborn herring gulls than is a tow-dimensional pointed strip of cardboard with a red dot painted on it.

This is important to note that the relation between cue and behaviour changes with time and experience.

Jack Hailman found that older laughing gull chicks are much more selective in their response to models than younger ones. Although 1- or 2-day old gulls peck equally at almost any pointed object presented to them, they soon begin to refuse models that do not closely resemble laughing gull heads. As a result of their social interactions with their parents, the young birds acquire information, both auditory and visual, that leads them to identify their parents as individuals. Eventually they learn to beg only from their mother and father.

Biased Learning

Animals (*e.g.*, male thynnine wasps and baby gulls) may have a repertoire of actions that they exercise upon encountering the appropriate sign stimuli, but that the results of performing an instinctive behaviour may provide the animal with information that it uses to modify its behaviour, creating a kind of flexible instinct. On the other hand, learning may be less flexible than one tends to imagine.

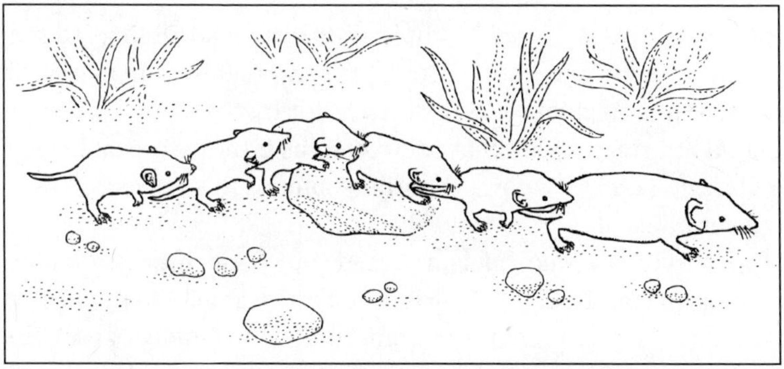

FIG. 4.10: Imprinting in shrews. Young shrews from caravan early in life, having the odor of their mother, which they will follow.

Imprinting is a kind of learning that reveals the *preprogrammed* nature of learned behaviour. Imprinting an imprinting-like behaviour are now known to occur in many other birds. For example, the foster-reared galahs imprinted on their pink cockatoos, foster parents, and as adults associated only with pink cockatoos, not with members of their own species. Imprinting also takes place in some mammals.

Learned Kin Discrimination

When a baby shrew or gosling imprints on its mother, it has learned to recognize a close relative. Imprinting is then a proximate mechanism for kin discrimination. It is defined as *the differential treatment of members of the same species in a way that depends on their genetic relatedness.*

The ability to respond differently to individuals depends on their degree of genetic similarity occurs in a variety of animals in which parents care for their offspring or in which other relatives interact cooperatively. Kin discrimination of siblings often is the result of a simple rule thumb: *Treat individuals differently if you have been reared with them.* Thus, for example, young spiny mice placed in a test arena will seek out each other's company, but if given a choice, will prefer to huddle with individuals with whom they associated in their litter as opposed to individuals with whom they have no prior experience.

In nature, this preference would ordinarily lead siblings to remain with fellow **siblings**, but if one experimentally creates a litter composed on nonsiblings that are cared for by the same female, these unrelated littermates will treat each other as if they were siblings. This *discrimination error* shows that the young of this species learn who their littermates are.

The proximate mechanism based on odor may promote kin discrimination in Belding's ground squirrels. Paul Sherman studied this phenomenon. He captured some pregnant females and shipped them to Warren Holmes's laboratory. When two females gave birth close in time, Holmes switched some of the pups to create four classes of juveniles:

- Siblings reared apart.
- Siblings reared together.
- Nonsiblings reared apart.
- Nonsiblings reared together. Foster pups were readily accepted by the adult females.

When the juveniles had reached the postweaning stage, pairs were placed in an arena and given a chance to interact.

Animals that were reared together, whether siblings or not, generally treated each other nicely, whereas animals that had been reared apart were likely to react aggressively to one another. This shows that the little squirrels learn something from the experience of growing up together, and that they use this information in their social relations. The most remarkable finding of these experiments was that biological sisters reared apart engaged in a significantly lower rate of aggressive interactions than nonsiblings reared apart. In other words, sisters have some way to recognizing one another, perhaps an odor similarity, that is not dependent on the experience of sharing a mother and a burrow. In fact, even half-sisters with the same father reared apart in captivity are nastier toward unrelated females than to their paternal half-sisters when permitted to interact in a test arena or in the field.

Holmes and Sherman have given the label *phenotype matching* to the mechanism responsible for the discrimination capacity of female Belding's ground squirrels and other animals like them. These creatures apparently learn something about their own phenotype, their appearance or odor or some other cue, and then discriminate among others on the basis of how similar those individuals are to them. Such a mechanism can have the effect of causing individuals to behave differently toward other in a manner correlated with their kinship status.

Language Learning

Imprinting and learned kin discrimination illustrate how specialized learning abilities can be. Language learning is highly flexible form of leaning at the other end of the spectrum form imprinting. After all, the mechanism underlying language learning can accommodate all of the roughly 4000 different languages that occur (or occurred) worldwide. But despite this diversity, there are any number of special constraints that structure the way in which a language is learned, no matter what the language is.

A human vocal apparatus can produce number of sounds, a total of only about 40 speech sounds (*phonemes*) are used to construct the thousands upon thousands of words in all human languages; many of the same phonemes appear in different languages. The brains of human infants have properties that facilitate discrimination among phonemes, and thereby facilitate language learning.

Very Young Babies

Very young babies are able to tell the difference between such similar pairs of consonants as *b* and *p*. If tapes of artificially synthesized sounds are played, baby will perceive by English-speaking adults as *ba*, *ba*, *ba* to babies form English-speaking households, after first giving each infant subject a pacifier wired to record its sucking rate. The infants sucking rate typically increased sharply when the tape started playing, but with repetition of the sound, the infants habituated to it and their sucking rate fell. When a new syllable is presented, such as *pa* or even one featuring a novel, but very similar, consonant sound that Thai speakers use but that does not occur in English, the infants became aroused and their sucking rate promptly accelerated. Thus, the perceptual mechanisms needed for the subtle discrimination of speech sounds have already developed in the infant's brain by the time it is born. Soon after birth all young humans go through a stage in which they babble, producing a variety of unstructured sounds. They seem to match the sounds, they make against their stored memories of language sounds they have heard. Their ability to make fine discriminations among similar consonant and vowel sounds surely aids in this matching process.

Young Child

If a young child is congenitally deaf and cannot hear spoken language, it cannot acquire information about speech sounds. It will go through a babbling phase but eventually will stop producing sounds altogether. However, if such children are exposed to sign language users, the quickly develop facility in the use of this visual language following much the same developmental schedule as that followed by hearing children as they acquire a vocal language.

As a child learns a language, whether Hindi, English, the pattern he/she follows in predictable. The child first uses one-word sentences (*No*; *Go*; *Mama*), then always enters a two-word stage (*Dada come*; *Bring me*). This phase endures for some time before the child enters the third phase; **telegraphic speech**, in which sentences consist of nouns without plurals and verbs without tense endings-speech stripped to its essentials. Finally, young children begin to elaborate their control over the grammar of speech (or sign language), acquiring the rules that give language its meaning.

Without a knowledge of these rules, language communication would be impossible. The ability of some one to communicate with other occurs because there are only certain ways subjects, verbs, predicates, verb tenses, and prepositions can be used in Hindi/English. Young children can acquire the necessary grammar skills without ever receiving formal instruction in them. As a result, some persons have hypothesized that the human infant's brain provides the child with a special capacity to extract grammatical rules just by listening to the speech of others.

Special Features of all Forms of Learning

Language acquisition superficially appears to be a remarkably flexible kind of learning. It is highly structured by the special proximate mechanisms and reside in the brains of all but a tiny handful of humans. The same point can be made even about operant conditioning.

Any action that an animal could perform, workers in the field soon began to discover contradictory cases. For example, one can readily condition a white rat to do some things, like running in a running wheel, by sounding a warning noise and giving it an electric shock if it fails to start running promptly. After a rat has had some experience with hearing the sound and receiving a shock while standing in the wheel but not while running, it will make the appropriate association and start running whenever it hear the warning cue. But a rat cannot be conditioned to stand upright in the running wheel using the same procedures. Rats that happen to rear up just after the sound are not shocked; despite this, they fail to make the association between this behaviour and avoidance of electrical punishment. The frequency with which they perform the response when they hear the warning signal actually declines over time.

John Garcia and his co-workers have examined the ability of white rats to learn to avoid various sensory cues that are associated with punishing consequences. Punishment like, X-ray radiation, mimics the effects of poisoning by causing a buildup of toxic products in irradiated tissues and body fluids. Even tiny doses of radiation induce mild nausea, which the animal associates with any unusual-tasting liquid or food it has recently consumed. If a rat consumes a food or fluid with a distinctive taste and then is exposed to minute amounts of radiation, it will refuse to ingest anything with that flavor at a later time. The degree to which the food or fluid is avoided is proportional to:

- The intensity of resulting illness.
- The intensity of the taste of the substance.
- The novelty of the substance.
- The shortness of the interval between consumption and illness.

Taste-aversion learning can be seen as an example of classical conditioning, in which X-ray irradiation (the unconditioned stimulus) always elicits illness and suppresses consumption of food or liquids (the conditioned response). The taste of the food or liquid acts as a conditioned stimulus that the animal pairs with X-ray irradiation, and the conditioned animal reduces food or fluid intake whenever it experiences the distinctive taste. However, taste-aversion learning is special. For example, only a single bout of radiation is needed to condition a rat to avoid food with a certain taste, unlike the more widely studied cases of classical conditioning in which repeated trials are usually needed before the animal forms the conditioned association.

THE EVOLUTIONARY BASIS OF BEHAVIOURAL DIVERSITY

Humans tend to think that highly flexible learning. It is inherently superior to other kinds of behaviour, especially "simple" innate responses, because of unusually well-developed capacity for the more flexible forms of learning. Ecological conditions may favor the ability to acquire, store, and use experiential inputs to modify behaviour. Learning presumably costs something, and one of the costs probably is the energy needed to manufacture and maintain those elements of nervous systems required to store information and use it to change an animal's behaviour.

If the large brain of humans is related to our great ability to learn, as many people have argued, then the physiological expenses of human learning are great indeed. Although the brain makes up only 2 per cent of our total body weight, it demands 15 per cent of all cardiac output and 20 per cent of body's entire metabolic budget. A large brain boosts energy expenditures.

The human brain is sensitive to oxygen deprivation, a fact that has been responsible for the shortening of many lives. Moreover, it is also developmentally vulnerable to genetic accidents; many of the known single-gene effects on human behaviour involve severe brain damage resulting form a single mutant allele. Finally, our reinforcement networks, although often rewarding or punishing us in biologically appropriate ways, may malfunction, an event that causes various kinds of debilitating mental illness. A less massive brain, more simply constructed, might be less expensive to maintain and less susceptible to injury and operative failure.

Simple rules of behaviour are not only probably cheaper in physiological terms, but they are also highly effective in situations in which there is a reliable relationship between a particular cue and a specific, productive response. Surely it is no accident that instincts are characteristic of very young animals.

Biased Learning

Biased nature of animal learning is that these features reduce the risk that an animal will learn the wrong things or learn irrelevant information. The ability to learn from experience is useful if it helps an individual to adjust to variable conditions that could not have been anticipated prior to its birth, such as the location of food and dens, or precisely what edible prey species are available, or exactly what its parents look like, or what language is spoken in its home. Specific learning mechanisms help focus an animal's attention on the key variables.

In species whose males and females have different-sized home ranges, the sex that typically travels the greater distances should exhibit superior spatial learning ability.

Studied were made on three species of small rodents by Steven Gaulin and Randall Fitz Gerald. They examined in one species, the meadow vole (*Microtus pennsylvanicus*), that males have home ranges more than four times as large as those occupied by each of their several mates. In contrast, both prairie and pine voles (*Microtus ochrogaster* and *Microtus pinetorum*) are monogamous and share the same-sized living space. When tested in a variety of mates, which the animals had to solve in order to receive food rewards, males of the wide-ranging meadow vole consistently made fewer errors than females of their species. But in both the prairie and pine voles, there was no difference in the spatial learning performance of males and females, which have similar home ranges and so are confronted with equivalent spatial learning problems in their natural lives.

The hypothesis that learning abilities reflect selection for fitness-enhancing skills has been tested in another way with these voles. If male meadow voles have been under stronger selection for spatial leaning capacity than female meadow voles, then males might be expected to devote more brain tissue to this specific task. In some vertebrate animals, a particular brain structure, the hippocampus, is believed to play an important role in spatial learning. As predicted, male meadow voles devote a significantly greater proportion of their brain volume to the hippocampus than do females of their species.

The general hypothesis presented here on the adaptive value of learning is that selection favors specific learning abilities as solutions to specific ecological problems.

Some (but not all) animals may gain useful flexibility by adjusting their diets to whatever happens to be available to them or by learning the features of the environment where they happen to live. By the same token, social animals face an unpredictable but highly important social environment in which an individual's ability to adjust to the behaviour of others may greatly affect its reproductive success. Knowing who is dominant to whom, remembering what individual *X* did to individual *Y*, and keeping track of how relationships between others are changing require learning an cannot be anticipated with preset responses.

CHAPTER 5

Methods of Studying Behaviour

INTRODUCTION

For studying the behaviour of any animal we should concentrate our attention on the types of responses it gives to its natural surroundings. The important thing about an animal is what it does, and when we have described this it is possible to analyze the environmental change, which cause it to act, the physiological pecularities which changes its behaviour and the various individual consequences of its reaction. The physiological pecularities are associated with the activity of neurons. Following are the methods of studying behaviour.

METHODS ASSOCIATED WITH NEUROPHYSIOLOGICAL APPROACH

The neurophysiologic approach involves analysis of neural function; the neurophysiologist removes, stimulates and records the activity of neurons. By placing an electrode on the nerve leading from some sense organ and making a recording, the experimenter can determine what kind of sensory inputs are available to the animal. By monitoring neuronal activity, he can determine what stimuli will actually generate action potentials in a given sense organ. In this way, he can distinguish between animal that is incapble of detecting a particular stimulus and another animal that can detect the stimulus but simply is not responding under the given test conditions.

Electrical Stimulation

Complex patterns of behaviour can be produced by electrical stimulation of certain parts of the central nervous system. Although the enormous complexity of the central nervous system makes it difficult to interpret the results of such experiments, the location of the neural pathways involved in the control of certain movements can be established. When an electrode is implanted in the brain of an anaesthesized animal, and the animal is allowed to wake and move around freely, it can be stimulated successively with impulses of a different strengths. Observation of the relation between the area stimulated and the behaviour observed in the animal provides some insight into the operation of the brain. In the electrical stimulation of attack behaviour, the rooster is stimulated by electrodes implanted in a particular part of its brain. It starts to move towards the keeper and as stimulation is continued it attacks.

By Sensory Input

In the second method, the investigator makes systematic changes in the sensory input of an animal and observes the changes in output in some segment of its behavioural repertoire. He then makes a dia grammatic representation of the relationship between input and output, usually relying upon feedback loops and other cybernetic phenomena.

Brain Lesions

For studying animal behaviour, K.S. Lashley performed experiments on the effect of brain lesions on learning. He investigated the retention of maze learning after parts of the cortex had been removed. In one of his experiments he used a maze with eight blind alleys on the way to the goal box. All the rats were trained to their maximum performance and then a part of their cerebral cortex was removed equally and symmetrically from both hemispheres. When the rats had recovered from the operation, they were re-tested in the maze and their errors scored over a number of re-learning trials. The lesions amounting to some 10% of the cortex have little effect but beyond these errors, begin to rise. The maze learning depends on a variety of cues-visual tactile and olfactory. The engram for these are located in the cortical region of the brain and by lesions these engrams are disturbed so also in the learning ability.

Drug Administration

It is a neurophysiological method to study behaviour. Experiments with mice show that puromycin which inhibits the protein systhesis, interferes with the consolidation of memory. Long-term memories can be normal in puromycin treated animals, but short-term memory is affected. The short-term memory is stored by neural activity and this is followed by a storage phase involving protein synthesis. This storage phase converts the short-term memory into stable. When puromycin is injected in the learning phase, it affects processes that are necessary for the formation of memories. Investigations indicate that memory might have a basis in the synthesis of RNA-that engrams might consist of specific sequences of nuclceotides in the RNA molecules. There have been reports on the transfer of specific conditioned reflexes of Planaria and fish by the administration of RNA extracts. Studies by Hyden suggest that there are changes in the structure of RNA in specific neurons that are involved in specific kinds of learning-for example in the neurons of the vestibular nuclei of rats that have undergone training in a task involving balance.

The olfactory cues play an important role in homing in a salmon. The salmon smells distinctive aroma of his home river remembers it and subsequently home in on it. Salmons have been prepared in the laboratory with electrodes in their olfactory lobes to record neuronal activity and with a catcheter in the nasal orifice. When water from the salmon's home river is perfused through the fish's nose a clear burst of nerve impulses is detected in the olfactory lobe. When water from other rivers is perfused through the nose little or no electrical activity is detected in the electrodes buried in olfactory lobe. The experimenters prepared an RNA extract of the olfactory lobe of a salmon that homed in on river A and injected that into the olfactory lobe of a salmon that homed in on river B. Within 48 hours the olfactory lobe of this second salmon showed a clear burst of electrical activity recorded by the indwelling electrode. When water from river

A was perfused into the Salmons nostril. This suggests that some sort of memory was transferred from one salmon to another via RNA extract.

METHODS ASSOCIATED WITH PSYCHOLOGICAL APPROACHS

These are: (i) Skinner box (ii) Shuttle box

By Skinner Box and Shuttle Box

In addition to these methods of studying behaviour, which might be described as neurophysiological because they actually concentrate on the neuronal circuitry underlying behaviour, there are two widely used methods of studying behaviour itself. The psychological school of behaviourists, led by B.F. Skinner at Harvard, has attempted to establish general principles of behaviour and especially of learning. Skinner's studies of training rats using immediate reward or reinforcement when the task has been accomplished, has the basis of programmed learning. It is the goal of these studies, carried out in the laboratory, to control all the experimental variable so that the effect of one can be measured. One of the central concepts that emerged from studies by the comparative psychologists was stimulus-response theory. This attempted to explain a behaviour as a series of reactions to stimuli.

Although the importance of stimuli and responses in determining behaviour patterns is clearly apparent, animals are more than a collection of sets of stimulus response reactions. The experimental psychologist confines his subjects to carefully defined experimental conditions, such as a maze or a shuttle box, in which the subject learns to move from one side to another to avoid an electric shock, or a skinner box, in which it learn to press a lever or peck at a key to get a reward of food or drink.

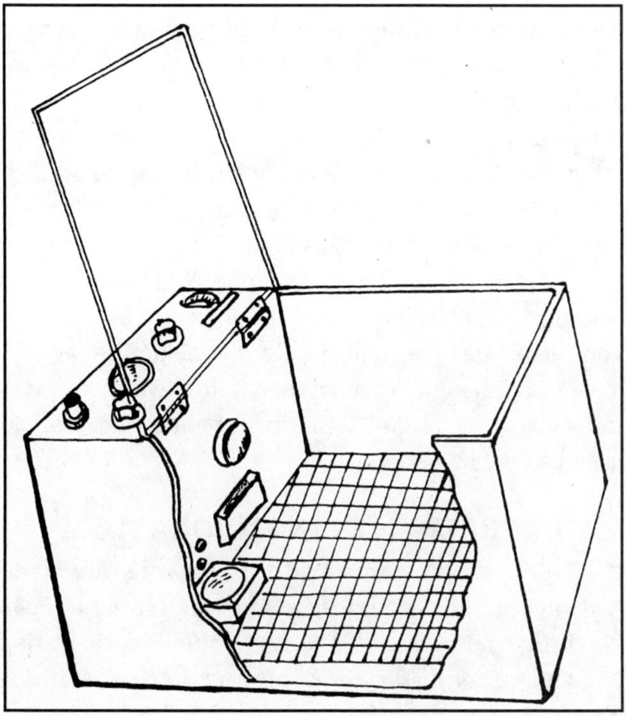

FIG. 5.1: Skinner box.

OBSERVATION IN NATURAL HABITAT

Another system of behavioural studies, founded in the late 1930's by Konrad Lorenz and Niko Tinbergen. The ethologists insist that animal behaviour be studied under conditions. They have explored the rich variety of adaptive behaviour patterns shown by birds, fish and insects and have been especially concerned with analyzing the factor controlling social behaviour, including aggressive, reproductive and parental behaviour.

Field Observations

This is the best method of studying animal behaviour. In the natural habitat an animal performs its behaviour without any disturbance J.T. Emlem did an experiment with the behaviour of cliff swallows. These birds build their nests out of mud in protected spots under cliffs and the eaves of houses. J.T. Emlem, wanted to find out whether these birds showed any tendency to defend their own nests, but in order to do this he had to make sure that the same birds always come back to the same nests. He broke down the wall between the nests and observed that the birds begin to fight each other. After some time they begin to repair the broken wall and become peaceful. They also start brooding their eggs in the nest. This simple experiment illustrates one important technique in field experiments. Which arises out of the nature of experimental design.

We can also observe and study agonistic behaviour, sexual behaviour, or epimeletic behaviour (care-giving behaviour), et-epimeletic behaviour (care-soliciting behaviour), allelomimetic behaviour and social behaviour

EXPERIMENTS IN LABORATORY

Although the field experiments and observations are realialtic but there are always all sort of interruptions and variable environment factors which interfere. One of the basic theories that arises out of observation and experiments on behaviour is that it is affected by many factors.

This is evident in experiments with heredity and environment. In the laboratory we can study different behaviour patterns. We should consider all possible environmental factors, which affect the behaviour pattern. To avoid misleading results we must take following precautions:

Time

The time of day and time of year are important and it is better to plan an experiment so that experiment and control animals are tested simultaneously.

Individual Differences

Every individual behaves differently from every other one because of heredity and previous experiences. The ideal experiment is one in which the same individual is both experimental and control but this is not possible if it is necessary to observe the experimental and control simultaneously. The favorite type of experiment is that of paired comparisons, in which an experimental and control animal are matched as accurately as possible in a pair. Heredity can be controlled by using inbred strains and the same sex. Previous environmental factors can be matched by taking animals which are of the same age and born of the same parents. This is easy to do with those animals which produce more than one offspring at the same birth.

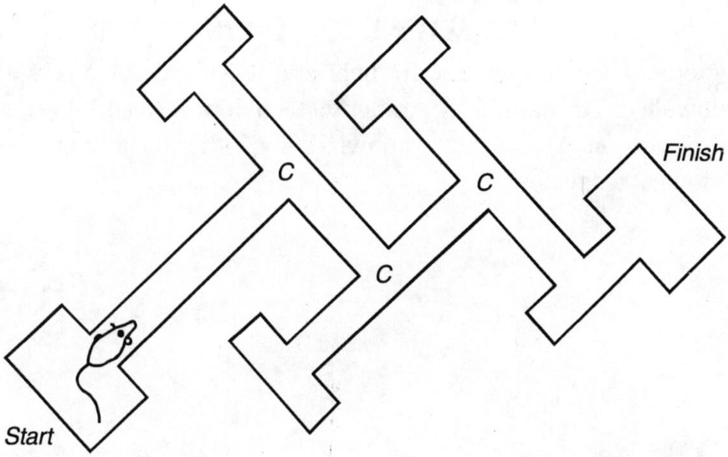

FIG. 5.2: Shuttle or simple maze. C = indicates choice points.

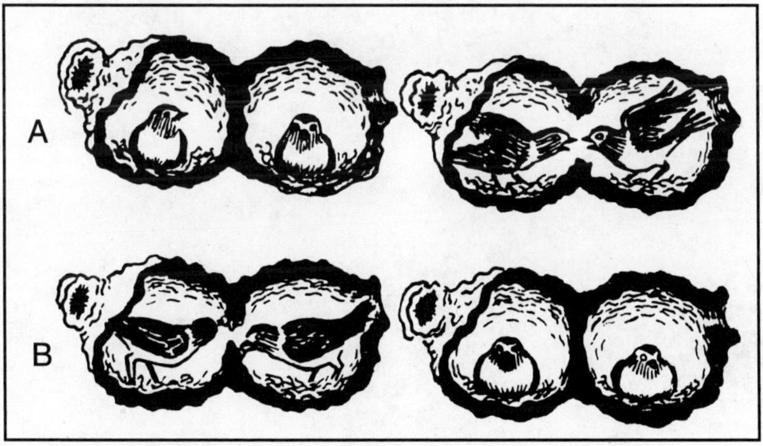

FIG. 5.3: Field experiment in cliff shallows.

Social Environment

This can be kept stable by raising animal in isolation. Animals frequently react towards an experimenter as part of the social environment and that their relationship with him may affect the outcome of the experiment. The laboratory rats will perform better on maze if they are accustomed to handling ahead of time rather than being suddenly seized by a stranger.

PHYSICAL FACTORS

The factors such as temperature light and noise are obvious and can be controlled. The careful experimental technique succeeds best when it is based on a thorough knowledge of the basic behavioural adaptions of a species.

CHAPTER 6

Genes, Genetics and Behaviour

GENOME AND GENE

Each organism possesses a genome that contains the biological information needed to construct and maintain a living example of that organism. Most genomes, including those for all cellular life-forms, are made of DNA (deoxyribonucleic acid) but a few viruses have RNA (ribonucleic acid) genomes. DNA and RNA are polymeric molecules made up of linear, unbranched chains of monomeric subunits called nucleotides. Each nucleotide has three parts: a sugar, a phosphate group, and a base.

Understanding the information contained in genome sequence will be the major challenge of the early 21st century. The genome is the entire DNA content of a cell, including all of the genes and all of the intergenic regions. The human genome contains approximately 80 000 genes but the coding regions of these genes take up only 3% of the genome. The yeast genome contains 6000 genes and has a more compact organization. The genomes of some plants are dominated by repetitive DNA sequences. Prokaryotic genomes are small with very little space between genes.

There is no such thing as a common genome structure. There are major differences between the genomes of bacteria, viruses and organelles on the one hand and the nuclear genomes of eukaryotes on the other. In eukaryotes there are major differences in the types of sequences found, the amounts of DNA and the number of chromosomes.

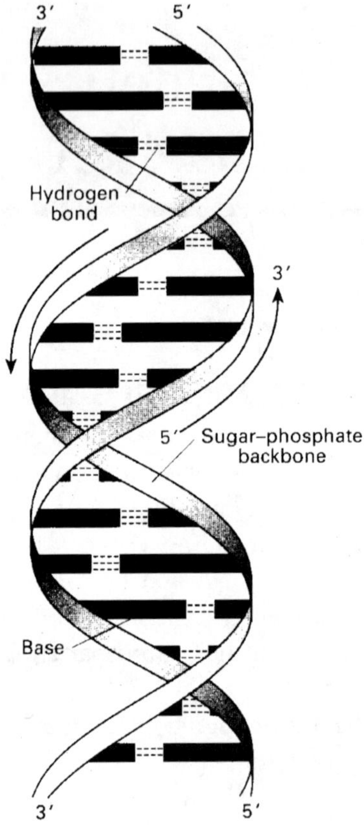

FIG. 6.1: DNA molecule -the basic tool for genetic studies.

THE GENE

The term coined by Johannsen (1909) for the unit of heredity, that is, the hypothetical entity which determines the development of a particular character. The word gene was derived from De Vries's term pangen, itself a derivative of the word pangenesis which Darwin (1868) had coined. At one time it was assumed that the hereditary units defined by mutation, recombination, and function were the same, but with the discovery that they are not, the term gene now applied to the unit of unction, that is the cistron.

Gene, Environment and Behaviour

Behavioural traits are the result of an interaction between the genetic programme and the environment. All behaviour patterns have both, a genetic and an environmental component. Without genotype there could be no behaviour. The genetic blueprint contains instructions that interact between genotype and environment and are the basis for construction, proliferation and specialization of cells. Genetic information is worthless if it cannot acquire the materials with which to build enzymes, which in turn act on other environmentally acquired substances to form tissues, nervous system, and a complete animal with behavioural capabilities.

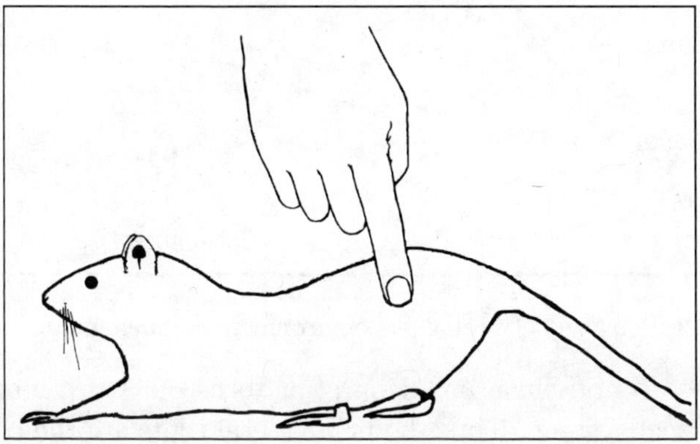

FIG. 6.2: A sexual difference in behaviour. Female rats, but not males, adopt a specific pre-copulatory position in response to pressure on the flank when they are sexually receptive.

The genes are the blue prints for the assembly and regulation of proteins, which are the building block of our bodies. Each gene codes for a specific sequence of amino acids that the body assembles to form a protein. If the smallest part of this chain is altered, the entire protein can. The genes do not magically blossom into behaviour. They are the stretches of chemical bonds that code for protein production or regulate the activity of other genes. Therefore, all aspects of animal behaviour as well as our bones are a part of this process. Proteins do not directly cause behaviour. For example one gene (G2) codes for a particular protein (P2), that protein does not cause a particular type of behaviour. Proteins interact with other physiological intermediateries (I2), which may be other proteins, such as endocrine secretions or neurotransmitter, or any other proteins. Environmental factors (E2) are also involved. These influences can ultimately and indirectly influence behaviour in certain direction. Therefore, the genes do not directly cause behaviour but work indirectly via physiological systems.

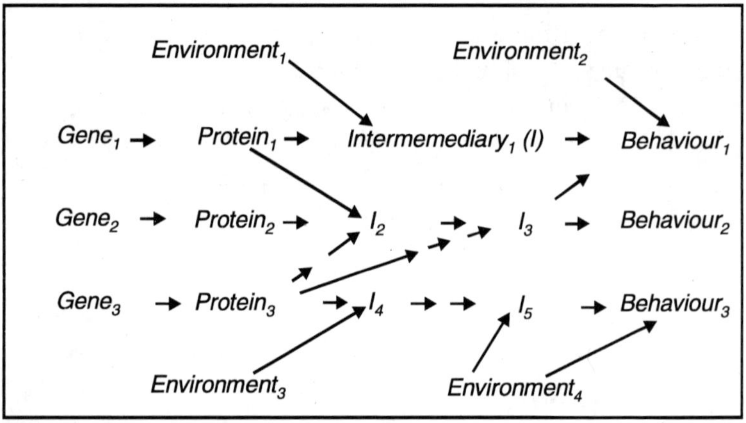

FIG. 6.3: Relation between gene, environment and behaviour.

Genes do not cause behavioural patterns but work indirectly via physiological systems. Thus the behavioural traits are the result of an interaction between genetic program and the environment. All behaviour must have genetic and environmental components.

Genes and Behaviour: The Connection

The connection between genes and behaviour is indirect and complex and therefore not easy to envisage, however, the connection exists and it is important on both the proximate and ultimate levels.

For understanding proximate mechanisms of an individual's ability to behave, it is necessary understand the relation between an individual's genetic information and the development of the various system (neural, hormonal, muscular) that make behaviour possible. At the ultimate level, evolutionary change in behaviour cannot occur unless there are hereditary difference among individual that affect their behaviour and reproductive success. As a result, demonstrating that genetic differences can be responsible for behavioural differences among individuals is essential if we are to have confidence that behaviour can evolve.

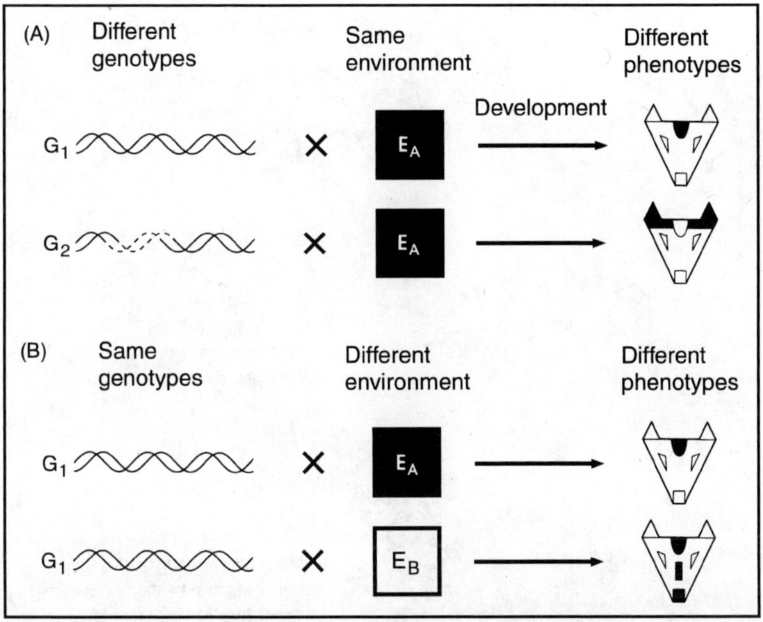

FIG. 6.4: What causes individuals to differ?. The development of an organism's trait (its phenotype) depends on the interaction between genetic information and environmentally supplied materials. Differences between individuals in either **(A)** their genes or **(B)** their environments can lead to the development of different phenotypes.

The hypothesis of behavioural differences between individuals are caused by differences in the genetic information that they possess, because behavioural differences in an individual developed in different environments. The behavioural development involves an interaction between an individual's **genetype** (genetic makeup) and the environment in which it exists to produce that individual's phenotype (its observable characteristics).

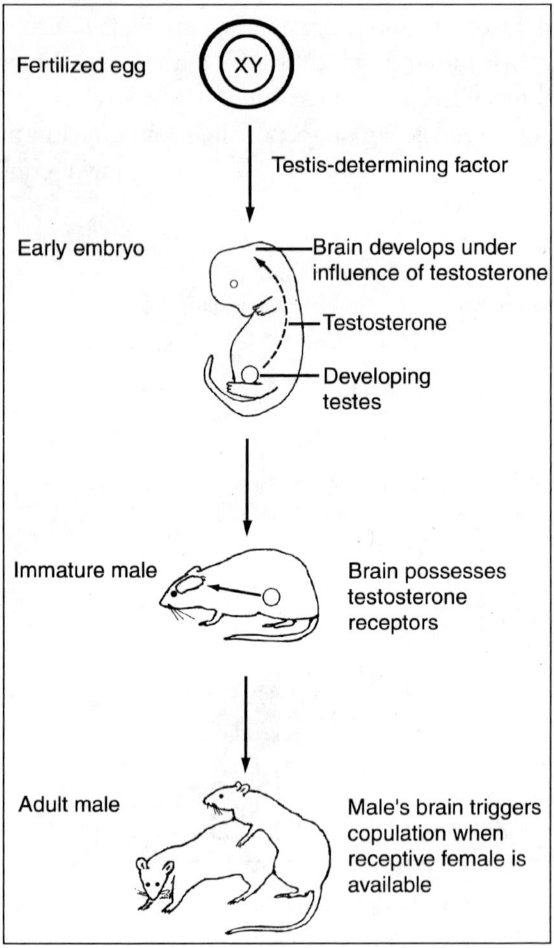

FIG. 6.5: Development of male copulatory behaviour in the laboratory rat is dependent upon genetic information carried by the Y chromosome and upon various environmental influences, including hormones present in the developing embryo.

To understand the above hypothesis, studies on galah chicks raised by pink cockatoo foster parents were conducted. Most galahs produce the same distinctive galah contact call, but these few (crossfostered) individuals do not. In this case, the behavioural difference between the two kinds of galahs almost certainly stems form the difference in the acoustical and social experiences of the birds and not from any genetic difference between them. All the galahs that produce pink cockatoo contact calls have been reared by pink cockatoos; all those that produce galah contact calls have been reared by galahs. There is no reason to suppose that those baby galahs that happen by pure chance to be adopted by pink cockatoos differ genetically form the rest of their species in ways linked to the development of contact signals. Therefore, one can rule out the hypothesis that this particular behavioural difference stems from different hereditary influences on development.

Genetic Difference and Behavioural Differences

The behavioural differences between members of two **funnel web spider** populations have been studied. Individuals found in a relatively lush streamside habitat in Arizona are slow to respond to prey that land on their webs, whereas spider of the same species that happen to live in the dry desert grasslands in neighboring New Mexico sprint out onto the web apron as soon as a prey appears.

The differences between spiders in the speed with which they attack might stem purely form environmental differences.

For example, the streamside spider might be less hungry than those living in the harsher, drier grasslands. Further studies were conducted by Ann Hedrick and Susan Reichert. They took spiders from both areas into the lab and reared a new generation to maturity under identical conditions. They observed the following observations:

The offspring of the streamside parents still were slow to respond to prey, taking about a minute on average to come after a cricket placed on the web apron.

The offspring of grassland parents reacted in less than three seconds on average, even though they had received just as much food as the laboratory descendants of streamside spiders.

The above results negate the environmental differences hypothesis while supporting the view that genetic differences are responsible for the different speeds of attack exhibited by individuals from the two areas.

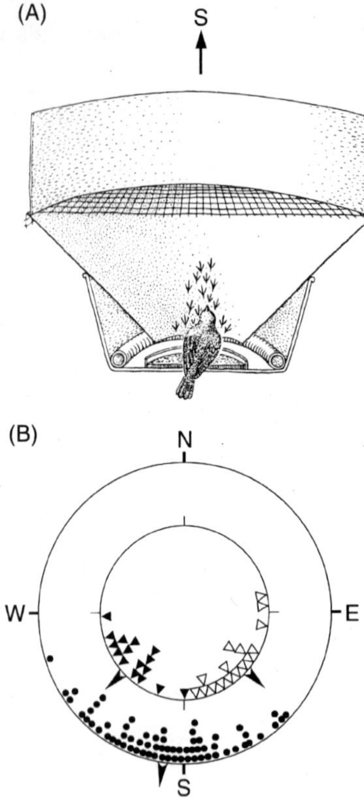

FIG. 6.6: Test for differences hypothesis. **(A)** A funnel cage of the sort used to determine the migratory orientation of captive birds. The cage is shown cut in half. The bird is able to see the night sky through the wire mesh ceiling in the cage, and as it jumps from the floor of the cage onto the surface of the funnel, it leaves marks on the paper covering the funnel. The marks permit the measurement of the bird's preferred direction ((due south in this example) as it attempts to migrate. **(B)** The inner ring of the circle diagram shows the directions taken by southwest-ward-orienting birds (dark triangles) and southeast-ward-orienting birds (open triangles) in funnel cage. The outer ring shows the direction taken by hybrids blackcaps (with one southeastward- and one southwestward-orienting parent), which was intermediate to that of their parents' respective groups (black circles). The large arrows show the mean direction taken by each of the groups of birds. (Helbig, A. J., 1991).

The difference between the members of the two populations may be due to the intensity of bird predation on funnel web spiders, which is much higher in the streamside habitat than in the grasslands. Given a high predation risk, streamside spiders that exercise caution in leaving their safe retreat to venture out after a struggling prey may live longer and reproduce more than those that exhibit less caution.

Similar to the behavioural difference between members of different funnel web spider populations, the behaviour of blackcap warblers also varies form region to region.

Blackcaps (bird) breeds in Germany and migrate to a great distances twice a year. They move between Europe to Africa via Spain in the spring and fall, but there are nonmigratory blackcaps as well, including those living in Cape Verde, an archipelago off the west coast of Africa, where they stay year-round.

The hypothesis of genetic differences between German and Cape Verde blackcaps was studied by Peter Berthold and colleagues based on their different migratory tendencies. They predicted that birds with one German and one Cape Verdean parent would exhibit a different migratory pattern than either parent. This prediction was based on the assumption that *there is at least one gene in blackcaps whose presence affects the migratory tendency of individuals*.

The simplest case would require a single gene that we might call *M*, which comes in two forms, or alleles, *M1* and M2. The German birds might possess the genotype *M1/M1* and the Cape Verdean birds might possess the genotype *M2/M2* (Birds and most other animals have two copies of each gene in their genotypes, one donated by the individual's mother in her egg and the other coming from the father in his sperm).

If the behavioural differences between the parents with respect to migratory behaviour stem form their genetic differences, then the *hybrids* should receive distinctive alleles form each parent, making them genetically intermediate (if we consider the simplest one-gene case, their genotype with respect to the *M* gene would be *M1/M2*). If the hybrids' migratory behaviour fell between that of their two parents, that result would be consistent with the genetic hypothesis.

Berthold tested this hypothesis. He first captured birds form Germany and Cape Verde, then paired German males with Cape Verdean females and *vice versa* in laboratory and produced *hybrid* offspring. He tested migratory behaviour in the parent birds and the hybrids. He did so by placing the blackcaps in special cages with electronically activated perches that record whenever a bird lands upon them. During the fall migratory period, caged German blackcaps jumped back and forth between perches every night for many weeks, averaging about 370 hours of migratory restlessness. During this same period, Cape Verde birds slept quietly through the night without exhibiting any restlessness. As expected, hybrid blackcap offspring showed a reduced migratory tendency compared with their German parent but much more migratory activity than their Cape Verdean parent. They averaged about 260 hours of nighttime hopping, a result that supports the hypothesis that the hereditary makeup of a blackcap influences its tendency to migrate.

- **Genetics and Flight path in Blackcap:** Andreas Helbig examined hereditary differences of birds form two different migratory populations in regard to flight paths during migration.
- **German blackcaps** fly in a southwesterly direction to Spain and then on to Africa.
- **Austrian blackcaps** fly in direction of southeast across Turkey to Lebanon and Israel before turning due south to Ethiopia and Kenya.

Behavioural Differences based on Single-Gene Differences

Behavioural differences between individuals living in different populations with genetic differences within a single population have been studied in geneticist's favorite insect, the fruit fly *Drosophila*.

Some fruit fly larvae (called rovers) are highly **active** when feeding on yeast cells while others (called sitters) are not. Marie Sokolowski and her associates used genetic techniques to create two genetically uniform strains: Members of one strain invariably exhibited the rover phenotype, traveling about four times as great a distance on a yeast-coated Petri dish during a 5 minute test than members of the sitter strain. When adults of the two strains were allowed to reproduce together, they created offspring (the F1 generation) all of which were rovers during the larval phase. When these larvae matured, they interbred, creating an F2 generation with a ratio of rovers to sitters of 3:1. The Mendelian genetics supports the hypothesis that rovers carry one or two copies of the **dominant form** of a gene affecting larval foraging behaviour, whereas sitters have two copies of the **recessive form** of this gene. So here is a case in which the difference between the two behavioural types stems from a difference in the information contained in a single gene, now known to be located on the second of the four chromosomes that fruit flies possess. The two behavioural types occur with in population of *Drosophila melanogaster* around the world; the genetic differences may be maintained because of natural variation in microhabitats as well as greater parasite pressure on the more conspicuous rover larvae.

Many other single-gene effects have been identified in fruit flies, although most of these have not been found in natural populations. Instead, researchers have first exposed populations of adult flies to conditions that cause genetic mutations (which are generally damaging), then scanned for behavioural oddities among the flies, before finally performing the necessary breeding experiments. Some mutant alleles have been named to reflect their behavioural consequences, among them stuck (males with the mutant gene fail to dismount after the normal 20 minutes of copulation), coitus interruptus (males with the allele disengage after just 10, not 20, minutes of copulating), and bang-sensitive. Other mutant alleles affect the daily activity pattern of fruit flies, which normally follow a schedule that repeats every 24 hours.

Using the techniques of molecular genetics, two research teams have shown that each of the mutant alleles differs form the typical, or wildtype period gene (*per+*) by just one pair of nucleotides in a chain of DNA composed of more than 3500 such pairs. For the *per°* form of the gene, the single alteration in the DNA molecule results in the production of a protein chain that contains about 400 amino acids, instead of the 1200 appearing in the wild-type protein. This mutation causes the cell's machinery to stop *reading* the gene's information prematurely.

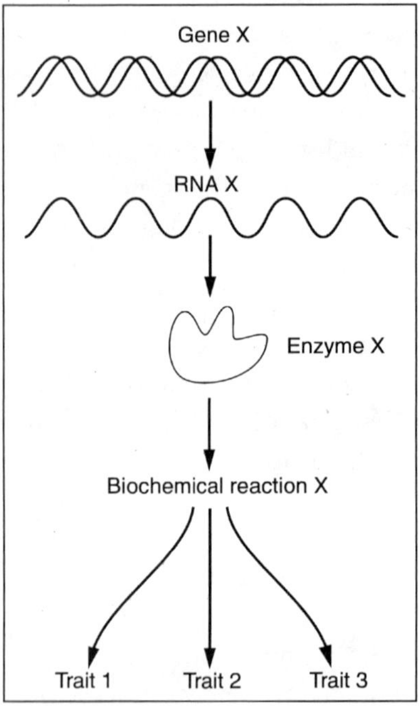

FIG. 6.7: Pleiotropy. A gene may have multiple effects on the development of an individual (*e.g.*, gene X codes for RNA molecule, which codes for an enzyme which catalyzes a particular biochemical reaction contributing to the development of several different traits).

The information contained in the *pers* and *prel* alleles is used by the fly's cells to make a protein chain with the full 1200 amino acids. However, the mutant chains differ from the wild-type protein by a single amino acid (a different substitution for each mutation). Even this small alteration causes dramatic behavioural differences in the activity pattern of the flies.

The *per* gene does more than influence the daily activity cycles of fruit flies, this phenomenon called **pleiotropy**. The gene also affects the courtship song of male flies, which they produce by vibrating their wings to produce one pulse of sound after another in a long chain of pulses. (Fig. 6.7).

Many genes are involved in determination of development of a single character is **polygeny**. When a single-gene effect does occur, it does not mean that there is one gene for the courtship song of a fruit fly, another for the activity cycle, and still another for feeding behaviour. Single-gene effects on behaviour occur because one gene's product somehow influences a complex developmental process that requires the regulated interaction of dozens or thousands of genes. A mutant allele's effects may be analogous to giving a worker on a long assembly line an improper tool.

Testing the Genetic Difference Hypothesis: Twin Studies

How genes influence the development of human behaviour is a controversial matter. Human twins have behavioural differences, and may be due to genetic differences.

Hereditary differences are found between **fraternal twins**, but not between **identical twins**. The identical twins share the same genotype.

Identical (**monozygotic**) twins are derived from the very same fertilized egg, which divides and gives rise to two genetically identical embryos.

Fraternal (**dizygotic**) twins are produced form two different fertilized eggs with different hereditary information. Fraternal twins are no more similar genetically than any other pair of siblings; they share 50 per cent of their genes in common on average.

Behavioural development is influenced not only by the genes of an individual inherits but it is also dependent on his/her surrounding environment and experiences. These factors may be more similar for identical than for fraternal twins, perhaps because parents and other people treat identical twins especially alike because of their nearly identical appearance. The shared environmental influence may be the reason when identical twins behave in similar manner.

Genetic Difference and IQ Differences

Identical twins are also more similar than fraternal twins in their scores on IQ tests (Table 6.1). When identical twins are reared together, the correlation between their scores is usually between 0.5 and 0.9. If the IQ scores of pairs of identical twins were always exactly the same, the correlation would be 1.0. If the correlation were zero, the score of one twin would be utterly useless as a predictor of the score of the other. As it turns out, if one twin has an IQ of 115, the odds are excellent that the other will be close to this score (say, between 110 and 120), and there is only a very small chance that the other twin would score 95 or 135.

A close IQ similarity is found between identical twins reared apart, which is that their adoptive homes were more similar than those selected for fraternal twins that were reared apart irrespective to adoptive home environment, *e.g.*, socioeconomic status, education level of both adoptive parents, intellectual orientation of the household. Home environments channel the intellectual development of the separated identical twins along similar lines, leading ultimately to very similar IQ scores.

TABLE 6.1: Familial correlations for IQ scores: Predicted versus actual correlations

Category	Predicted Correlation*	Number of Studies	Actual median correlation
Identical twins reared together	1.00	34	0.85
Identical twins reared apart	1.00	3	0.67
Fraternal twins reared together	0.50	41	0.58
Siblings reared apart	0.50	69	0.45
Non biological sibling pairs	0.00	5	0.29
Parent-biological child	0.50	32	0.39
Parent-adopted child	0.00	6	0.18

*Predicted correlations are based on the assumption that the differences between individuals are solely due to genetic differences between them.
Source: Bouchard and McGue [1981).

Why IQ is Not Genetically Determined

The fact that the heritability of IQ scores is substantial is sometimes interpreted to mean that intelligence is "genetically determined."

Leaving aside the serious problems of establishing the relation between IQ and intelligence (about which much ink has been spilt), this interpretation is incorrect. The results of the familial comparisons within population outlined above show just one thing: genetic differences among the people studied to date contribute greatly to the differences in the score they achieved on IQ tests.

The above conclusion does not mean that IQ is *genetic* or *genetically determined*, or *inherited* and doed not require environmental influences for its development. Taking IQ tests requires. A brain is the product of a breath takingly complex interaction between the genetic information in a fertilized egg and the environment. It includes the nongenetic materials in the egg's surroundings. These materials are utilized by the growing embryo and are absolutely essential for the construction of brain tissue. Moreover, as the brain develops and begins to generate electric activity and receive messages form outlying sensory receptors linked to it, it is creating and receiving "experiences" that are vital for its further development.

If environmental differences did not contribute to the development of differences between people, then the correlation between the IQs of identical twins would be expected to be 1.0; but it is less than 1.0. Identical twins are not behaviourally identical because their development is shaped by somewhat different environments. Each twin experiences slightly different surroundings in the womb, each consumes somewhat different foods, and each has its won unique set of social interactions (this is especially true of twins separated early in life).

The Response to Selection

The various techniques described thus far have illustrated how it is possible to test the hypothesis that behavioural differences between individuals, including member of our own species, arise because the individuals differ genetically. The behavioural trait also respond to selection and becomes more common in a population through selective breeding.

Geneticists have conducted experiments on artificial selection on fruit flies, laboratory mice and rats. The direction of evolution on these experiments is under the control of persons who allow some individuals with a certain attribute to breed (raising their fitness) while preventing others with a different form of the trait of interest from breeding (reducing their fitness to zero). If there is a genetic basis for difference between the two categories of individuals, then the selective breeding regime should change the genetic makeup of the experimental population, leading to a group dominated by individuals with the fitness-promoting attribute. However, if there is no genetic basis for a difference between individuals, then selection of certain types cannot cause evolutionary change within the population, because those individuals that reproduce do not pass on a distinctive allele or alleles to their offspring, which, therefore, cannot inherit the genetic basis for a particular attribute. Because artificial selection experiments mimic the action of natural selection, they have great significance for person interested in the possibility of behavioural evolution under natural conditions.

Carol Lynch conducted experiments with house mice, which build nests of soft grasses and other plant material in nature. Under laboratory conditions these mice happily accept cotton as ideal for their nests. The amount of cotton a mouse collects can be quantified as the number of grams pulled into a nest cage over a 4-day period. In the starting generation in Lynch's experiment, individuals moved between 13 and 18 grams of cotton into their cages from an external cotton supply.

Lynch tried to develop three lines:

1. *High line* by interbreeding males and females that collected a relatively large amount of cotton.
2. *Low line* by crossing males and females that gathered relatively little cotton.
3. *Control line* by crossing males and females chosen at random from the population.

The offspring so produced were reared under conditions identical to those of their parents, eliminating environmental variation as a variable that might affect their behaviour. When the offspring of the three groups became adults and were examined with respect to the amount of nest material they collected in 4 days. The most avid collectors in the *high line* were permitted to breed, creating a second selected generation, as were the least eager cotton collectors in the low line.

Lynch repeated these procedures over 15 generation, with the eventual result as follows:

- *High line* mice gathered about 40 grams of cotton for their nests on average.
- *Low line* mice only brought in 5 grams on average. The 15th generation control mice performed at about the same level as their ancestors (about 15 grams).

These observations offer evidence that genetic differences occur among the mice in the original population, differences related to nest building. These results enabled Lynch to create evolutionary change in the laboratory through selective breeding.

Fundamentally similar results have been achieved in selection experiments with many other animals like male fruit flies and crickets.

EFFECTS OF GENES ON PHYSIOLOGICAL BASES OF BEHAVIOUR

Geneticists have established that some behavioural differences between the members of a species are caused by genetic differences. But just how can possession of a specific allele or alleles influence nest building or calling duration or IQ scores or daily activity cycles?

Gene does not make a trait; typically it codes for a specific kind of ribonucleic acid that in turn carries the information needed to construct a particular protein.

For example, the *amy* gene (responsible for amylase synthesis) contains information for making a protein called amylase. This salivary enzyme catalyzes the reaction that breaks down large complex molecules of glycogen into its sugar subunits. About 50,000 genes besides the *amy* gene and most of which code for proteins, the large majority of which are enzymes. In other words, we have the information needed to make about 50,000 different enzymes that facilitate about 50,000 different biochemical reactions. Each type of reaction plays some role in the operation of our bodies; some biochemical reactions have behavioural consequences for us.

There is a definite relationship between the enzymatic product of a gene and psychiatric disorders, for example monoamine oxidase (MAO). The activity of this enzyme varies over a broad range among individuals. Very high and very low activity levels characterize particular families and are presumably related to the presence of specific alleles. In families with low MAO levels, the incidence of suicide and attempted suicide is eight times that of families who members have high MAO levels.

Genes and Nervous Systems

Comparative physiological studies of mutant and normal individuals are also being pursued with animals that have nervous systems. For example, *Drosophila* fruit flies with the Shaker allele continue to move their legs rhythmically, even when anesthetized, unlike normal flies. This allele causes nerve cells to develop in ways that affect their permeability to potassium ions. As a result the cells fire more readily than normal cells, affecting eh mutant fly's locomotion.

Genes and Grater Snake Behaviour

At the proximate level, an individual's genetic makeup affects the enzymes its cells can produce. The enzymes present in an individual influence the rates at which certain biochemical reactions occur, regulating how cells develop and function and thereby affecting the cellular basis for particular behavioural abilities. The alleles with reproduction-enhancing information spread through populations and evolution of this sort may occurr in nature (?).

Arnold worked with a garter snake, *Thamnophis elegans*. This snake is found over much of western North America in a wide variety of habitats, including both foggy, wet coastal California and the drier, elevated, inland areas of that state. There are marked differences in the diets of snakes living in the two areas (referred to hereafter as *coastal* and *inland*). There is a difference in the feeding behaviour of coastal and inland garter snakes.

Arnold was interested to know any genetic differences between them. He took pregnant female snakes form the two populations into the laboratory, where they were held under identical conditions. When the females gave birth a litter of babies (garter snakes produce live young rather than laying eggs), each baby was placed in a separate cage away form its littermates and its mother to remove these possible environmental influences on its behaviour. Some days later Arnold offered each baby snake a chance to eat a small chunk of freshly thawed banana slug by placing it on the floor of the young snake's cage. Naïve young coastal snakes usually ate all the slug hors d'oeuvres they received; the inland snakes usually did not. In both populations, slug-refusing snakes did not even make contact with the slug food, but ignored it completely.

Arnold selected another group of isolated newborn snakes. This group had never fed on anything and offered them a chance to respond to the odors of different prey items. The newborn snakes flick their tongues and even attack cotton swabs, which were dipped in fluids from some species of prey (toad tadpole solution). By counting the number of tongue flicks that hit the swab during a 1-minute trial, Arnold measured the relative responsiveness of inexperienced baby snakes to different odors. (Snakes have an organ in the roof of the mouth that analyzes odors carried to it by the tongue. When the animal's tongue touches a source of chemicals, it carries some molecules back to this organ, which plays a role in prey recognition).

Populations of inland and coastal snakes reacted about the same to swabs dipped in **toad tadpole solution** (a prey of both groups), but behaved very differently towards swabs daubed with slug scent. Within each group there was some variation in response, but most inland snakes ignored the slug odor, whereas most coastal snakes responded strongly to it. Because all the young snakes had experienced the same environments, the differences in their willingness to eat slugs and to tongue-flick in reaction to slug odor had to have been caused by genetic differences among them.

On the basis of tongue-flick scores of siblings, Arnold determined that within each population only about 17 per cent of the differences in *chemoreceptive responsiveness* to slug odor stemmed from genetic differences among individuals. The low heritability of tongue-flicking within the coastal or the inland population means simply that most of what little **phenotypic variation** exists within each population. It is caused by subtle environmental variables. This makes sense if past selection has eliminated much of the genetic variation that affected the development of feeding behaviour in coastal snakes and in inland snakes as well.

If the feeding differences between the two populations arise because most coastal snakes having different allele or alleles than most inland snakes, then crossing adults from the two areas should generate a great deal of variation in the resulting group of *hybrid offspring*, more variation than is found in either parental population.

Arnold conducted that the differences between populations have a strong genetic component and suggested evolutionary basis for these differences. He further suggested that:

The geographic difference in the feeding behaviour of the snakes which may be due to their proximate genetic basis (different alleles predominate in the two populations).

The proximate physiological basis (the chemoreceptors that detect certain molecules associated with both slugs and leeches are more prevalent in coastal populations).

Their ultimate ecological an evolutionary basis (inland snakes must contend with potentially dangerous leeches whereas coastal snakes are exposed on to edible slugs.

Arnold's study of snake behaviour genetics provides a model of how to integrate proximate and ultimate levels if analysis in behavioural research.

CHAPTER 7

Brain, Nerve Cells and Behaviour

The behaviour patterns we observe in the animals are adaptive. They respond to appropriate stimuli in an effective manner and feed themselves, find shelter, mate and display different behaviour patterns. For the display of behaviour patterns, animal perceive stimuli by receptors and transmit it to various body parts and to effect response through effectors, which make the nervous system. Along with the endocrine system, nervous system coordinates and integrate the activities of various parts of the body. This makes possible the integrated control of internal environment, which is called homeostasis. The nervous system brings quick coordination by means of nerves where as the endocrine system does so by secreting hormones.

Neural mechanisms constitute a proximate cause for behaviour. Understanding how nerve cells operate, singly and in groups, provides a basis for understanding how animals perceive and react to their environment. Different species have different neural mechanisms and therefore perceive different things and behave differently as well. The specialized nature of animal nervous systems is apparent in feature-specialized detector neurons, cells that play key roles in discriminating perceptions. Stimulus filtering is a universal attribute of feature detection and perception. The design of an animal's receptors limits what information the receptors can collect and relay for further processing.

A knowledge of natural history can help researchers identify key problems confronting a species and thereby provide clues as to what special proximate mechanisms the members of that species are likely to possess. The many differences among species in the design and operation of nervous systems reflect the effects of evolution. Proximate neural mechanisms exist because they provide animals with the ability to detect and respond to environmental cues in ways that advance individual reproductive success.

BRAIN: STRUCTURE

The vertebrate brain is divisible into prosencehalen, mesencephalon and rhombencephalon which appear early in the embryonic development of vertebrates as three primary vesicles. Each of these three regions of the brain are further sub divided so that the typical vertebrate brain has five divisions. The prosencephalon have, secondary brain vesicles called telencephalon and diencephalon. The mesencephalon has a cavity called cerbral aqueduct. The rhombencephalon has metencephalon and myelencephalon as secondary vesicles. All these divisions have specialized structures and each structure makes its own contribution to the functioning. The brain has sensory and motor structures with great association area between them.

Myllencephalon

It is the hindmost part of the brain, its derivative is medulla oblongata which is an extension of the spinal cord into the brain. It contains the continuation of the sensory and motor columns of the spinal cord. It has its own dorsal and its own ventral sensory and motor nerves entering and leaving it. It is the centre for the autonomic reflex control of circulation, heart and lungs.

Metencephalon

It includes pons and cerebellum. Pons takes part in the regulation of respiration and other vital regulations. The cerebullum is the complex structure serving in the coordination of movements and maintenance of posture, tone and equilibrium. The degree and extent of movements are determined by cerebellar feedback control. The cerebellum has cerebellar hemispheres. It receives fibres from the sensory system.

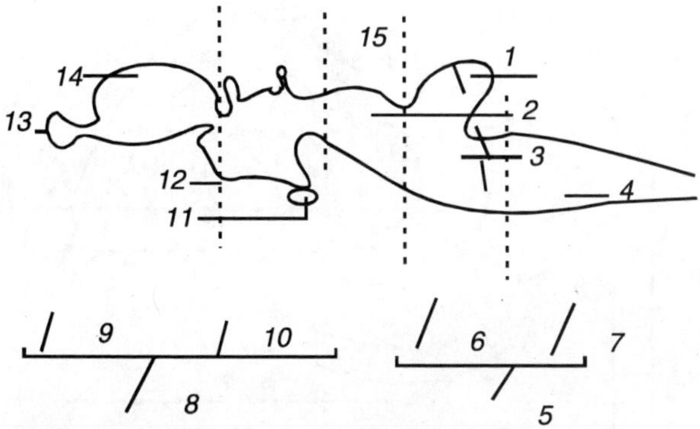

1. Cerebellum *2. Tectum*
3. Pons *4. Medulla Ooblongata*
5. Rhomben Cephalon *6. Metencephalon*
7. Myelencephalon *8. Prosencephalon*
9. Telencephalon *10. Diencephalon*
11. Pituitary *12. Optic Stalk*
13.Olfactory Bulb *14. Cerebral Hemisphere*
15. Mesencephalon

FIG. 7.1: Main divisions of vertebrate brain.

Mesencephalon

It includes cerebral peduncle and tectum. The latter is divisible into superior colliculus and inferior colliculus. The cerebral peduncle is divided into dorsal and ventral area.

Diencephalon

It is a part of fore brain in this the thalamus is located in dorsal region and hypothalamus beneath it. The thalamus serves as the relay station. From it, all types of impulses (except olfactory) are relayed to the cerbral cortex. Through the ascending reticular activating system, the thalamus is involved in wakefulness and alertness. The thalamus forms part of limbic system and plays a role in emotional behaviour. The thalamus has connections with the hypothalamus and so is associated with autonomic control of viscera. The hypothalamus is the main centre for controlling visceral activities.

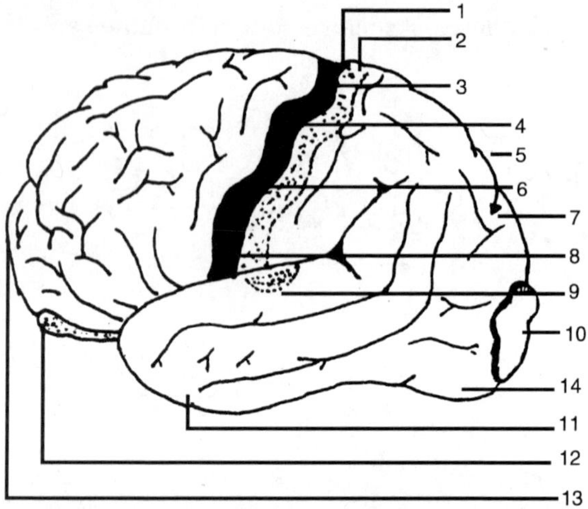

1. CENTRAL SULCUS
2. SOMATIC SENSORY AREA
3. LOWER LIMB AREA (MOTOR)
4. TRUNK AREA (MOTOR)
5. PARIETAL LOBE
6. UPPER LIMB AREA (MOTOR)
7. PARIETO OCCIPITAL SULCUS
8. HEAD AREA MORTOR
9. AUDITORY AREA
10. VISUAL AREA
11. TEMPORAL LOBE
12. ALFACTORY BULB
13. FRONTAL LOBE
14. OCCIPITAL LOBE

FIG. 7.2: Lateral view of mammalian brain showing cerebral hemisphere motor and sensory control areas.

Telencephalon

It includes cerebral cortex, corpus striatum and rhincephalon. The cortex receives projections of fibre from lower part of the brain by way of nuclei in the thalamus and it, in turn, sends efferent fibres back to the lower centres.

The projections are of two types, firstly those that come from the sense organs in the form of specific projections, every sensory event perceived is sent upto the cortex, so there are sensory areas on its surface. Secondly there are non specific projections in the cortex which come from reticular formation of mid and fore brain.

This reticular formation receives collaterals from all sensory fibres and serves to arouse the cortex. The efferent fibres leading from the cortex come from motor area, which control all muscles of body.

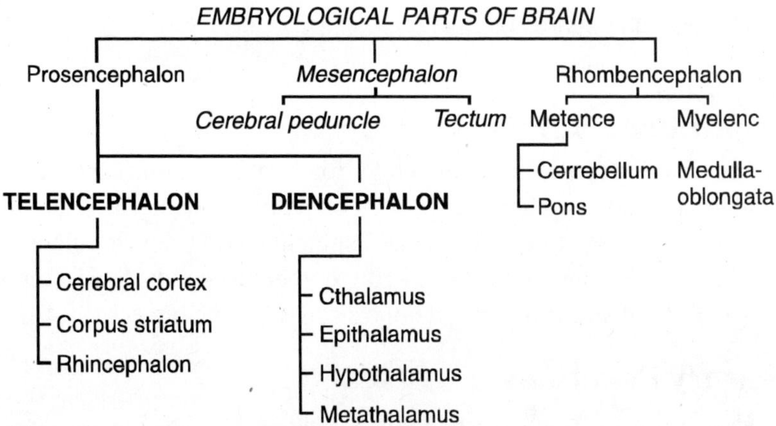

FIG. 7.3: Embryological parts of brain.

BRAIN-LESION				
Parietal lobe	⟶	Function Languaage Planned movement Spatial orientation	⟶	Lesion Defect in speaking
Frodntal	⟶	**Function** Emotional response Social behaviour	⟶	**Lesion** Antisocial behaviour Impaired memory
Occipital lobe	⟶	**Function** Analysis of vision	⟶	**Lesion** Visual agnosia
Temporal lobe	⟶	**Function** Auditory perception Speech, Olfaction	⟶	**Lesion** Poor memory Defective auditory perception

FUNCTIONS OF CEREBRAL CORTEX

Motor Functions

- Regulation of tone, posture and equilibrium
- Regulation of automatic and associated acts.
- Control of autonomic nervous system.
- Inhibitory control over lower motor centres.

- Control of eye movements
- Control of speech

Conditioned Reflex

The cerebral cortex is responsible for the formation of reflexes through the development of new connections with different sub cortical centres. For the establishment and development of conditioned response or reflex through specific conditioned stimuli, special cortical and sub cortical centres are responsible.

Sensory Functions

- Perception of touch, pain, heat and cold.
- There are audio-sensory centres which are responsible for pitch and loudness.
- Hippocampl gyrus is responsible for olfactory perception.
- Occipital lobe perceives all visual-impulses
- The speech centres are located in temporal lobe.

Intellectual Functions

Cerebral cortex is responsible for memory intelligence, judgment and planning. There are association area (psychic area) responsible for these functions.

Hypothalamus and Behaviour

E.G. Walsh (1964) in his book *Physiology of Nervous System*, mentioned that the hypothalamus which is a small centre in the brain, plays a dominant role in functional architecture of the body. It is difficult to think of any function of the body that is not dependent directly or indirectly upon the hypothalamus. There are nuclei in the hypothalamus but they are not so well defined as in the thalamus. There are several fibre tracts entering and leaving and these put the hypothalamus into connection with the cerebral hemisphere and also with the posterior parts of the brain. The important feature of hypothalamus is its intimate connection with the pituitary gland. This endocrine gland, which controls the whole hormonal system of the body, develops from the fusion of down growth of the embryonic hypothalamus, with an upgrowth from the roof of embryonic mouth cavity. The pituitary which joins it to the hypothalamus has nerves and blood vessels.

Structure

Hypothalamus consists of the following nuclear masses:

A. **Anterior group:** They are in relation with optic chiasma. (i) medial preoptic nucleus (ii) lateral re-optic nucleus (iii) supra optic nucleus (iv) supra chiasmatic nucleus (v) paraventricular nucleus (vi) anterior thalamic nucleus

B. **Middle group:** They are situated in close relation with infundibum. (i) ventromedial hypothalamic nucleus (ii) dorsomedial hypothalamic nucleus (iii) Lateral hypothlamic nucleus (iv) posterior hypothalamic nucleus (v) arcuate nucleus.

Posterior Group

They are in close relation with the third ventricle: (i) nucleus intercalatus (ii) pre-mammillary nucleus (iii) supra mammillary nucleus (iv) medial mammillary nucleus (v) lateral mammillary nucleus.

The hypothalamic nuclei receives a number of projections from different parts of the brain. Free interconnections also present between hypothalamic nuclei.

Functions of Hypothalamus

Hypothalamus has a regulatory influence on the autonomic nervous system

1. **Effect on parasympathetic activity:** The parasympathetic centre lies in the anterior part of the hypothalamus. Its stimulation causes slowing of heart rate, vasodilation, lowering of blood pressure, salivation, increased peristalsis and contraction of urinary bladder.

   The sympathetic centre lies in the posterior portion of hypothalamus. Its stimulation results in increased heart rate, increased blood pressure, and inhibition of peristalsis.

   Regulation of body temperature by anterior and posterior nuclei.

2. **Role in sexual behaviour:** Day, in 1941 observed that lesion on the ventral part of hypothalamus produces changes in sexual behaviour in male pigs towards female. Bard in 1940 has shown that lesion of the caudal part of the hypothalamus causes inhibition of oestrous cycle in animals.

   Stimulation of posterior hypothalamus by weak current causes prolonged sleep.

   Lesion in supramammillary area in animals causes loss of voluntary movements.

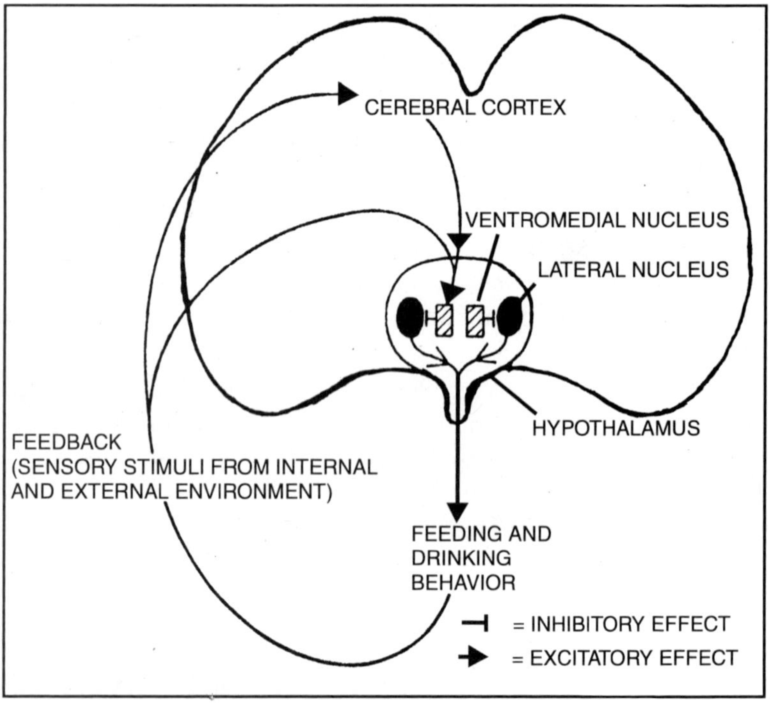

FIG. 7.4: Hypothalmic structures in the vertical cross section of Mammallian brain, showing their role in feeding and drinking. The sensory feedback may inhibit these behaviour pattern by activating the ventromedial nuclei, which inturn inhibit the lateral nuclei.

3. **Hypothalamus and Reticular system:** Hypothalamus is related to wakefulness through its connection with the reticular arousal system.

Hypothalamus regulates homeostasis, which affect the different behaviour patterns.

4. Regulation of eating and drinking behaviour: The hypothalamic nuclei in the tuberal region are concerned with the feeding. The "satiety centre"is identified in ventromedial nucleus and a feeding centre in the lateral nuclei. These centres are influenced by the glucose level in the blood. A lesion of the former results in excessive food intake, while the latter results in loss of appetite. The thirst centre is also identified in lateral hypothalamic nucleus.
5. **Hypothalamus and pituitary gland:** It has nervous connection with the posterior lobe and a vascular connection with the anterior lobe of the pituitary gland. By virtue of these connections it influences the secretion of this gland and through it the other endocrine gland.
6. **Hypothalamus and Limbic system:** It forms an important part of the limbic system of the brain. Elementary drives or motivation and visceral functions are associated with them.
7. **Hypothalamus and cyclic behaviour:** Certain functions of the body show cyclic pattern of activity in the 24 hours of a day. The hypothalamus control the cyclic activities and is said to function biological clock.
8. **Hypothalaamus and emotional behaviour:** Its connection with prefrontal cortex and thalamus plays role in the integration of visceral and somatic activities, feeling, mood and emotional behaviour.

Hypothalamic Nuclei and their Role

1. **Anterior Nuclei:** It regulate body temperature during heat by sweating and vasodilation.
2. **Posterior Nuclei:** It regulate body temperature during cold by shivering, vasoconstriction and epinephrine secretion.
3. **Median part of ventromedial nucleus:** Controlling effect on the feeding centre.
4. **Para ventricular nucleus:** Controlling effect on drinking
5. **Supra mammillary area:** Control of voluntrary movements
6. **Ventromedial nucleus:** Neuro endocrine control.

7. **Arcuate nucleus:** Neuro endocrine control.
8. **Posterior hypothalamic area:** Controlling effect on sleep, wakefulness.
9. **Ventral hypothalamic Area:** Sexual behaviour.

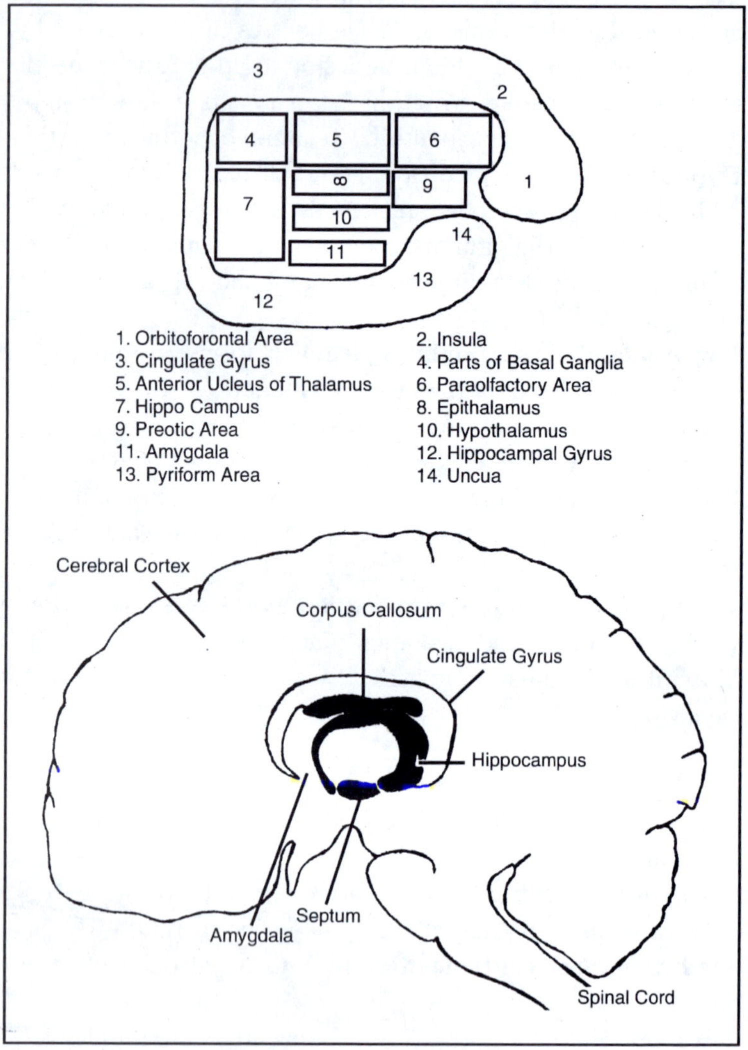

FIG. 7.5: (a – above) Limbic system, **(b - below)** Limbic system and its components in vertical section of Mammalian brain.

LIMBIC SYSTEM

It includes all limbic lobes of the cerbrum and the associated Structure II. subcortical nuclei such as the amygdaloid complex, sptal nuclei, hypothalamus, epithalamus, anterior thalamic nuclei, parts of basal ganglia and the midbrain reticular formation. It also includes other parts of the brain which are concerned with basic emotional drives.

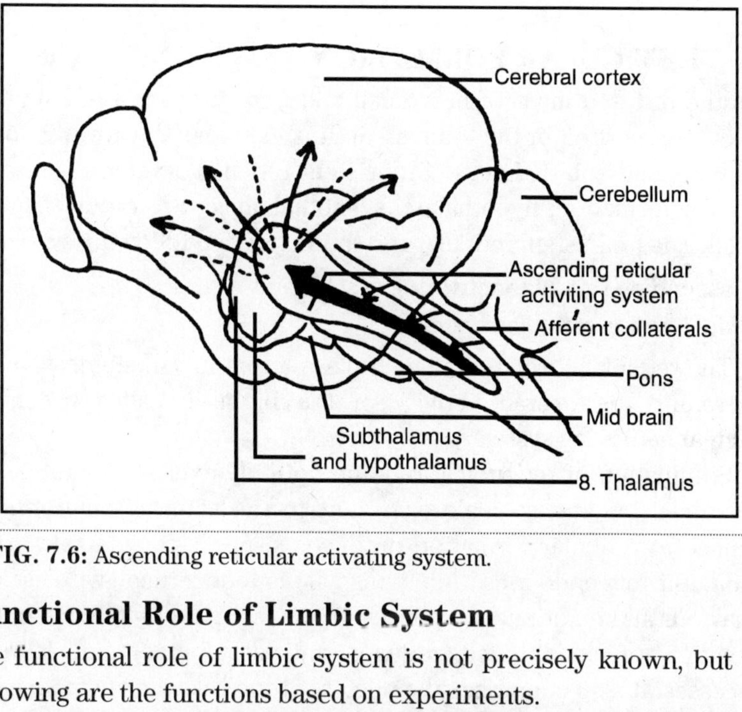

FIG. 7.6: Ascending reticular activating system.

Functional Role of Limbic System

The functional role of limbic system is not precisely known, but the following are the functions based on experiments.

Limbic system and behavioural responses: It is responsible for emotional reaction. The bilateral removal of temporal lobes (which include hippocampus and amygdaloid) in monkeys, is followed by an attitude of indifference and total loss of emotional response even of a basic nature such as fear threat, defence reaction. Some animals exhibit hyper sexual or perverted sexual behaviour.

1. This system is concerned with biological rhythms (cyclic behaviour), motivation and endocrine changes.

2. It integrates olfactory, visceral and somatic impulses reaching the brain.
3. It controls visceral functions associated with emotions. There are mediated through hypothalamus.
4. The bilateral removal of hippocampal structures in animals is followed by disturbance of shortterm memory.
5. Stimulation of amygdaloid nucleus may act as reward because pleasurable sensation is felt by the animal during stimulation.

RETICULAR FORMATION AND BEHAVIOUR

It is the diffused mass of nerve cell and fibre forming a reticulum in the central portion of the brain stem. It is extended downwards in the thalamus and sub-thalamus. Brain stem reticular system consists of reticular formation, hypothalamus, subthalamus and certain thalamic nuclei. The brain stem reticular formation has two following systems:

- ascending reticular activating system and
- descending reticular system

The reticular formation, which plays a role in wakefulness and in controlling the overall activity of the brain is called ascending reticular activating system.

Stimulation of reticular formation not only exerts wakefulness in the animal but it also makes an alert to the external environment. Damage to reticular formation produces sleep. It plays a role in the regulation of endocrine functions. It is concerned with sexual behaviour and emotional responses. It has regulatory influence on the formation of conditioned reflexes and development of learning processes. It also comprises the nuclear group responsible for feeding thirst and satiety. In this way, it plays an impotant role in the behavioural patterns.

NERVE CELLS AND BEHAVIOUR

Human Males

The relation between nerve cells and behaviour has a special neuronal basis for homosexuality in human males. The human populations is the existence of males which show little or no sexual interest in females but instead have a strong sexual preference for their fellow males. There is a genetic basis for the differences among men in their sexual preferences. Is there is any effect of hormones circulating in the mother's blood on the response of the embryonic brain and on the development of the trait?

Neuroscientist Simon LeVay suggested a hypothesis, according to it the brains of homosexual men possess distinctive structural and functional attributes different from those of heterosexual men. He predicted that there would be differences in the size of certain nuclei (anatomically distinctive aggregates of nerve cells) in the anterior hypothalimi of homosexual and heterosexual males. He based his prediction on earlier discoveries that the anterior hypothalamus plays a key role in regulating sexual activity in humans and other vertebrates.

LeVay further studied large differences between human males and females in the size of certain nuclei in the anterior hypothalamus and concluded that these cells are involved in sexual behaviour. He tested the neural hypothesis by acquiring the brains of a number of homosexual men who had died of AIDS. He prepared the anterior hypothalamic of these men for microscopic analysis and measured the size of the nuclei in question. He did the same with the brains of a group of men who were presumed to be heterosexual; men who had not died of sexually transmitted AIDS. He found that a nucleus called *INAH-3* was much smaller on average in the homosexual men than in the heterosexual men (where it is typically about the size of a grain of sand) but about the same size as the *INAH-3* in women.

These results support the hypothesis that specific clusters of cells in the human brain have great effect on the sexual orientation of adults. But the issue is far from closed. Ideally, the hypothesis that a small *INAH-3* causes a homosexual orientation in males should be tested against alternatives, one of which is that homosexual activity causes a reduction in the size of *INAH-3*.

It is still unknown that whether social interactions among homosexual humans cause changes in specific neurons within the hypothalamus, or whether a given set of cells in the *INAH-3* cause homosexuality. However, brain component is in some way responsible for causing homosexuality in males. Much work is needed to understand how these cells exert their proximate effect on the behaviour.

How do Moths Evade Bats?

Studies on noctuid moths (nocturnal insectivorous bats) have been conducted to know the causal relationship between nerve cells and behaviour with respect to how certain bats avoid their deadly enemies.

In warm summer evenings, bats hunt moths in many parts of the world and they require *a minimum amount of illumination, perhaps a 100-watt bulb with a reflector, and a fair amount of patience and mosquito replellent.* The bat catch a moth in its tail membrane and fly off with its catch, but if he/she were alert enough, the bat watcher would also see some flying moths turn abruptly even before a bat came rushing into view. Moreover, the observer might see moths dive or cartwheel out of the grasp of an approaching bat. These observations suggest that some moths have the ability to detect a bat at a distance and can make themselves difficult to capture.

Physical Properties of Sound

Sound is the result of pressure changes in a medium (usually air), caused by vibration or turbulence. The amplitude of these pressure changes is stated in terms of sound level, and the rapidity with which these changes occur is the sound's frequency. Sound level is measured in decibels (abbreviated dB), and sound frequency is stated in terms of cycles per second, or nowadays, Hertz (abbreviated Hz). Sound level in decibels is a logarithmic rather than a linear measure of the change in pressure with respect to a reference pressure level. A small increase in decibels can represent a large increase in sound energy. Technically, an increase of 3 dB represents a doubling of sound energy, and an increase of 10 dB represents a tenfold increase. The ear, however, perceives a 10-dB increase as doubling of loudness.

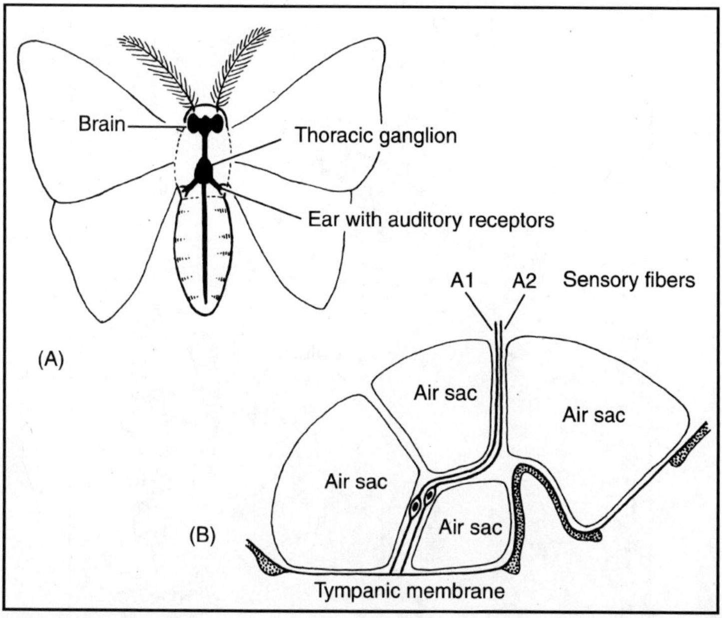

FIG. 7.7: Noctuid moth ears. **(A)** the location of the ear. **(B)** The ear's design, which features two sensory fibers (A1 and A2) lionkes to a tympanic membrane.

Another important aspect is the duration of the sound, and the way it is distributed in time. Continuous sounds have little or no variation in time, varying sounds have differing maximum levels over a period of time, intermittent sounds are interspersed with quiet periods, and impulsive sounds are characterized by relatively high sound levels and very short durations.

The way sounds are distributed in time is also important, in that intermittent sounds appear to be somewhat less damaging to hearing than continuous sounds because of the ear's ability to regenerate during the intervening quiet periods. However, intermittent and impulsive sounds tend to be more annoying because of their unpredictability.

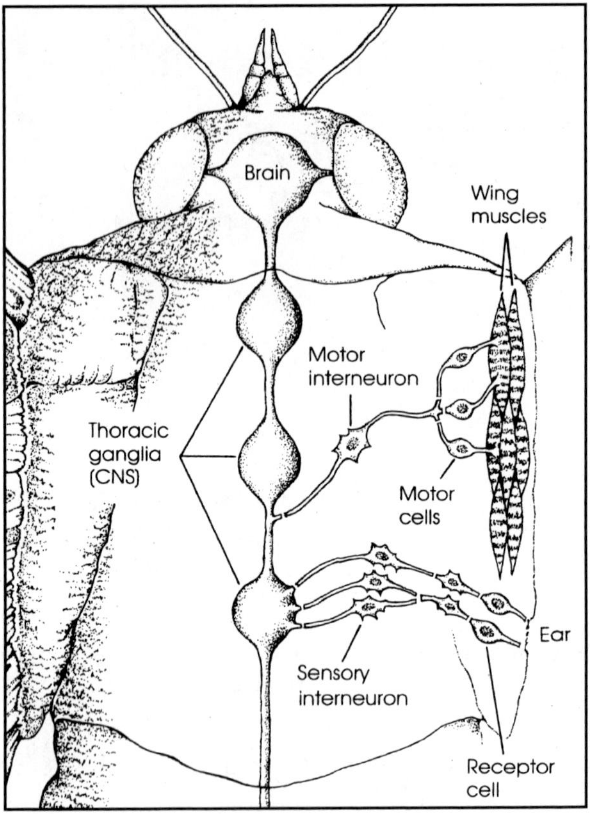

FIG. 7.8: Neural network of moth. Receptors in the ear relay their information to the central nervous system (CNS) via sensory interaction. Cells in the thoracic ganglia communicate decision to wing muscles via motor interneuron.

In bats, sound is produced by vibrating structures, such as the larynx. When a bat's muscles cause its larynx to vibrate, pressure waves are generated that travel out of the animal's mouth and through the air. These waves have a frequency. It is measured in kilohertz (kHz), and an amplitude, or intensity, measured in decibles (dB). A typical nocturnal, insectivorous bat vocalizes in the ultrasonic range, that is, with sound frequencies higher that 20 kHz, which we cannot hear. The energy in their calls is high, and the intensity of the pressure waves as they leave the sound-generating apparatus is substantial.

A nerve cell, or neuron, responds to stimulation with a change in the permeability of its cell membrane to sodium ions. In the moth ear, positively charged sodium ions enter the receptor cells at a point near the tympanum, altering the electrical charge differential, or membrane potential, of the receptor cell membrane. This change affects the permeability of neighboring portions of the membrane. In this way sodium ions enter at those sites and repeat the effect, causing changes in membrane potential to sweep around the cell body. Depending upon the intensity of the activating stimulus, the change in membrane potential may be great enough to induce a brief, stereotyped, all-or-nothing reverse in the electrical charge across the neural membrane. These changes, called **action potentials,** which means the neural messages are transmitted. An action potential travels the length of the neuron to the point of near contact (the **synapse**) with the next neuron in the network.

Neurons Communication

It is a common method is for the arrival of an action potential at a synapse to cause the release of a neurotransmitter chemical by one cell that diffuses across the gap separating it from the neighboring cell(s). These substances may affect the membrane permeability of the postsynaptic cells in ways that increase or decrease the probability that they will produce their own action potential(s).

Sensory Interneurons

The cells that relay receptor information to the brain (or its equivalent) are called sensory interneurons. Their messages can change the activity of other cells in the central nervous system, which in the moth consists of aggregates of neurons in the thoracic ganglia and other ganglia in the head. These cells can be thought of as decoders, analyzing sensory inputs and making "decision" about which reactions to order.

Motor Interneurons

Certain patterns of activity in the thoracic ganglia affect motor interneurons, whose action potentials in turn reach nerve cells that are connected with the wing muscles of the moth. When a motor neuron fires, the neurotransmitter it releases at the synapse with a muscle fiber induces changes in the membrane permeability of muscle cells. These changes regulate the contraction or relaxation of the muscle, with consequent effects on the movements of the wings the thus, the moth's behaviour.

Action Potentials and Information

The neurons of noctuid moths operate in basically the same way as the neurons of other animals. In all species with nervous systems, behaviour is the product of an integrated series of changes in cell chemistry, initiated by receptor cells and carried on by sensory interneurons, brain cells, motor interneurons and motor cells, and muscles. Since, these changes occur in an individual. Although there is nothing extraordinary about the basic design of noctuid moth neurons, they perform very special tasks for their owners.

STIMULUS FILTERING AND BEHAVIOUR

In natural environments, animals are exposed to a great array of acoustical, visual, and tactile stimuli, to name only some modalities of potential sensory inputs. Not all of this barrage of possible information is really useful to individuals as they attempt to survive and reproduce. Therefore, it is not surprising that animal nervous systems respond selectively, extracting relevant stimuli from the sensory barrage while ignoring most other stimuli. This process is known as stimulus filtering.

Stimulus Filtering by Vertebrates

Studies conducted with the help of ultrasound sensitivity in insects with specialized receptors and interneurons provide information on filtering. It activates special reactions for critical signals. Vertebrate neural systems generally are composed of vastly more numerous neurons than those of insects, but even so, they, have their specializations too. For example, the human ear does not respond to ultrasonic sounds that are routinely detected by a moth or cricket. Therefore, out auditory system performs stimulus filtering.

Sound Perception in Bats

Bat is an example of a vertebrate with a large, complex, neuron-rich nervous system. It has special feature-detection units. The bat's neuronal systems can detect and respond appropriately to key stimuli in its environment. For a sonar-using, flying bat, these key stimuli include the echoes coming from objects struck by its orientation calls-and, appropriately enough. The echo detector neurons have been observed in the Mexican free-tailed bat and mustache bats. The auditory system of a mustache bat is more complex and provides much more information that the ear of a noctuid moth. These cells respond more intensely to the second of two separate pulses of sound, one following the other in close succession, just as an echo would follow the vocalization pulse. Among these neurons are some that react to sounds at the very threshold of bat hearing if, and only if, the low-amplitude sound is preceded by a loud sound, preferably of the intensity and frequency of a typical Mexican free tail orientation pulse.

Same bat researchers have conducted elegant tests of the hypothesis that the brain maps of mustache bats help them identify the distance to a flying insect (target range) and the speed with which the prey is moving (target velocity), vital information if the bat is to intercept the prey.

Echolocating bats have **selective perception**. For example, the platypus can locate food by sensing the extraordinarily faint electric fields that their animal preys inadvertently produce. Certain electric fish take this skill one step further by producing a weak electric field and then detecting disturbances to the field caused by a prey's intrusion into it. These and other abilities, which humans cannot match. These animals have specialized proximate neural mechanisms, which gather and process certain kinds of information from the environment.

Visual Perception

Vision is so natural to us that it is easy to assume that what we see must be exactly what other animals see. The common toad of Europe has specialized visual system act acts similar to echo locating apparatus of a bat or the electric field detection mechanism of a platypus.

Imagine a brown beetle moving over dark soil in front of a toad. The beetle will cast a very small image on the surface of the retina as the light waves reflected from the beetle enter the lens and are focused on the back of the eye. The image moves over clusters of receptors. Some of these clusters will constitute the excitatory central area of the receptive field of one (or more) ganglion cells. These cells will fire and information will be sent to the brain.

The toad has ganglion cells that respond to changes in light intensity that reach the retina, changes typically caused by moving objects, whose movement affects how much light enters the retina at a particular point. From a toad's perspective, small moving images on its retina are much morel likely to be caused by its prey (nearby beetles and worms) or its enemies (distant herons or hedgehogs) than are large stationary images on its receptor surface.

Specialized Visual Perception

The optical illusions in toads has special features for detection of specific stimuli. Certain of our visual cells react exceptionally strongly to edges, actually enhancing the contrast between neighboring dark and light areas. There is no more light reaching our eyes from the white paper right next to the black squares that from the central grayish regions that are not bordered directly by black. But our brain tells us that there is, creating a useful illusion of the sort that contributes to our ability to see the outlines of objects.

The recognition of human faces by human brain depends on visual mechanisms. Evidence for this hypothesis is provided by a few unfortunate people who have suffered injury to a particular part of the of the brain's temporal lobe. These people can see things, they can recognize and name many objects, they can identify particular individuals by the sound of their voice or by familiar clothing, but when shown an image of their friends, their spouses, even themselves, they are at a complete loss.

The affected cells in human brain (in question) have something to do with the perception of faces, a task highly pertinent to the lives of these social primates. But demonstrating that there is a *correlation* between cello activity and presentation of a particular stimulus does not show that perception of the stimulus is actually *caused* by these particular cells, which might be incidentally stimulated by inputs from other networks of cells that are really responsible for the perception in question.

Mechanisms of Motor Control

The mechanism of neuropsychological and certain sensory systems have specialized elements for the detection of critical stimuli such as ultrasound, moving objects, or the visual cues associated with faces. Just as sensory detection reflects specialized features of nerve cells, so too does an animal's reaction to critical sensory cues.

For example, the cricket *Teleogryllus oceanicus* manages to turn away from ultrasonic bat cries when it is flying at night. This insect possesses **acoustical receptors** in its forelegs, some of which fire in response to sounds of 40 to 50 KHz. These sensory messages travel to a diversity of cells in the cricket's central nervous system. One such cell is a sensory interferon called *int*-1, one copy of which is located on e ach side of the insect's body. Ron hoy and his co-workers established that int-1 played a key role in the perception of ultrasound by playing sounds of different frequency to a cricket while recording the response of its int-1 cells. These cells became highly excited when the cricket's ears were bathed in ultrasound. The more intense a sound in the 40 to 50 KHz range, the more action potentials were produced, and the shorter the latency between stimulus and response-two properties that exactly match those of the A1 fiber in noctuid moths. It shows that high *int*-1 signal activity causes the cricket to respond to ultrasound.

Central Pattern Generators

A central pattern generatoris the functional cluster of cells contained entirely within the central nervous system that can generate the pattern of signals needed to produce a particular response. It regulates locomotion. The generators are widely distributed through the animal kingdom and have been especially well studied in certain invertebrates.

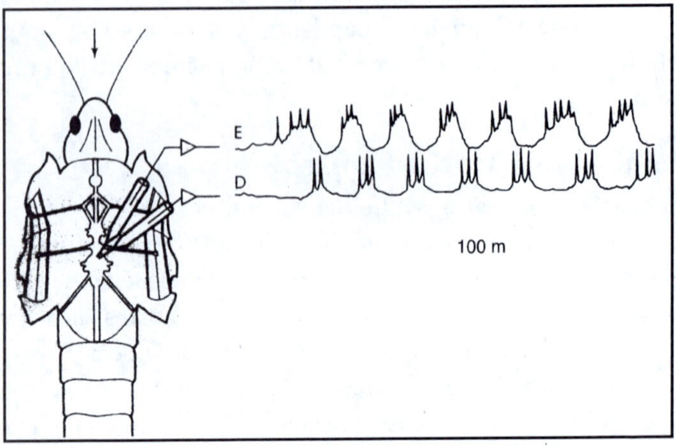

FIG. 7.9: Neuronal control of the flight pattern in grasshopper *Locusta migratoria*. A puff of air (downward arrow) on the animal's head activates neurons. In the thoracic ganglion of a restrained, partially dissected grasshopper. Simultaneous recording of an elevator neuron **(E)** and depressor neuron **(D)** reveal alternating bursts of action potentials and timed in the manner necessary to sustain the wing-beating pattern essential for flight.

Such systems do not require sensory feedback in order to produce their self-generated sequence of signals. For example, if one takes the brain stem and spinal cord from a lamprey (a primitive fish), the living tissue can still play out the rhythmic pattern of signals that would cause swimming motions in an intact lamprey. This result shows that within the brain stem or spinal cord, a central pattern generator exists that underlies the regulation of swimming behaviour in this species. This unit does not need sensory feedback in order to generate its functional set of commands (although in an intact animal, it does receive and use sensory feedback to adjust the basic swimming pattern in relation to particular conditions encountered by the lamprey.)

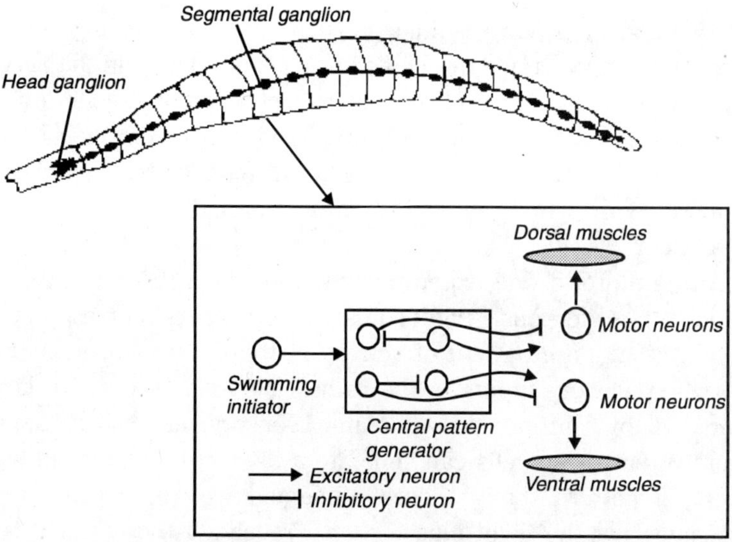

FIG. 7.10: Central pattern generator and swimming behaviour in the medicinal leech. The leech swims by undulating its segmented, wormlike body. Swimming movements are coordinated by neuronal complex found in each segmental ganglion. When activated by a swimming initiator cell in the nervous system, the four neurons in the central pattern generator produce an integrated series of signals that travel to key motor neurons attached to the dorsal and ventral muscles of the leech. These signals cause the muscles to contract in the precise pattern essential for functional swimming.

When the grasshopper *Locusta migratoria* flies, it will remain airborne only if its wings move up and down in a precisely timed fashion. The wing muscles of these insects are controlled by separate motor neurons that either elevate or depress them. An elevator neuron begins to fire soon after air blows onto the head of an immobilized, but living, grasshopper. The activity of this neuron begins an alternating cycle of elevator and depressor neuron signaling highly reminiscent of that just described for the dorsal and ventral flexion neurons of *tritonia* sea slugs.

If the alternating pattern of motor neuron activity stemmed from reciprocal inhibitory arrangements between the elevator and depressor neurons, then we would predict the existence of direct connections between the two types of cells. But just as is true for *tritonia* sea slugs, direct links do not exist, suggesting that the alternating pattern stems from a cell or cells elsewhere in the nervous system. Candidates for inclusion in a central pattern generator are some large interneurons in the thoracic ganglia of the grasshopper. These interneurons fire rhythmically at a frequency that matches the frequency with which the wings beat up and down in a flying grasshopper.

Furthermore, if one experimentally interrupts the activity of one of these interneurons, flight muscle activity is correspondingly delayed. Finally the pattern of activity in these interneurons persists even when sensory inputs to the central nervous system are largely eliminated by cutting the incoming sensory nerves. It appears therefore that these cells can generate a distinctive pattern of signal activity, a pattern that imposes fundamental order on the motor commands that the flight muscles must receive if the insect is to fly properly.

A very similar sort of mechanism has been discovered in a totally unrelated animal, the leech, an aquatic invertebrate that swims by waving its elongate body. The swimming undulation requires a precisely timed sequence of dorsal-ventral contractions of the muscles at various points along the body. A leech's wormlike body consists of many segments, each with its own set of dorsal and ventral muscles and its own central nervous system unit, or ganglion, which is linked to the ganglia in neighboring segments. If one electrically stimulates certain interneurons in an experimentally isolated ganglion, these cells "turn on" the central pattern generator, leading to a prolonged and precisely organized volley of signals from four cells on each side of the ganglion. Each of the four cells takes it in turn to fire for periods of less than a second in a rhythm that is synchronous with the pattern of muscle contractions that occur in given segment when the leech is swimming. The sequential pattern of firing is achieved in large measure through the inhibitory interactions among the four cells in the quartet. In addition, the central pattern generator in each ganglion possesses inhibitory connections with the central pattern generators in neighboring ganglia. Such an arrangement enables one segment to communicate with its neighbors in ways that generate a wave of muscle contractions and relaxations along the length of the leech's body so as to propel the leech forward through the water.

The mechanism by which leech swimming is controlled is highly complex, so much so that a complete wiring diagram would be mind-boggling. Nevertheless, just four cells in each central pattern generator play a major role in imposing a particular rhythm on the messages sent to motor neurons, which ultimately translates into organized movement instead of chaotic immobility. Just as sensory cells are not neutral reporters of environmental events, central neurons regulating movements have their own unique properties that "bias" behavioural outcomes in adaptive ways.

NAVIGATION

Although understanding the simple movements of a sea slug or a leech has been advanced by testing the central pattern generator hypothesis, the details of the operation of motor neurons are complex and are still not fully understood in most cases. These are many other locomotory abilities whose neural control is far more mysterious still. A premier example is the ability of some animals to navigate through unfamiliar terrain to reach a goal point, as when a migratory animal or a displaced bird returns home after a trip of hundreds of miles over a route that the individual has never followed before.

CHAPTER 8

Communication among Animals

INTRODUCTION

The study of communications, between animals has always interested ethologists. Darwin's book, The Expression of the Emotions in Man and Animals, (1872) was mainly about communication. Another study is by Julian Huxlley (1914) on the courtship of great crested grebe. Animals perform certain acts, which communicate message to another animal, for example, facial expressions of monkeys, monotonous sounds of insects, song of birds and dance of bees. All these acts are called communication signals and are stereotyped. In many cases one of the most important pieces of information that they transmit is species specific, for example when an animal is advertising for a mate it perform such signals, which are common throughout the species. Any individual that diverges from these signals, will be rejected by the members of the opposite sex as possibly belonging to another species.

Much of the communication of animal involves olfactory or audition vision although some species rely on other senses, such as electroreption used by some fish. The kind of sensory modality used for a particular signal depends to some extent on the information it conveys. In advertising for a mate, larger animals use sounds, as these travel rapidly. Smaller animals cannot produce sound of high intensities so they rely on pheromones. Some animals mark the boundary of their territory with scent gland or with urine relies on the persistence of the smell. If animals live together for a long time and can recognize each other as individuals, they can co-operate and develop relationship, which may vary from pair to pair depending on their experience of communication with each other.

FIG. 8.1: Darwin's observations on communication. **(a)** Friendly posture, **(b)** Angry posture.

Thus we can say that when an animal communicates, the message is encoded in signals, it may be olfactory auditory or tactile.

COMMUNICATION SIGNALS

Communication signals have adaptive value. One hypothesis is that most animals are preadapted to provide signals because their ordinary, everyday activities provided potential information. For example, when a water strider moves across the water's surface, it creates little waves that incidentally carry information about its presence. Water striders generate waves specifically to communicate with others, an action that could readily have arisen from the side effects of the movements of water striders in the past. Likewise, when animals urinate or defecate they produce materials that happen to contain visual or olfactory information. Hyenas actively mark the boundaries of their territories with dung and urine, which clearly announces the presence of particular hyenas, and warns intruders to stay away or risk dismemberment at the jaws of the clan.

Similarly, just by passing the tissue of a tree through her digestive tract, a female bark beetle generates some volatile metabobic by-products that carry information about her existence and location. If this information happened to facilitate the location of a female by a male, she could derive a benefit from an incidental effect of her feeding and excretory activities, and so could the male that tracked her down more efficiently by attending to this information.

Signals are provided by the actions of animals that are affected by **nervous systems** have properties that reduce the frequency of *conflict behaviour*, but such behaviour may still occur. Thus, two rival herring gulls that meet at the border between their territories may attempt both to attack and to escape from their opponent. The resulting conflict may cause a male to raise his head back as if he were about to peck at his opponent without actually carrying out the action (an *intention movement*). Or the male may redirect his attack onto a safe object, violently stabbing a clump of grass rather than the stimulus (the rival male) that aroused his aggression in the first place.

Conflict behaviours could have been involved in the origin of certain now-stereotyped display behaviours that gulls use to signal to others. Arising as an incidental effect of the neural systems controlling attack and escape behaviour, certain conflict behaviours could have accurately signaled a heightened readiness to attack, deterring one male from entering the other's territory, to the benefit of both (the deterred male avoided a beating, the resident saved his energy). Under these circumstances, a communication system might have had its beginning, to be subsequently modified in ways that have led to a modern system of complex visual displays.

Adaptive Value of a Signal

Spotted hyenas are highly social animals that live in permanent bands often containing several dozen members. Clan member do many things together, including killing zebras and other large game. When some clan members rejoin their group after a temporary separation, they are likely to erect their penises, which they then present to their companions for nuzzles and sniffs. You may be surprised to learn that female spotted hyenas participate fully in this activity, for they too have something that looks exactly like a penis! In fact it is difficult for a human to determine the sex of a hyena without being able to inspect its genitalia at very close range, not the easiest inspection to perform on your average hyena, which is generally reluctant to cooperate with inquisitive biologists.

The observation that female hyenas have a mimetic penis and engage in elaborate "penis"-sniffing rituals raises fundamental evolutionary questions: what is the history behind the behaviour, and what is the adaptive value, if any, for females that participate in the activity? We will deal with the historical question first.

No fossil evidence exists on how the pseudopenis of female spotted hyenas came into being and how its ritual use developed over time. We turn therefore to comparisons of the structure and behaviour of the relatives of the spotted hyena, which is one of four species belonging to the Hyaenidae, a family that is placed in the mammalian order Carnivora along with some other families, including the dogs and cats.

The only species in the entire order whose females have a pseudopenis is the spotted hyena, although inspection of the anogenital region occurs in many carnivores, including hyenas other than the spotted hyena. Therefore, males of the ancestral hyena probably used their penises as devices for communication in certain social interactions, among other things.

But how did female spotted hyenas come to be endowed with a pseudopenis for use as a social signal? A possible answer is provided by anatomical studies of the hyena's pseudopenis, which reveal that it is a highly enlarged clitoris. Thus, the historical question becomes, How did the spotted hyena clitoris become penislike?

It is well known from comparative hormonal studies that testosterone has key effects on the masculinization of mammalian embryos. The tissues of a very early stage mammalian fetus that are destined to become reproductive organs develop into testes and penis if the embryio is male and manufactures testosterone. If the embryo is female, the hormone testosterone is absent, and ovaries and the secondary sexual characteristics of females will develop. The same tissues that develop into a penis under the influence of testosterone become a clitoris in the absence of the hormone.

In 1973 R.F. Ewer hypothesized that female spotted hyenas must differ hormonally from typical mammals. Recent studies have confirmed this point, most notably in documenting that the ovaries of females produce testosterone and other androgens. When a female hyena is pregnant, her embryonic offspring, male and female alike, are exposed to high levels of an androgen that is converted to testosterone in the placenta and passed on to the developing fetuses. The male hormone activates the basic mammalian system for developing male traits, thereby masculinizing young females, producing an enlarged and penislike clitoris.

We can test the hypothesis that the origins of the female spotted hyena's enlarged clitoris lie in the masculinizing effects of testosterone by predicting that females of other mammals, when exposed to testosterone early in life, will also exhibit a penislike clitoris. Supporting examples exist even in humans. A few pregnant women have received medical treatment that happened to expose their embryionic female offspring to high testosterone levels. These children did indeed possess a greatly enlarged, penislike clitoris upon birth.

It is conceivable, although unlikely, that an embryonic mutant female spotted hyena living long ago happened to produce or be exposed to precisely the correct amount of masculinizing male hormone to develop a near-perfect pseudopenis. If so, the trait could have originated from a single mutation that yielded a developmental result identical to the current trait.

On the other hand, the transition from the ancestral state (a relatively small clitoris) to the current state (a large pseudopenis) may have occurred over many millennia as modifying mutations gradually led to a more perfect mimetic penis in females with fewer costly side effects. Along these lines, it is pertinent that human females accidentally exposed to male androgens and embryos are sterile as adults, an illustration of the point that large, random changes affecting development are unlikely to produce reproduction-enhancing results.

No matter whether the current pseudopenis is the product of a single change or multiple modifications, the trait probably originated from the novel use by a mutant female of the basic mammalian rules of genitalic development that she inherited from her ancestors.

An Adaptive Signal?

At least one mutant allele that altered the hormonal environment of female embryonic spotted hyenas spread through the population in the past. All of today's spotted hyena females possess this allele, or more recently modified versions of it, and probably other later-appearing mutant genes as well. Together these genes contribute to the development of the secondary sexual characteristics of female hyenas. As a result, all of todays spotted hyena females possess a pseudopenis and the ability to use the structure to communicate with others.

The fact that at least one mutant allele affecting secondary sexual characteristics spread through this species in the past indicates that the allele promoted the reproductive success of the individuals that possessed it. A novel trait (like the spotted hyena's pseudopenis) could persist only if possession of the mutant gene underlying the attribute conferred a selective (reproductive) advantage on the individuals that possessed it. If it did not, the trait would disappear as the mutant allele that induced development of the attribute eliminated itself from the gene pool through its association with reproductive failures. To understand the maintenance of the original enlarged-clitoris trait, we must therefore under stand why the bearer of the gene that led to the development of the trait gained higher fitness than the then-typical females of her species.

Why would a spotted hyena female with masculinized external genitalia have more descendants than her "normal" or typical female counterparts? There is every reason to believe that the trait would have reduced a mutant female's fitness, rather than increasing it. To inseminate a female spotted hyena, a male must deposit sperm in the female's vagina, which can currently be reached only via the enlarged tubular clitoris in females. Copulation in modern spotted hyenas gives the appearance of being difficult to achieve, thanks to the decidedly tricky coupling arrangements that are required.

An even more potentially costly aspect of the penislike clitoris to the individuals that possess it becomes apparent at the time when a female gives birth to her pups. Because the female's reproductive tract terminates in the clitoris, her babies must pass through the clitoris in order to be born. Imagine a human male giving birth through his penis and you have some idea of the problems this poses. Those of us who have seen a hyena give birth in person or on film will never forget it.

To offset the apparent costs of a pseudopenis, there must have been substantial benefits associated with the mutant allele(s) responsible for its development. One possibility is that the hormone-induced pseudopenis was employed right from the start as a communication device in ways that generated fitness benefits. An alternative hypothesis, however, is that the pseudopenis trait was initially a costly side effect of a mutant allele that provided other highly adaptive effects, perhaps increased aggressiveness.

We may never know whether the first female with an enlarged clitoris gained a net fitness benefit as a specific consequence of this trait or whether the pseudopenis caused a fitness loss that was more than compensated for by some other effect of a fitness-enhancing allele. But we can potentially examine whether the psuedopenis is *currently* employed in ways the raise female reproductive success.

One hypothesis is that the pseudopenis is used adaptively in the spotted hyenas' frequent *greeting ceremonies* to communicate with other hyenas. Many behavioural ecologists define an evolved communication signal as one that conveys information to another individual, with both signaler and receiver deriving a benefit from the transaction. If giving the signal *or* responding to it reduced individual fitness, selection would favor nonsignalers or nonreceivers. A key question, therefore, about any potential communication signal is, what benefits might the signaler gain by transferring information to others that compensate it for the costs of its action? And what benefits might a receiver gain by receiving the information and permitting it to influence its behaviour?

Spotted hyenas live in large bands, hunt big game, and compete fiercely with one another for meat from the animals they kill. Competition for dominance in the group is of paramount importance because dominant, or alpha, females and their offspring gain more food that subordinate ones. The sons of alpha females "inherit" their mothers' high dominance status. When fully mature, these male offspring emigrate to another clan of hyenas. If the son of a dominant female becomes the top male in his new clan, he will enjoy exceptional reproductive success because only the dominant male mates.

Thus, the social system of spotted hyenas rewards dominant females. Females are heavier and more aggressive than males, whom they dominate in their clans. The dominance interactions among females and between the sexes may be mediated in part by penile displays. This hypothesis generates the prediction that the tendency of an individual to present its erect penis or pseudopenis to others in a greeting display should be related to its dominance status. It is. Subordinate females and cubs are far more likely than dominant ones to take the initiative in these displays. This result is consistent with the hypothesis that subordinates gain by transferring information of some sort to more dominant individuals by way of penile (and pseudopenile) displays. Just what this information might be remains to be identified, although observers of spotted hyenas in the wild have all agreed that the greeting ceremony appears to promote cooperative behaviour among the participants.

The possible hypothesis may be drawn to the physiological (perhaps hormonal) state of an individual and can be assessed by olfactory or gustatory inspection of the erect (blood-engorged) penis or clitoris. Subordinate females may benefit reproductively in the long term by frequently signaling to dominants that they have not adopted the hormonal condition that will cause them to challenge the status of dominant members of the troop. Dominants can afford to tolerate do operative subordinates, permitting them to enjoy the benefits of social life in the clan, provided that they do not pose an immediate threat to their social status and reproductive potential. Long-lived subordinates may eventually be able to assume dominance upon the demise or decline of their superiors. Although the appeasement hypothesis remains to be tested.

How the Receiving Signals are originated

Our focus has been on signal producers, but from the perspective of signal receivers as well, perceptual abilities that evolved in another context may sometimes have enabled individuals to detect and interpret incidental activities of others in ways beneficial to both parties. The ability to detect waves in water may have originally assisted water striders in locating insect prey struggling on the water surface. But once in place, these same perceptual systems may have also been productively employed in receiving signals from fellow water striders.

The possibility that elaborate communication systems may have had their origins in the preexisting properties of animal nervous systems has led to the **sensory exploitation hypothesis**, in which a mutant signal becomes established in a population because it enables a signaler to exploit an already evolved preference or bias for that signal in a receiver.

For example, males of the tungara from (*Physalaemus pustulosus)*. They can produce whining calls that may or may not be followed by one or more *chucks*. Females prefer males that incorporate the *chuck* as finales to their calls, moving to these males for mating while ignoring rivals that happen to be generating only the whining component of the call.

There are a number of species of frogs closely related to the tungara frog, and males of some of these species *never* produce chucks. Yet when females of *Physalaemus coloradorum*, one of the non-chucking species, are exposed to various artificial calls under laboratory conditions, they move toward those taped signals of their species that have a chuck added to them in preference to taped calls without chucks. This result suggests that a preference for chucks arose in the common ancestor of *Physalaemus* frogs *before* chucks originated. When the first mutant male of *P. pustulosus* to add a chuck to his call appeared, he apparently tapped into a preexisting sensory bias in females that had evolved for some other reason. The female preference for his signal yielded reproductive gains that helped propel the mutant gene through later populations.

This conclusion would be more convincing had females of *Physalaemus coloradum* been given an opportunity to compare taped calls with some arbitrary sound added to them against taped calls augmented with a chuck. According to the sensory exploitation hypothesis, calls with chucks should be far more effective in attracting females than calls with some other comparable sound tacked on.

Sensory Exploitation Hypothesis

This hypothesis has been explored with a few other species besides *Physalaemus* frogs. Analysis of a cluster of fish species in the genus *Xiphophorus* suggests that the ancestor of these species lacked the logn swordtails that appear in males of some member of the genus. Females of the swordtail species *X. helleri* prefer males with relatively long tails but so do females of the platyfish *X. maculates*, a species whose males naturally lack the elaborate extension of the lower part of the caudal fin.

OLFACTORY COMMUNICATION

In Nonchordates

Silk moth has an olfactory network. It can smell through its antennae. The adult male of this species has large bushy antennae covered with sensory hairs. These hairs have a coat of cuticle and are innervated by sensory neurons. The cuticle is porous and the neurons associated with these structures respond to certain molecules that enter the hair through pores. When the substance comes in contact with the membranes of the receptor cell, it generates a receptor potential.

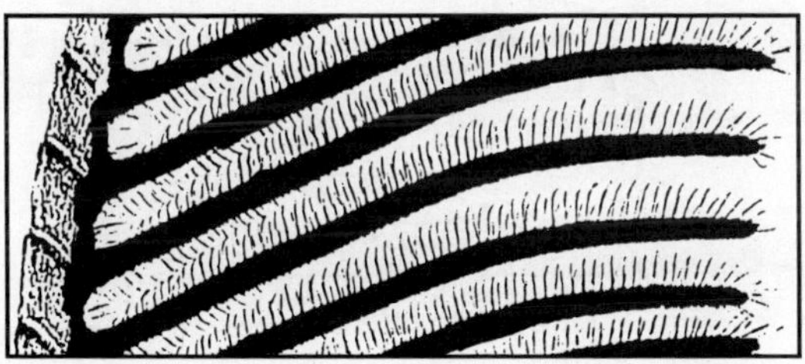

FIG. 8.2: Antenna of male silk moth with sensory sensilla.

The volatile chemical, makes its way through a pore in the cuticle of the hair and migrate through a liquid substance surrounding the receptor, and changes the permeability of sensory neuron.

Dietrich Suchneider, explained that adult male receptors are sensitive to one chemical, 10-Trans-12-cis-hexa-decadien-1-oL. With the help of this the male is able to locate and mate with the female. The adult female sits calmly in one spot and release a minute amount of chemical, which drifts downword and disperses. Some molecules reach the males antenne, enter the pores in sensilla, move through the liquid surrounding the receptor and alter the membrane of this cell.

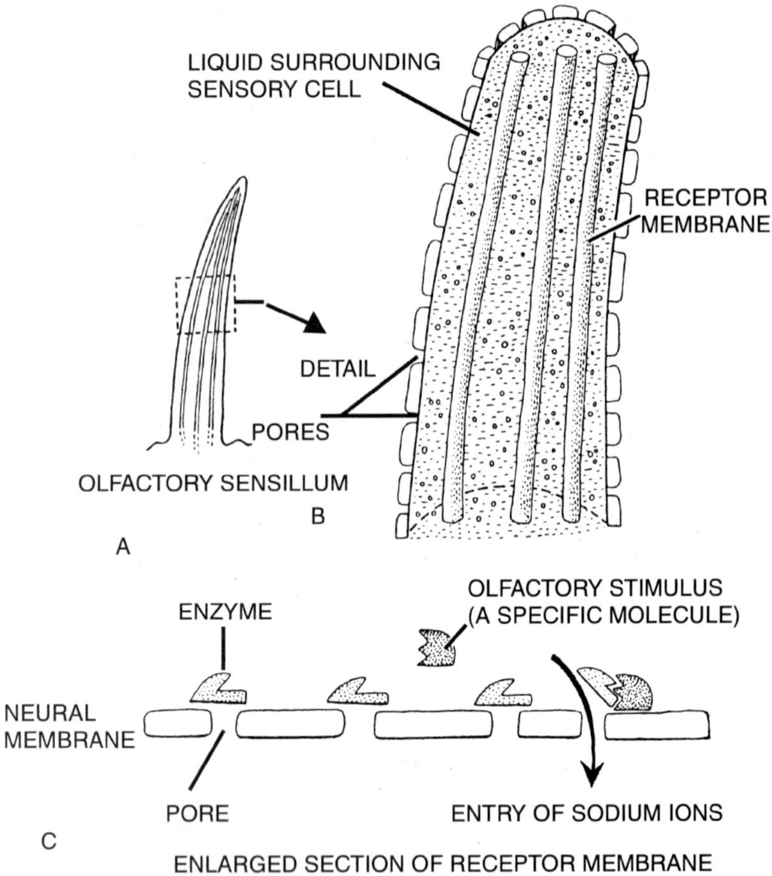

FIG. 8.3: (A) Single plfactory sensillum, **(B)** Detailed structure of sensillum, **(C)** mechanism of olfactory communication.

Thus the olfactory perception is well developed in silk moth. The chemical substance acts as a signal for particular behaviour patterns.

Most of the insects release an olfactory pheromone (chemicals substance) which has the advantage of dispersing over a long distance. The molecules that are used as reproductive pheromones have long chain of carbon molecules. They are species specific. There are disadvantages associated with the use of an olfactory message. Its effectiveness is highly dependent on wind conditions. The females act only as signallers and the males as receivers. The chemical substance secreted by the female acts as an olfactory stimuli for the male.

In Vertebrate

Olfactory communication has been studied by J. Petter (1962), and Kaufmann (1962) in the primates. The prosomians show several behaviour patterns, they have throat and chest glands that are used for marking. Some species of lemurs rub branches with the secretions of specialized glands located on the fore arms and in the armpit. The skin on the feet face and in the ano-genital region is richly supplied with sweat and sebaceous glands, their functions are olfactory communication.

Primates have a number of behaviour patterns associated with urination and defecation that appear to serve communicatory end. The tree shrews, which have methods of spreading urine over their surrounding loris, will moisten their paws with urine and distribute it over themselves and their environment. Olfactory communication plays little role in distance communication in monkeys. It arise clearly in females at the onset of estrus when the urine seems to convey information about their condition to the males in the group. The odor of a female in estrus (macaque) is detectable and the males of many species sniff at the genitalia of estrous females.

Individual recognition by olfaction also occurs in many mammals, particularly to show relationship between mother and young.

FIG. 8.4: Auditory communication in birds. Male bird in the centre is singing on his territory.

ACOUSTIC COMMUNICATION

In Nonchordates

The male cricket chirping by its burrow emits a complex pattern of auditory stimuli with specific properties. A mature unfertilized female cricket of the same species gains information from the males song. Her nervous system permits her to identify a mate of her own species since the male of different species have different songs. The song announces the sex of cricket and location of the male in the environment. All these factors increase the possibility that sexually motivated female cricket will approach, locate and mate with the male of her own species. The same auditory signals are available to other males and serve to increase the probability that they will avoid rather than approach the singer. The singer is announcing that he is a territory holder and will defend his holdings against other males.

In Vertebrates

The male of many species of birds have characteristic territorial song. It is a call, which announces that the individual is a sexually mature male and the area occupied by it is a defended area. This song permits identification of the birds. The songs are species specific. The birds are tuned to the vocalization produced by adult male of their own species and will remember these sound, while ignoring those produced by males of other species. The birds brain have selective system or template for the acquisition of information which are necessary for song learning. Birds can recognize the song because they have recognizable dialects.

The auditory communications have advantage and disadvantage. The male bird in the centre is singing in his territory. Advantage occurs to him if his song attracts a female or repels rival male. His song may be ignored by other species but may also attract predators, which is a disadvantage of singing.

In tree frog (*Eleutherodactylus coqui*) male and female frogs differ in their auditory systems. During the breeding season, males produce a mating call consisting of two notes, an unmodulated pure tone co note at about 1000 HZ, followed by an upward-modulated qui note spanning the range of frequencies from 1800 to 2200 HZ. Male and female react differently upon hearing the call. If a resident calling male hears a near by frog give a co-qui, he will respond with single co note, he may later attack the intruding male. The co is used in inter-male communication, and qui note is used in male attraction.

In Primates

Many primates shake branches in the course of aggressive display, generating noise that may communicate something to the opponent. Some produce sounds by striking the ground or the base of trees with the palm of hand or foot. In chimpanzee, these slaps are organised into drumming Gorills make sounds by beating the chest.

VOCALISATION IN PRIMATES

Primates have means for generating vocalisations of a wide variety of types. Rowell described nine sounds which are acoustic signals, communicating message to another animal.

1. **Roar:** Loud noise made by the confident animal when threatening another of inferior rank.
   Pant-threat is similar to roar, but broken up into short syllables, made by a less confident animal wanting the support of rest of the group in its attack.
2. **Bark:** Given by a threatening animal insufficiently aggressive to move towards the other, like the bark of dog.
3. **Growl:** Similar to bark broken up with short sound units.
4. **Shrill:** Bark alarm call of the group.
   Screech has an abrupt pitch change up and then down, made when threatening a higher ranking animal.
5. **Geckering:** A screech similar to screech, but broken by syllables, made by an animal being threatened by another.
6. Scream Shortlr than screech and without rise and fall. Made by a losing primate in a fight while being bitten.
7. **Squeak:** It is a very high pitched noise made by a defeated primate at the end of an agonistic act

TACTILE COMMUNICATION

Little is known about the tactile worlds of animals, but certain behaviour patterns represent the tactile communication. The most characteristic behaviour pattern involving tactile communication is grooming, in which one animal manipulates and mouths the fur of another, also removing the particles of dirt. The tree shrews use the teeth and tongue for grooming. Hands are used by monkeys and apes. The grooming is prominent in species in which dominance relations an play important role. The tactile signals in grooming, maintain peace and cohesion in primate societies. Tactile signals a play role in reproductive behaviour. The tactile signals generated by feet and teeth that inflict pain, elicit either a like reaction or submission and function to repel or overcome the recipient. When the signals are used in a hierarchically organized group, they serve to maintain status in the group.

COMMUNICATION AMONG BEES

Animals often communicate by behaviour patterns which mutually affect one another behaviour, typically, the behaviour concerned either reproduction or agonistic. One of the classic examples of nonaggressive, nonsexual communication is the means by which honeybees direct other members of the colony to the source of food. If the food source is more than a hundred meters away from the hive, the forager bee performs a waggle dance instead of a round dance. In addition to the information that is normally transferred by the round dance, the Waggle dance also expresses the distance and an indication of direction to the goal. In the Waggle dance the bee runs a short straight distance and makes a curve alternately to the right and then to the left in half arc returning each time to the starting point. The angle of the straight lime to the plumb line corresponds to the angle of the food source in relation to the sun's position. The straight run part is accompanied by sidewise wagging movements and a rasping noise. The raspy noise is produced from repeated stamping vibrations. The sound production is controlled by breast musculature. With certain peep tones, the follower bees are able to stop the dancer and to dinduce it to release a food sample. The speed of the dance expresses the distance to the source, greater distance indicated by slower dances.

ROUND DANCE

With rapid rocking steps the forager bee moves in circles which are often so tight that only one comb cells lies inside. She runs around the six adjacent cell, suddenly turning and running in the opposite direction. One or two full circles may separate each reversal of direction. The round dance signifies that a rich source of food lies in the vicinity of hive.

Honeybee Dances

Worker honeybee possess a highly complex behaviour, their dances, which have been interpreted as the symbolic means by which foragers communicate with others in the hive, providing them with information about the distance and direction to good supplies of pollen and nectar. For example, when a forager bee has fond a rich new food source (a patch of flowers, a watch crystal filed with honey) a distance from the hive, it will often return to the hive and either perform a *round dance* or a *waggle dance* on the vertical surface of the comb.

All populations of the honeybee perform round and waggle dance, the logical group to examine first is the genus *Apis*, to which the honeybee (*Apis mellifera)* belongs. The three other *Apis* species are tropical bees, and all except. All *Apis* species have both round and waggle dance displays. *A. florae* perform dance displays on vertical surfaces. In contrast, *A. florae* dances on the horizontal surface of a comb built in the open over a limb. To indicate the direction to a food source, this bee simply orients her waggle run directly at it. Because this is a less sophisticated maneuver than the transposed pointing done in the dark on vertical surfaces, it is probably a relatively ancient form of dance communication.

A man watching dancing bees (in special observation hives) can derive a surprising amount of information form these activities. If the bee executes a round dance, she has found food fairly close to the hive, say within 50 meters of it. If, however, the worker performs a waggle dance, she has visited a nectar or pollen source more than 50 meters distant. By measuring following:

The number of times the bee runs through a complete dance circuit in 15 seconds, or the length of the straight-run portion of the dance, or

the frequency with which sound bursts are produced while dancing, a human can tell approximately how far away the source is. For example, the fewer the number of dance circuits performed over 15 seconds, the more distant the site.

Moreover, by measuring the angle of the straight run with respect to vertical, a bee-watcher can tell you the direction to the food with respect to the sun. Apparently, a foraging bee on the way to a discovered food source notes the angle between the food, hive, and sun.

During a waggle dance (not during round dances), she transposes this information onto the vertical surface of the comb when she performs the straight-fun portion of the dance. If the bee walks waggling straight up the comb, the nectar or pollen will be found by flying directly toward the sun. If the bee waggles straight down the comb, the food is located directly away from the sun. A patch of nectar-producing flowers positioned 90° to the right of a line between the hive and the sun triggers waggle runs oriented at 90° to the right of vertical on the comb, and so on. In other words, sun compass information is converted into a symbolic code based on gravity.

Dance displays of bees encode fairly specific information about the distance and direction to good foraging sites was reached by Karl von Frisch after 20 years of experimental work. His basic research protocol involved training bees (which he daubed with dots of paint for identification) to visit particular feeding stations, which von Frisch had stocked with rich sugar solutions or honey. By watching the dances of his trained bees, he saw that their behaviour changed in highly predictable ways depending on the distance and direction to a food source.

Von Frisch believed that the worker bees in a hive could derive information from the dances of successful foragers. Because it is normally dark inside the hive, these other bees do not watch a dance from a distance but instead follow her about on the comb as well as sense vibrations produced by her. Von Frisch found that a trained dancer from a given feeding tray appeared able to recruit others to go to this specific site. He concluded that, by walking after a dancing bee within the hive, others were informed about the location of distant food. If true, the adaptive value of dancing would be clear because workers would be able to locate rich patches of food more quickly than by searching on their own. They would be able to extract these resources before other nectar or pollen feeders, providing their queen mother with the raw materials to make more offspring, thereby advancing their own genetic success.

Bee workers learn form the dances *per se* where to hunt for food. A mechanical or robot "bee" can apparently induce recruits to search for food in a particular direction offers some evidence in favor of the proposition that workers derive useful information from the dances. Most researchers find it implausible that the dance movements are totally irrelevant to the bees, given that they carry energetic costs to the dancer and given that human observers can accurately decode the distance and directional information that they contain.

Here, however, we are not concerned with the current adaptive utility of the dances, if any, but instead with how such elaborate and complex activities might have originated and subsequently changed to attain their current form.

CHAPTER 9

Orientation

INTRODUCTION

It is the adaptive behaviour in which animals responding to environmental changes, have to coordinate and orient their movements in relation to external stimuli. The orientation depends on the sensory capabilities of animals. Mittelstaedt (1973) considered orientation in the absence of external stimuli as idiothetic orientation in contrast to orientation utilizing environmental information which he refers to as allothetic orientation.

Orientation within the home area can occur by means of scent trails (ants), echolocation (bats), or electrical discharges (Mormyridae). Bees orient by using the suns position which is called sky-compass orientation, or by using polarized light called light compass orientation. The tidal sand flea *Talitrus saltator*, which may orient to the sun during the day, is also able to use the moon at night for assessing the correct route, which is called lunar orientation. It was reported by Papi and Pardi (1959). The migratory birds can orient according to celestial bodies (sun lunar and star). Magnetic field orientation has been reported by Wiltschko and Wiltschko (1975). Many fishes and larvae of water beetles (*Dytiscidac*) orient according to the impinging light source. Dytiscus larvae, which must surface to breath, will drown if the aquarium is lighted from beneath. Since they move towards the source of light it is dorsal light orientation. Many fishes swim with their back toward the light inside caves; where the light is reflected from the floor, these fish swim upside down.

ORIENTATION: TYPES

Taxes

In taxes the animal's body takes up a particular direction. It may be combined with locomotion so that the animal moves towards or away from the source of stimulation. These responses are called taxes. Taxis can be explained by following examples.

The grayling butterfly (*Eumenis semele*) flies towards the sun in its escape from predators. If one eye is blinded its escape reaction will consist of flying in circles, exhibiting the dependence on bilateral optic stimulation. It is not necessary that all taxes depends on equal bilateral stimulation, the same butterfly will continue to pursue female in a straight path after unilateral blinding. The light compass reaction of ants and bees is a taxis.

The homing ants will change their direction in accordance with the change in the position of the Sun even when they are captured and kept in the dark boxes. Even when sun is not visible, these insects are sensitive to the plane of polarization of the light from the sky, therefore, they will orient accordingly

Loeb, studied the taxis in fish. According to him taxis may cause forced orientation in which the animal's adaptation is simple and automatic. In some cases, taxis may be a part of more complex pattern of behaviour so that the natural orientation may depend on more than one taxes. For example, in *Crenilabrus rostratus* the up right orientation of fish depends on photic and gravitational taxes. If light comes in from the side of a tank rather than from above, certain fish may orient at an angle upward or downward. If the effects of gravity are removed by destroying the labyrinth of the inner ear, the fish will orient perpendicularly with light from the side and even ventral side up if light comes from below, this was observed by Niko Tinbergen.

In higher animals, taxis can be observed under very limited conditions. The new born rat which has its eyes closed will show a fixed orientation to gravity when it is placed on a wide inclined plane. Its natural tendency is to climb upward against gravity. The climb is not straight up the incline but is at some angle to the left or to the right and the size of angle is determined by the steepness of the in cline. The steeper the incline, the greater the angle of climb. But when the rats eyes open, its behaviour become variable. The adult rats show tendency to climb upward, they quickly learn to escape from the inclined plane.

H. S. Jenning (1900) pointed out that all animals show great variability in behaviour and are not fixed completely in orientation responses. The reason is that the living organism is responsive to more than one aspect of its environmental and internal state at any given instant and may be making many adoptions at once.

CLASSIFICATION OF TAXIS

Kuhn (1919) classified the taxis and his classification was extended by Franenkel and Gunn (1961). He recognised following types of taxis

Anemotaxis

Orientation and locomotion are in relation to the wind direction. If it is a transverse orientation, it is called anemomenotaxis.

Astrotaxis

Orientation to heavenly bodies, also called star orientation.

Chemotaxis

An orientation reaction in free moving animal induced by a chemical stimulus. When a capillary tube containing a substance such as glucose, is placed in a medium having *E. coli*, the bacteria alter their pattern of locomotion in such a way that they congregate near the source of substance.

Geotaxis

A reaction in response to gravity. If the *Drosophila* is placed in a vertical glass tube that is stoppered on both ends, a *Drosophila* will move towards the upper end of the tube. Turn the tube upside down, and the fly will again move upward. In this way the *Drosophila* can be driven from end to end for hours.

Klinotaxis

It is a simple form of directed movement in which the side-wise movement of the anterior part of the body results in a continuous testing of the position of the orientation stimulus in space. For example, maggots of flies.

Menotaxis

It is an angular orientation in relation to the stimulus source. The animal maintains a certain imbalance in the response of each side of the body to the stimulus. One can also describe this diagonal or cross orientation as a telotaxis: the animal simply fixates the stimulus with a lateral fixation receptor of the sense organ. This can be observed in bees, and hermit crab.

This adaptive response was studied by Schneirla (1933) in ant. This involves orientation of a constant angle to the direction of the source of stimulation. The path of homing ant is guided by the direction of the sun. If the direction of the sun is changed by the use of a mirror the ant changes the course or direction accordingly.

Phobotaxis

Orientation in a stimulus situation in which aversion occurs. Paramecium that enter water with a high carbondioxide content stop, turn and continue their movement. The turns are not directed in relation to the stimulus, only through trial and errors does the Paramecium succeed in avoiding danger zone.

Phototaxis

Orientation movements to the light are called phototaxis. If the movements are towards the light, it is positive phototaxis and if away from the light it is negative phototaxis.

Tropotaxis

It is a turn in the stimulus field. Thus the animals regulate their activities in spatial relationship with the environment.

Kinesis

In this response the stimulus produces a change in the speed of movement or in the rate of turning and this changes the position of the animal in relation to the source of stimulus. For example, Woodlice (*Porcellio scaber*) tend to aggregate in moist places. This is due to an influence of the relative humidity on the locomotory activity of the animals: as the humidity increases the proportion of animals which are motionless increases. The animals therefore become aggregated in the damper region.

KINESIS: CLASSIFICATION

Orthokinesis

The change in conditions produces retardation of movements, so that the animals aggregate in one direction. Such an influence on the liner velocity is called orthokinesis. For example the swimming movements of ammocoete larva of the lamprey changes with light intensity.

Klinokinesis

When the rate of turning is affected by external stimulation, the response produced is called klinokinesis. The Planaria, aggregate in the darker parts of its habitat, although the locomotion continues. The animals do not leave dark regions once they reach them. This is because of two following factors:

The animals change direction as they swim along and the rate of change in direction is increased by an increase in light intensity.

They response to an increase in light intensity due to rapid adaptation.

CHAPTER 10

Migration

INTRODUCTION

Migration between two divergent habitats on a seasonal basis is represented by many animals, including locusts, Salmon, birds, bats and fishes. Some species undertake migration as parts of exploration. In some species, population explosion leads to dispersal migration. Exploratory migration is common in vertebrates so the seasonal or periodic migration in response to change in environmental conditions between two different habitats is called migration. Animals that migrate, move some distance from one location to another at one time of the year and then go back to the original area at another date on a regular annual cycle. This migratory behaviour has evolved in response to several different ecological pressures. Thus seasonal movement of a large number of animals as a habit to have advantage of favourable environmental conditions offered in another habital is called migration.

MIGRATION: BIRD

Description

It is the most puzzling case of animal orientation, in which long distance flights are undertaken by birds during migration and long range feeding expeditions. It was studied by Kramer (1957) and Matthews (1968). They studied sensory clues which permit orientation of this type. Matthews suggested that diurnal birds could obtain the necessary information from observation of sun's arc, provided they could remember the characteristics of the sun's arc at home. The migration of starlings was studied by Kramer; he explained that sensory clues are involved in this. During the migration season birds show intense activity. Starlings remain oriented so long as they can see the sky and sun is not observed. If the direction of the sun is changed by the mirrors the orientation of the starling changes. The direction of the sun changes with the time of day but the direction of migration does not changes so the birds must be able to correct for the movement of sun.

It must have an internal chronometer. This has been shown by experiments by Hoffmann. The chronometer depends on the light-dark cycle. Matthews (1968) suggested that the bird measures the sun's altitude and the rate of change of altitude. The exact method by which the sun is used, is still not clear. The nocturnal migrants cannot obtain their direction by the sun, they orient, according to the star orientation. It was observed that birds become disoriented when the stars are hidden by cloud Emlen (1967) studied the orientation of migratory restlessness of Passerina Cyanea caged in planetarium. Experiments indicates that birds can orient by clues obtained from planetarium. It has been explained that night migrant show navigational abilities when exposed only to stars.

RECENT INVESTIGATIONS

Bird migration presents a complex series of problems because the orienting stimuli have not been identified but Schmidt-Koenig (1979) has shown that birds are sensitive to the following stimuli.

Ambient Pressure

Birds are sensitive to atmospheric pressure, a sensory ability that may provide them with an accurate physiological altimeter.

Infrasound

Sound with a frequency of less than 10 hertz is called infrasound. Infrasound travels a very long distance and natural sources of infrasound like surf can be used by birds as a navigational aid (Kreithen 1978).

Odor

Avian species have long been thought to have poor sense of smell but experiments using cardiac-conditioning have confirmed the results from physiological methods in proving that olfactory sense in birds is used in navigation.

Magnetic Compass

Responses to magnetic fields have been shown to occur in many species. Bookman (1978) proved magnetic sensitivity of birds. In birds it appears that it is the declination of earth's magnetic field that is important in providing directional sense.

Sun Compass

Birds can use the sun as a compass for navigational purpose. Mc Donald (1972) proved that birds can estimate the sun's altitude by measuring shadows rather than the sun directly.

Star Compass

Some birds show typical directional migratory restlessness at night. This directionality is related to stars, explained by Soure (1955).

MIGRATION: PURPOSE

The birds migrate in order to have better surroundings for food, breeding and nesting. The migrants also explore new areas for nesting purpose. Migration helps migaratory birds to avoid adverse climatic conditions. During winter, migration from higher altitudes and latitudes provides protection from cold. In the temperate regions, immigrants get more food and better conditions.

Migration: Fish

Many fishes, like avian species perform periodic migration. Fishes may descend from rivers to the sea as in the case of ceels (*Anguilla*) it is called katadromous migration or they descend from sea to rivers as in the case of salmon which is called anadromous migration. Some fishes of warm tropical seas perform latitudnal migration moving north in the spring and south in the autumn example *Sphyraena*,

Xiphius glandus. Because of the typical habits of the *Anguilla*, no body knew where they lay their eggs and how the young once are looked after. In 1905 Johan Schmidt studied the life history of lel.

CATADROMOUS MIGRATION

This type of migration is furnished by *Anguilla vulgoris* and *A. rotrata*. The life cycle of European lel (*A. rostrata*) has four stage, which are as follows:

First Stage

Eggs are laid in the Sargossa sea, they hatch in the spring as leaf shaped larvae called Leptocephali. At the end of their first year they attain the size of 25 mm and reach the Atlantic and then begin to swim on the surface. In the second summer they reach mid Atlantic. Ultimately they reach the west of Europe.

Second Stage

When the Leptoepchali stop feeding and become pencil shaped, they are called elvers.

Third Stage

The elver moves to the rivers and grow in size and their colour changes to yellow. The males prefer to live in estuarine water.

Fourth Stage

When the young lel become sexually mature it becomes a bright silver lel. It spends 8-10 years in fresh water, the female prefer to live more in fresh water. After this they again leave for sea. Schmidt found that Europeon lel and American lel hatched out -50o 60'W longitude, 22o-29' N latitude at the depth at 900 ft this is the area which lies south east of Bermuda, near Sargosso sea. The Leptocephali larvae of American eel, drift towards the American coast and cover the distance in two years. They metamorphose and become elevers which enter the mouth of the rivers on the eastern coasts of North America.

ANADROMOUS MIGRATION

Arthur Hasler (1960) studied the migratory behaviour in salmon. Pacific salmon (*Oncorhynchus*) hatch in streams of western U.S.A. and Canada. After the smolt stage of development, they swim to the Pacific Ocean. After two years at sea they become sexually mature and migrate back to the exact stream where they were spawned. The journey to the coast is followed by means of a sun compass. At the coast, they have to select the correct river and correct tributary stream within the river system. Hasler, discovered that during the smolting period the fish become imprinted upon the olfactory characteristics of their native stream. During their return journey they are able to discriminate between the Water coming from their native stream and that from other tributaries. They are recognizing landmarks. The scent of their birth place flows all along the migratory route, so it is not necessary for the young salmon to remember landmarks all along the outward journey. If the salmons are transferred to another stream after the period of imprinting, they return to their native tributory and not to the stream down which they pass on their outward migration. It has been proved that the geophysical environment such as magnetic field at earth, can act as the orienting stimuli.

INDIAN MIGRATORY FISHES

Hilsa (sardine family) is a habitant of the Bay of Bengal. It ascends to estuaries of the Ganges during breeding season, and than moves to fresh water. Chanos is present in the coastal waters of the Arabian sea. These migrate annually towards the river mouth for spawning. Bombay duck (Harpodon) shows migratory trends for feeding purposes.

CHAPTER 11

Social Organisation in Primates

INTRODUCTION

The cohesiveness and co-ordination of animal societies is an important feature, which establishes certain relations among the members of the society. Social organisation refers to populations and not to individuals and defines the nature of interactions between members of a species. The social organisation is spceies-specific. In the vertebrates this may vary with changing conditions. The inter dependence of animals of a society lays the basis of mutual co-operation. This co-operation is not restricted to highly social animals. Tigers, which usually live and hunt alone in large territories, avoid control with others, this feature is responsible for cohesiveness so any interaction between one individual of a species and another is called social behaviour.

According to Tinbergen the true society includes more than a mated pair or a mother and her offspring. The members inter-communicate and have some social relationship with an another. The social behaviour determines the social relationship. Two things are necessary for the differentiation of behaviour into social relationship.

The ability of an animal to discriminate between different individuals.

Some kind of behaviour, which can be differentiated by biological factors. For example, an animal must be able to tell the other animal apart and must be capable of either fighting or escape behaviour before dominance order can be established. When the behaviour between two individuals has become differentiated by either biological or psychological means and has become regular and predictable, we can say that a social relationship has been set up.

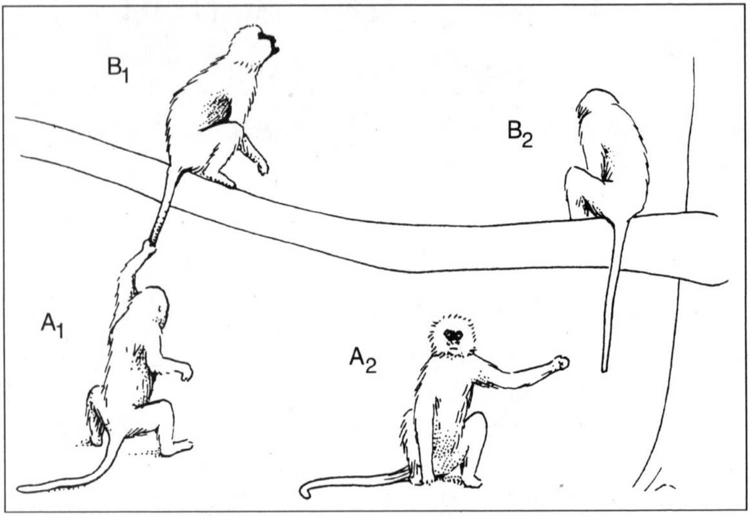

FIG. 12.1: Sophisticated social learning ability in vervet monkeys. After witnessing an aggressive interaction between two individuals from two different genetic lineages (A_1 and B_1) within a troop, other monkeys from those two lineages (A_2 and B_2) are more likely to fight even though they were not involved in the original conflict. Vervets apparently know who is related to whome.

ADVANTAGE OF SOCIAL BEHAVIOUR

Forces of natural selection will shape an individuals responses within a group so we can expect that all animal groups confer on advantage on the members that constitute them.

In a group there is co-operation for several activities in case of threat by another group, the whole group acts and opposes, so a group can survive where a few individuals could not.

Protection from predation.

Experiments indicate that the hormonal cycle of mammals is affected by the presence of males, this is concerned with stimulation and synchronization of breeding. This is an important factor which may make group life advantagenous.

Animals maintain their breeding rate below the maximum. The regulatory mechanism is present in their social system. Because groups are stable and to a large extent reproductively isolated from other selection has operated on the groups themselves, weeding out those which did not adapt to match their resources. It was studied by Wynne.

Social group have good communication and interaction between individuals. They communicate by means of olfactory, tactile and acoustic signals.

SOCIAL BEHAVIOUR IN HOWLING MONKEYS

Ray Carpenter (1931) made an extensive study of social behaviour of howler monkeys of Panama. He first looked at the motor and sensory abilities at these monkeys. They live in groups in the tree tops and their hands, feet and tails are developed for grasping. Their feet are almost like human hands. They use their eyes more than any other sense organ and are very active during the daytime. Howling monkeys show all behavioural adaptions-ingestive, eliminative, investigative, shelter seeking and reproductive. Very small amount of fighting behaviour is a peculiar feature of this animal. When chimpanzees or rhesus monkey would fight, the male howing monkey gives out a loud roaring cry and the female makes a high pitched yap. Allelomimetic behaviour is very promiment. They have following types of social relationships:

Female Young Relationship

It is a very prominent relationship. The female responds to the young monkeys, carrying it every where during the first year, picking it up, if it falls on the ground, inorder to protect it the female crounches over the young. She also feed the young. When the infant falls, she cries and when it is restored to arms, she makes pleasent sound.

Female-Female Relationship

The adult females stay close together and do not fight with one another.

Young-Young Relationship

Young monkeys have a good deal of contact with each other. They chase each other through the trees, sometimes biting and wrestling. They also perform playful acts, and fighting displays, so some sort of weak dominance relationships are developed.

Male-Female Relationship

The estrus period in female is of several days; when she is in heat she will approach any male and initiates reproductive behaviour. The male stays with her until sexually satiated. After this the female moves along to another male. When the group moves, the male always lead.

Male-Young Relationship

Generally the old males are in different to the young but if a young monkey falls down a tree, the males of the group will howl until it is rescued. Some times the old males pick up the young monkeys.

Male-Male Relationship

The males of a clan (large family group) do not fight but they roar at any other individual that comes near. The males of a group stick together. If one male is successful in obtaining food he will give clucking noise so that the others will follow him.

The total number of possible relationship can be obtained by a mathematic formula, which is as follows:

$$n\,(n-1)/2$$

here n = number of individuals in group. Suppose, there is a group of five, then the possible relationship would be ten. It shows that complexity of social organisation is related to the size of the group. Thus each additional number of a group adds a number of relationship in the group.

Social Organisation in Other Primate Societies

The social organisation is different in other primate groups. The howling monkey societies have care dependency behaviour by females, allelomimetic behaviour and sexual behaviour. Other primates such as Baboons, Rhesus, chimpanzee and Anthropoids, have some different behaviour patterns.

Baboons

Social behaviour and social organisation in baboons was studied by Washburn and Irven De vore. Baboons live in smaller sized social groups and have ecological relationship with their natural surroundings. They live in grassy plains. The group of baboons have fifty to one hundred individuals which wander in an area of two miles in diameter.

FIG. 12.2: Social organization in baboons. Atroop on March. Female in oestrus shown by dark hind parts.

Behavioural Development in Abnormal Conditions

The ability of a nerve cell of a fruit fly to compensate for its physical displacement is a prime example of development homeostasis, the capacity of an important structure to develop even in an abnormal environment. If developmental homeostasis applies broadly to behavioural attributes as well, then animals experimentally deprived of normal social interactions early in their lives will still develop reasonable normal social behaviour.

The classic experiments of Margaret and Harry Harlow on the development of social behaviour, in rhesus monkeys are examples for such behaviour. These experiments were conducted in an era when there was less sensitivity to the question of animal rights; readers can decide for themselves whether the harsh treatment of infant monkeys in these experiments yielded information of sufficient importance to justify the research. In one such experiment, the Harlows separated a young rhesus from its mother shortly after birth.

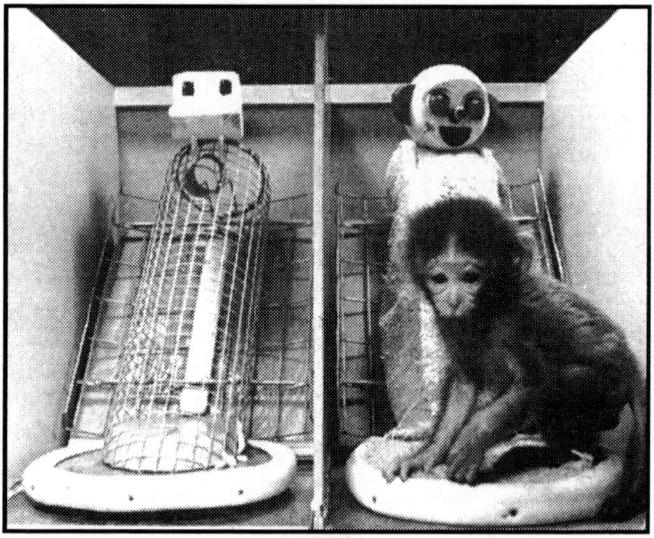

FIG. 12.3: Social deprivation experiment. The isolated baby of resus prefers the terry cloth surrogate mother to wire cylinder surrogate, although only the wire surrogate can provide milk.

The baby was placed in a cage with an artificial "surrogate" mother, which might be a wire cylinder or terry cloth figure with a bottle from which the baby was able to nurse. The baby rhesus gained weight normally and developed physically in the same way that nonisolated rhesus infants do. However, it soon began to spend its days crouched in a corner, rocking back and forth, biting itself. If confronted with a strange object or another monkey, the isolated baby withdrew in apparent terror.

The social isolation experiments demonstrated that the young rhesus needs social interactions to develop normal social behaviour. But what kind of social experience-and how much-is necessary? The hypothesis that interactions with a mother are sufficient for full social development of rhesus monkeys was not supported by the finding that infants reared alone with their mothers failed to develop truly normal sexual, play, and aggressive behaviour.

An alternative hypothesis is that young rhesus monkeys need social experience with other young rhesus if they are to develop normal social behaviour. To test this hypothesis, the Harlows isolated some infants form their mothers but gave these infants a chance to interact with three other such infants for just 15 minutes each day. At first, the young rhesus monkeys simply clung to one another, but later they began to play. In their natural habitat, rhesus babies start to play when they are about 1 month old, and by 6 months they spend practically every waking moment in the company of their peers. Even so, the 15-minute play group developed nearly normal social behaviour under extremely abnormal experimental conditions. As adolescents and adults, they were capable of interacting appropriately with other rhesus, showing typical social and sexual behaviour and not exhibiting the intense aggression or withdrawal of animals that had no social contacts as infants.

More recent experiments show that socially isolated rhesus infants can develop normal social behaviour even in the absence of social interactions with others of their species. William Mason reared some rhesus monkeys with mongrel dogs as surrogate mothers. Through their social interactions with this highly interactive companion, the monkeys came to develop close-to-normal social behaviour, despite having an extremely atypical "mother".

DOMINANCE SUBORDINATION RELATIONSHIP

The adult males are organized in a dominance-subordination relationship, with the most dominant male in the centre of the group and the others (less dominant) spaced out around him. At the edge of the group are the youngest males. At the time of attack, they give alarm calls and males rush over and threaten the intrunder. They spend night on certain sleeping trees. The male's position in the dominance order depends on his strength and ability for fighting. All the females are sub-ordinate to males. When the troop moves the females and infants remain in the centre, for the safety.

RELATIONSHIP

There are no permanent male-female relationship, it appears when the females are in estrus. The dominant male does large proportion of mating but females canpass from one male to another without competition between males.

RHESUS MONKEYS

Their social organisation is similar to that of baboons. There are no families but the offspring of a particular rhesus mother stay close to her. As the troop moves, the females and young males are always in the lead. The most dominant male is the leader of the group. He has the veto power, because the whole troop act according to his direction. Grooming behaviour is of common occurrence.

CHIMPANZEES

They do not live in permanent troops. They form temporary groups which wander over ranges at several square miles and may last for few hours or days. The group may have all males, all females, adult females and their infants or a combination of male and female. The mother and their young infants stay together.

CHAPTER 12

Human Behaviour

Human beings are an evolved animal species. Human sociobiology employs evolutionary approach to generate testable hypotheses about our behaviour based on the assumption that what individuals, to tends to propagate their genes.

The study of human sociobiology has been marked with intense controversy, in part because of confusion surrounding the goals and methods of the approach. Sociobiology does *not* demand acceptance of the notion that if a human behaviour is adaptive, it is developmentally unchangeable or socially desirable.

HUMAN BEHAVIOUR AND ADAPTATION

Human behaviour is full of fascinating puzzles for biologists. To take one minor example, there is the practice of donating blood-to-blood banks, something that occurs fairly regularly on college campuses in North America, among other places. Behaviour of this sort has the appearance of altruism because the loss of blood carries a possible fitness cost to the donor, albeit a very small one, while providing a fitness benefit, possibly substantial, to a recipient. The striking thing about the exchange is that the donor and recipient are very unlikely to be related and indeed, are very unlikely ever to meet.

Human has helpful and self-sacrificing nature, *e.g.*, blood donation. Blood donating is a recent cultural phenomena. A people who gives blood do so to help others, not for a disguised benefit to them selves. Giving blood is fine way of suggesting that one is so altruistic that he is willing to give up a most dear possession for a perfect stranger. This could yield payoffs in the future, not from the stranger but from those who live and interact with the donor and who view him as potentially more cooperative and helpful than others who are not known to be so altruistic. Humans possess a psychic mechanism that encourages us to engage in low-cost *do-goodery*. This hypothetical proximate mechanism makes useful good when we help others, even pure strangers, provided that the personal cost is low. This is one of the examples of human nature.

THE SOCIOBIOLOGY

The adaptationist approach to human social behaviour is often called sociobiology. E.O. Wilson suggested the theory of sociobiology for human behaviour. Sociobiology is not a novel discipline, nor is its subject matter limited to human beings. Sociobiology offers a way to analyze behaviour at the ultimate level.

The sociobiology is gene dependent and many persons are under the impression that a sociobiologist's goal is to discover genes for various human behaviours like altruism and aggression. In order to employ an adaptationist approach to the behaviour of any species one has to assume that the behaviour of interest has evolved. In order for behaviour to evolve it must have a genetic foundation, and in the past individuals with different alleles must have exhibited different behaviours that affected their inclusive fitness. Critics of human sociobiology have claimed therefore that it is not acceptable to talk about the possible adaptive value of human behaviour because no one has ever demonstrated precisely which genes underlie particular behavioural traits in humans.

The proximate role that genes play in the development of human behaviour are interesting and valuable. But one does not have to know everything there is to know about the proximate causes of a behaviour in order to test hypotheses about its adaptive consequences.

Sociobiology are also of opinion that humans rarely, if ever, are seem to be motivated to do the things because of a desire for reproductive success. Critics of sociobiology often claim that certain cultural practices, like blood donating, circumcision, prohibitions against eating some perfectly edible foods, and a celibate priesthood, seem most unlikely to advance individual fitness. If some human practices currently reduce fitness, then sociobiology cannot be correct according to these critics. Sociobiology also provides scientific justification for immoral social policies. The critics claimed that to say a trait is adaptive is to imply that is both genetically determined and good, and therefore *cannot* and should not be changed. There is no doubt that scientific investigation can be employed in ways that often surprise, and even horrify, the investigator. Einstein's basic research on the relation between energy and matter contributed to the development of atomic weapons, much to his dismay; Darwin's theory of evolution has been misunderstood and misused by some persons to defend the principle that the rich are evolutionarily superior beings, as well as to promote unabashedly racist plans for the improvement of the species by selective breeding of humans.

Sociobiology is a discipline that attempts to explain why social behaviour exists, not to justify the behaviour. This distinction is easily understood in cases not involving humans. Biologists that study infanticide by male lingers or the HIV virus are never accused of approving of infanticide or the AIDS diseases. To say that something is biologically or evolutionarily adaptive means only that it tends to elevate the inclusive fitness of individuals with the trait-nothing more.

Moreover, a hypothesis that a behavioural ability is adaptive does not demand that the characteristic be "determined" by genes, for the very good reason that there are no genetically determined traits there are no alleles for altruism or aggression or any other trait, in the sense of a gene that encodes the characteristic and produces it no matter what. Behavioural development depends on the interaction between the genetic recipe and the environment of the developing individual. Change the environment and you may well change the behavioural outcome.

A classic example in human biology involves language acquisition, a clearly adaptive ability for which there must be a genetic foundation. Among the many genes that we possess are some that code for enzymes that play a role in the development of a brain with certain specialized components that facilitate language learning. But these genes for the language trait require all sorts of environmental inputs, both in the form of the building block for enzyme production and neuronal development and in the form of acoustical experience, in order for the trait to appear in a person. Alter the environment and the nature of the characteristic can change, point that is most obvious in the diversity of different languages, which reflect the different acoustical environments that children experience in different cultures around the word.

A STRATEGY FOR DEVELOPING SOCIOBIOLOGICAL HYPOTHESES

Sociobiology offers a framework for the development and testing of ultimate hypotheses about social behaviour. Using this approach on human social activities has proved to be difficult, however, and there has been much debate on the proper procedures.

Human behaviour poses a special challenge for analysis and becomes apparent when one realizes how differently humans behave in cultures around the world. How can it be said that humans tend to behave in ways that elevate their fitness when there are polyandrous, polygynous, and monogamous societies, cultures in which females make important political decisions and others in which males dominate females, human groups for which warfare is a constant fact of life and other groups that never fight?

Although human cultures are diverse, behavioural variation occurs within many other species as well. Recall the discussion of alternative tactics and strategies, which one saw that conditional reproductive behaviours appear in many species. Recall the dunce with it multiple mating systems and the lion with its alternative forms of male coalitions. Perhaps cultural diversity among humans can be treated as an admittedly complex manifestation of battery of conditional strategies possessed by people everywhere, strategies that provide us with the flexibility to adopt whatever behavioural tactics may confer the highest fitness in the particular environment which one finds ourselves.

ADOPTION

The various cultures in the world encourage the practice of adoption to such an extent that about 30 per cent of the children are adoptee. The adoption practices of these cultures had no relation what severs kinship.

Adaptive Decision-Making: Human Sexual Behaviour

Why humans sometimes adopt children? Following are the examples of different categories of explanations for human behaviour:

First, the behaviour in question may currently have an average positive effect on the indirect or direct fitness of the individuals that engage in the activity.

Second, the trait may not currently tend to raise fitness but it did so in the past under different environmental conditions.

Third, the characteristic is not now and never was adaptive *per se* but instead is a reflection of psychic mechanisms that have an overall positive effect on fitness, despite sometimes causing incidental nonadaptive or even maladaptive effects.

Why might we use sexual selection theory to develop hypotheses about human sexual behaviour? For the same fundamental reason that the theory is used to analyze the behaviour of lions and dun nocks, namely, that the potential reproductive rate of human males is so much greater than that of females. Whereas the time and energy needed for egg production, pregnancy, and postnatal care severely limit the number of offspring a woman can produce in her lifetime, males can quickly replace sperm donated to one female. Male reproductively success can be greatly advance by acquiring multiple mates, either through polygynour marriage (a culturally sanctioned option in the large majority off all cultures) or through extramarital copulations. In fact, the variance in male reproductive success generally exceeds that of females.

Given the realities of human reproductive physiology, we would expect males to compete for females (if sexual selection has shaped the evolution of our behaviour), because sexual access to females (and their eggs) limits male reproductive success. We would expect females to exercise choice among potential partners, because there should be many willing candidates and because any variation among males the could affect female fitness would favor female selectivity.

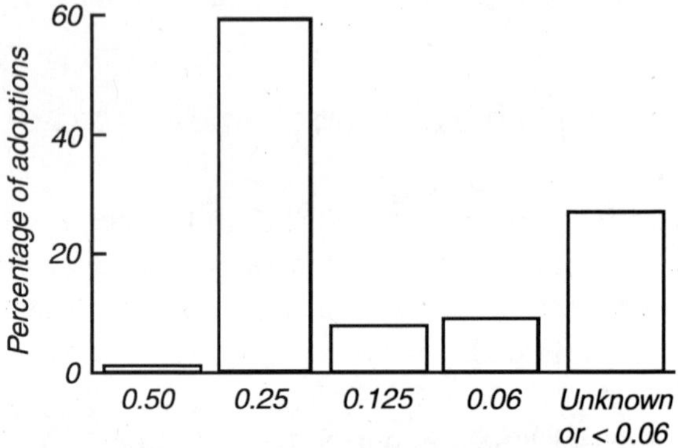

FIG. 13.1: The indirect fitness hypothesis for adoption can be tested by examining the coefficient of relatedness between adopters and their adopted children. In 11 island societies in the Pacific Ocean, adopters tended to care for fairly close relatives, supporting the position that adoption may have generated indirect fitness gains for many adopting individuals.

Male Competition for Mates

The evidence that males in all societies compete for access to females is abundant. Although sexual competition among males takes a host of forms, most of them nonviolent, the competition can become physical.

Martin Daly and Margo Wilson indicated that many homicides in modern societies are directly or indirectly linked to competition among men for women. Another dramatic manifestation of male competition for mates if the greater willingness of men than women to engage in sexual activity that is not culturally sanctioned. For example, married men are more likely to be unfaithful than are their wives. Imagine a married man who helps rear two children with his wife, but who also fathers another child by another woman whom he does not assist. If this child survives, the male has increased his fitness 50 per cent without making any additional parental investment. In contrast, a woman who has an offspring as a result of an adulterous liaison cannot avoid making a major parental investment in the child.

She will nurture the fetus and in all likelihood she will also care for the baby. The physiological ceiling on the benefits from multiple mating for women makes copulation outside marriage less advantageous for females and therefore is less likely to be practiced by them, so an evolutionary cost-benefit argument goes.

Donald Symons suggests that one can test the hypothesis that the sexual psychology of men has evolved to promote the pursuit of multiple mates by making a prediction about the proximate causes of male and female sexuality. He argues that male brains may be expected to have evolved in ways that provide men with psychological drives and desires that increase the likelihood that they will seek out multiple copula Tory partners. The value that males place on sexual variety for its own sake will, he predicts, be absent or much-reduced in women because of sexlinked differences in the operation of male and female brains.

Males commonly patronize female prostitutes, whereas women almost never pay men to copulate with them. Males, not females, support a huge pornography industry in western societies because men, not women, are willing to pay even to look at nude individuals of the opposite sex. Note that in modern societies these aspects of male behaviour probably are maladaptive; prostitutes almost universally employ effective birth control or undergo abortions when pregnant, and payment for pornographic materials is unlikely to do much for a man's reproductive success. The pornography industries take advantage of the male psyche. But maladaptive responses may reveal what people really care about, giving us insight into the nature of the human psyche, which evolved when birth control and playboy were not available.

Donald Symons noted that in western society the behaviour of male homosexuals is very different from that of lesbians. Not only is male homosexuality much more common than the female variety, but males until recently were likely to have a progression of partners. Whereas their female counterparts far more often had long-lasting, stable relationships. Sysmon's argument is that male homosexuals were free to express the proximate mechanisms that motivate males in general to achieve sexual variety.

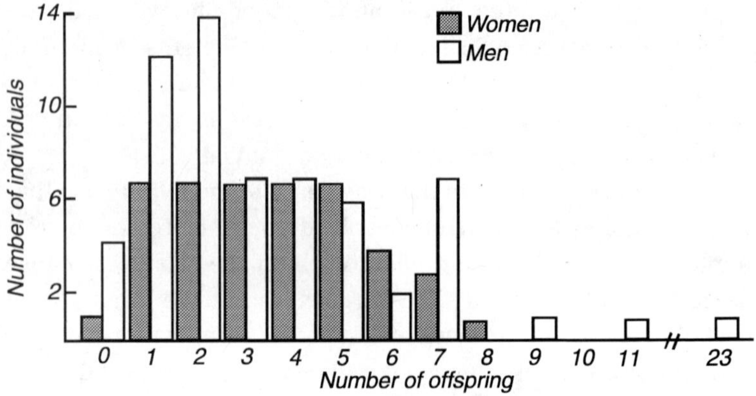

FIG 13.2: Reproductive success of men and women: data from a Xavante Indian population in Amazonia. A few men in this polygynous society had exceptional reproductive success, whereas many left few or no surviving offspring. Most women had moderate reproductive success.

COERCIVE SEX

The competition among males for sexual partners is also apparent in the readiness of some males to engage in coercive sex, including criminal rape. Despite the fact that rape is often severely punished, nevertheless this behaviour has been reported from various studies to date.

Intimidation Hypothesis

This hypothesis clearly relies on a form of group selection, as it is the oretical base. Brownmiller implies that some males are willing to take the risks associated with rape, which is a capital crime in many cultures, in order to provide benefit for the rest of male society. This argument suffers from all the logical problems inherent in a *for-the-good-of-the-group* hypothesis.

If the evolved function of the trait is to subjugate for all women, then the rapist element in male society can be predicted to target older, dominant women (or young women who aspire to positions traditional subordinate role of women. This prediction is not met. Most rape victims are young, poor women. The evidence strongly suggests that the intimidation hypothesis cannot be correct.

Nancy Thornhill proposed that rape is an optional tactic in a conditional sexual strategy. The sexual selection in the past favored males with the capacity to commit rape *under some conditions* as a means of fertilizing eggs and leaving descendants. According to this view, rape in humans is analogous to forced copulation in *panorpa* scorpion flies, in which males excluded from more productive avenues of reproductive competition engage in a low-gain, high-risk alternative. Male panorpa that are able to offer material benefits to females do so in return for copulations; males that cannot offer nuptial gifts attempt to force females to copulate with them. Human males unable to attract willing sexual partners might also rape as a reproductive option of last resort.

TABLE 13.1: Alternative ultimate hypotheses on why some human males commit rape, and some prediction derived from these hypotheses

Hypothesis	Predictions
Rape is nonsexual, purely violent at (proximate hypothesis) that is adaptive for all men as a tactic designed to subjugate all women (ultimate hypothesis)	The population of rapists and their victims will be similar to populations of criminals and victims involved in other violent crime. Rapists will target women in positions of power, or those who choose nontraditional careers.
Rape is an adaptive tactic derived from neural mechanisms controlling an adaptive conditional male strategy	Victims of rape are likely to be in their peak reproductive years. Victims of rape will sometimes become pregnant by the rapist. Rapists are likely to be unmarried, poor men.
Rape is an incidental effect or by-product of adaptive neural mechanisms controlling male sexual behaviour.	Victims of rape from all strata of society. Rapists will be individuals with an unusually high sex drive.

The argument that rape might serve a sexual function has angered some persons who feel that such a claim justifies rape and excuses rapists. Others have argued against the hypothesis on the grounds that rapists are motivated by a desire to attack, injure, or humiliate women.

At the proximate level, some rapists might well be driven by desire to attack women violently, but if this behaviour sometimes resulted in the fertilization of raped women, one could legitimately discuss its ultimate sexual function. And raped women do sometimes become pregnant, even in modern societies where many women employ chemical birth control technology. In the past, when reliable birth control pills and abortion procedures were not available, it seems likely that rapists would have had a higher probability of fathering children through forced sex.

There are several hypothesis to account for rape, this is beyond the scope of this book.

FEMALE MATE CHOICE

Given the potential importance of male parental care to the survival of human children, we would expect females to exert choice in favor of mates that possess or control useful resources. When it comes to selecting a marriage partner, women in Western societies consistently give high marks to *good earning power* in a potential mate, whereas men attach much greater value to *physical attractiveness*. Now it could be that those difference is simply an artifact of modern culture, an arbitrary tradition passed down from generation to generation. This is a testable hypothesis-but it fails its test, because the same difference between the preferences of men and women appears in a host of societies, including many non-Western ones. This result supports the argument that human females are especially likely to develop a proximate psychological mechanism that encourages them to marry good providers for them and their offspring.

MALE MATE CHOICE

In species in which both sexes may make large parental investments, mate choice by males is expected to evolve with respect to providing material benefits to a partner. Human males typically are called upon to make investments in the offspring of their wives.

A survey of college student about what their absolute *minimum* requirement would be with respect to the intelligence of persons with whom they would have different kinds of sexual relationships. Both men and women had similar standards with respect to a potential date, but whereas women had higher standards for a one-night sexual relationship. Men lowered their requirements for such an interaction. When it came to selecting potential spouses, once again men and women had similar preferences, and ones that were higher than for any other category of sexual relationship, as they both desired marriage partners of well-above-average intelligence. This finding generates the untested prediction that women of above-average intelligence have more surviving offspring than those of below-average intelligence (or did in the past under other conditions).

One factor that indisputably affects a women's potential for producing surviving offspring is her age; the peak fertility of human females lies between age 23 and 28. A 40-year-old woman is not only less fertile, but she also only a few reproductive years left before menopause occurs. Because female fertility and residual lifetime reproductive value are strongly correlates with age. Sociobiologists have predicted that males everywhere should prefer youthful females as mates.

Physical Attractiveness

The emphasis that males place on *physical attractiveness* of potential mates is consistent with this prediction, given that young adult women are generally considered more attractive than older women. A preference for young fertile women with a large residual lifetime reproductive value should express itself in an increasing disparity between a male's age and that of his preferred partner as the male grows older.

Young males in their twenties expressed an interest in partners of their own age, give or take 5 years, but males in their sixties specified a preference for women 5 to 15 years younger than they were. Women desire for partners from 5 years younger to 10 years older, no matter whether they themselves were young or old.

Again it is possible that this response was simply a reflection of all cultures with its own arbitrary societal norms. In India, males, as they age, prefer females that are increasingly younger than themselves, whereas females consistently prefer somewhat older partners.

A surveys made in 37 countries ranging form Zambia in Africa to Taiwan in Asia to Venezuela in South America, males everywhere declared a mean preference for spouses younger than they were. In contrast female respondents without exception opted for a spouse older than they were. These mean preference correspond to reality when it comes to actual marriages in 27 to 37 countries for which the appropriate data exist. On average, men marry women that are younger than they are.

FIG. 13.4: Paternal care by uncles. Uncles invest in the care of their sister' children in many societies. Here children of the Ifaluk culture of the western Caroline Islands butcher a pig with their mothers' brothers. Ifaluk children live with their unmarried uncles.

The male preferences are adaptively linked to the reproductive capacity of potential wives is shown in another way by the willingness of pisigis men to pay more bride wealth for brides that have reached puberty sooner. Early maturing women in this society do in fact have more children than women that mature later.

PARENTAL CARE

The sexual preferences of men and women result into the production of children. Both males and females can potentially provide parental care for their offspring, but there is great variation among individuals with respect to how much care they actually offer a given offspring.

For example, sociobiologists have predicted that married men will be especially careful about the allocation of their paternal investment, providing it freely only to progeny likely to be their genetic offspring. In keeping with this prediction, men in modern society that suspect or know that their wives have committed adultery often cite this factor as the reason for divorce, with its consequent reduction or elimination of male paternal care, whereas women that initiate divorce are much less likely to identify adultery by their partner as the reason for their action. Concern about paternity is so obsessive in many cultures that husbands of rape victims may divorce their unfortunate wives, an action accepted or even encouraged by a diversity of religious groups and legal codes.

CHAPTER 13

Wildlife Resources and Conservation

The term wildlife was first used by Willan Hornaday in 1913 in his book *Our Vanishing Wildlife*. Webster's Dictionary defines wildlife as living things that are neither human nor domesticated specially mammals, birds and fish hunted by man. Wildlife is a term that does not enjoy universally accepted definition. The term implies all things that are living outside direct human control and therefore includes those plants and animals that are not cultivated or domesticated. In its fullest meaning, wildlife encompasses insects and fungi, frogs and wild flowers, as well as doves, deer, and trees. Nonetheless, organizations concerned with wildlife generally favor the so-called "higher" forms of animal life.

Birds and mammals symbolize wildlife to most people and, of these animals, game species receive a disproportionately large measure of attention. However, only a small fraction of birds and mammals are regarded as game. The meaning of wildlife is implied in a definition that appeared in the first issue of *The Journal of Wildlife Management* (1937): *The practical ecology all vertebrates and their plant and animals associates*.

WILDLIFE MANAGEMENT

The Journal of Wildlife Management (1937) stated that, wildlife management along sound biological lines is part of the greater movement for conservation of our entire native fauna and flora.

Management clearly implies the influence and application of human manipulation. Wildlife management is the application of ecological knowledge to populations of vertebrate animals and their plant and animal associates in a manner that strikes a balance between the needs of those populations and the needs of people. Until the 1960s wildlife management was primarily game management, the husbandry and regulation of populations of birds and mammals hunted for sport. Wildlife management is changing, but its past remains relevant to the present and future. The practice of wildlife management is rooted in the intermingling of human ethics, culture, perceptions, and legal concepts.

Wildlife management emerged as a budding science in the 1930s, largely from the work, example, and writings of Aldo Leopold, Professor of Forestry at the University of Wisconsin. For wildlife management trained biologists are needed to census animal populations, to estimate the reproductive potential and harvest rates of grouse, to find ways of producing more upland game birds on farmland, to improve wetlands habitats for waterfowl, and to restore populations where wildlife had been extirpated.

A report entitled *Wildlife Conservation in India* (1970) of Indian Board for wild life states wildlife as the entire native uncultivated flora and fauna of the country. The wildlife (Protection) Act, 1972, also defines wildlife as any animal, bees, butterflies, crustacea, fish and moth and aquatic and land vegetation, which form part of any habitat. Any or all non - cultivated and non - domesticated life including both, plants and animal are called wildlife. At global level it is estimated that there exists 5-30 million species of living forms on our earth of these only 1.5 million have been identified. There include 3,00,000 species of green plants and fungi, 8,00,000 species of insects, 40,000 species of vertebrates and 3,60,000 species of microorganisms. India is enowed with a particularly rich biological full of vivid and beautiful accounts of wildlife. It comprises about 45,000 (15,000 flowering plants, 64 gymnosperms, 2,843 bryophytes, 1,012 pteridophytes, 1,940 lichens and 28,000 fungi). Nearly 4,900 of these species are endemic to India. The faunal wealth of India comprises of 81,000 species (5,000 molluscs, 57,000 arthropods, 2,456 fishes, 204 amphibians, 428 reptiles, 1,228 birds and 372 mammals) out of which 62% species are endemic to India. In addition, the country is very important Vavilovian Center of biodiversity and origin of over 167 important cultivated plant species, and some domesticated animals. To name a few the following crops arose in the country and spread throughout the world: rice, sugarcane, Asiatic vignas, jute, mango, citrus, banana, several species of millets, several cucurbits, some ornamental orchids, seceral medicinal and aromatics. Our country has been recognized as one of the world's top 12 megadiversity nations. This region is also a secondary centre of diversity for grain amaranthus, maize, red pepper, soybean, potatoes and rubber plant.

ALDO LEOPOLD (1887-1948)

Aldo Leopold is regarded as the father of wildlife management in the United States. Born in Burlington, Iowa. Leopold graduated from Yale in 1909 and began a career with the U.S. Forest Service in Arizona and New Mexico. However, his concerns went beyond forest management and included the preservation of wilderness. His efforts led to the Gila Wilderness Area in New Maxico, the first of its kind in the national forest system. In 1925, he became associate director of the Forest Products Laboratory in Madison, Wisconsin, but he left 2 years later to begin private consulting work. One of his major contracts was a survey of game populations in eight north-central states; his report won an Outdoor Life medal. In 1933, Leopold completed Game Management, the first textbook on the topic, and began to teach at the University of Wisconsin, where he remained until his death. His appointment as professor of game management was the first such position to be recognized by a university.

In 1935, Leopold helped organize The Wilderness Society and, in 1937, co-founded *The Wildlife Society.* He served as president for both the Wildlife Society (1939) and their Ecological Society of America (1947). A philosopher as well as a scientist, Leopold is perhaps best known for A Sand County Almanac, a collection of essays largely written at his "shack," a hideaway on an abandoned farm where he developed the concept of a land ethic (that is, land is a community of life whose health is vital and not solely a commodity for economic exploitation). One particularly famous essay, Thinking like a Mountain, reflects his changing attitude about the role of predators in natural systems. He also addressed the importance of biodiversity when he wrote, comparing natural communities to fine watch, *to keep every cog and wheel is the first precaution of intelligent tinkering.* Leopold may well have been the most influential figure to speak for conservation in the 20th century.

The Wildlife Society honors his memory with its highest tribute, The Aldo Leopold Award, presented each year since 1950 to a person who demonstrates distinguished service to conservation.

IMPORTANCE OF WILDLIFE

According to Aldo Leopold (1943) wildlife once fed us and shaded our culture. It provides us pleasure for leisure hours, but man has destroyed it by modern machinery. The need for wildlife conservation is necessary because it provides following advantages and benefits:

Ecological Balance

Conservation of life maintains a balance of nature through biogeochemical cycles, food chains, population controls by positive and negative feed backs. If a species is lost in long run, it may upset the natural balance and as a consequence makes the system vulnerable. It can be explained by following examples:

When all the herbivores animals in a forest are killed the tigers, lion, and enter human settlements and attack human beings and domesticated species.

Wild animal like lion, tiger, wolf, panther etc. occupy top position in the food chain. Decrease in number of carnivores would increase in number of herbivores, which will eat up most of vegetation, thereby disturbing the balance of nature structure and function.

Overfishing

Fishing at rates that exceed the sustained-yield cropping of fish species, resulting in a net population decline. For example, in the North Atlantic, herring has been fished to the verge of extinction and the cod and haddock populations are severely depleted. In the Third

World, use of huge factory ships, often by fisheries from industrialized countries, has depleted stocks for local people who cannot obtain protein in any other way. Ecologists have long been concerned at the wider implications of overfishing, in particular the devastation wrought on oceanic food chains. Massive sea-bird wrecks, in which Dead Sea birds are washed up on the coasts, their cadavers revealing signs of starvation, indicate a system in crisis. For example, in January 1994, tens of thousands of Dead Sea birds were washed up on the UK coastline of the North Sea. They are believed to have died of starvation as a result of overfishing. Estimates that the fishing catch could in principle be increased, perhaps to 100 million tones per annum, depend on better management of fishing programmes; it is estimated that, annually, 20 million tones of fish are discarded from fishing vessels at sea, because they are not the species sought. In Peru, overfishing and discharge of industrial and domestic waste pose a threat to Peru's anchovy fishery.

Economic Values

Timber, firewood, natural rubber, gums, resins, tannins, essential oils, spices, many drugs, silk, lac, honey, feathers, musk, ivory, leather, meat, egg, wool, milk are obtained from wildlife.

Wildlife is a source of income to recreation and tourism industry. The most popular tourist attractions are the wildlife sanctuaries and national parks. Wildlife of the country, thus may attract people from abroad and earn foreign exchange. The tourist industry of Kenya (East Africa), based on its wildlife, ranks third after coffee and sisal. Trade in live as well as dead animal not only supports thousands of people but also earn foreign exchange. For example, the market price of rhino horn was 20,000 US dollar per kg in 1990. The ivory of elephants, the glands of musk deer, the antlers of deer, etc., all command high prices. Many plants have medicinal value. For example, penicillin is obtained from Penicillium, quinine from Cinchona, morphin from opium and so on. A chemical obtained from the skeleton of shrimps and crabs may serve as a preventive medicine against the fungal infection.

Genetic Resources

All the domestic crops and livestock have originated from natural plants and animals. Genes from wild plant and animal can now be used to help breed better verities by the genetic engineers. Thus wildlife is an important genetic resource for characters like disease resistance, higher production, higher ecological amplitude etc,.

Biological Diversity

If wildlife is not disturbed by modern machinery that it maintains biological diversity which can be of following three types:

Types	
Genetic diversity	It refers to the variation of genes within species. This constitutes distinct population of the same species or genetic variation within population or varieties within a species.
Species diversity	It refers to the variety of species within a region.
Ecosystem diversity	In an ecosystem there may exist different land forms, each of which supports different and specific vegetation.

Aesthetic Values

Wildlife is also important from the view point of its aesthetic and recreational value for man. Recreation and enjoyment are essential to man's health. Aesthetic values such as the taste of wild berries, softness of moss bed and refreshing fragrance of wild flowers compel us to preserve them. A world without melodius birds, graceful beasts and thick forest would be poorer place for humans to live in. People feel pleasure and happiness in the presence of wildlife.

Education

Wildlife has its own effect on human beings. Visits to zoo, national parks, sancturies provides education to the students of schools and colleges.

Game Values

Wildlife has its worth as game also. In several western countries, million of people hunt or fish for recreation, spend in billions of dollars on these sports.

Scientific Values

Scientists of wildlife in biology and medicine are of direct value of humans. For example, sea urchins have helped greatly in understanding of human embryology, a desert toad in early determination of pregnancy, Rhesus monkeys in present knowledge of human blood groups and antlers of deer in determining the degree of radioactive contamination off natural environment. Monkey, Guinea pig, Rat and Frog are commonly used as experimental animal in medical research. Nine Banded Armadillo is being used prepare vaccine for leprosy because bacteria of leprosy easily grow on it.

IMPORTANT INDIAN FAUNA

India has varied faunal wealth. It has been estimated that in India about 81,251 animal species are available and out of these mammals (372), birds (1228), reptiles (446), amphibians (204), fishes (2546), mollusks (5050) and insects (60383), etc. are prevailing. Many of them have been listed as endangered (see schedule I of Wildlife Act of 1972). Following are some important mammals, reptiles and avifauna:

Indian Lion (*Panthera leo persica*)

The Indian (or Asiatic) lion, is now almost extinct from Asia except in the Gir Forest (Gujarat). The population of the lion in the Gir forest declined from 290 in 1955 to 177 in 1969. The Gir Lion project was started in 1972. As a result, the number of this species is now increased to about 300. The characteristics are: The Gir Lion National Park is well managed protected areas in the country that provides good facilities for visitors to see these unique animals in their natural habitat.

TABLE 14.1: Characteristics of Indian Lion

Body length	260 cm to 295 (male) 00 cm to 275 cm (female)
Tail	30 cm
Height	95 cm
Body weight	250 kg.
Colour	The coat of the lion is light brown in colour.

The male unlike female has a mane which grows on the head, neck and shoulders, making the lion only cat exhibiting sexual dimorphism. The lion lives in a small group (pride). It consists of up to 20 members and has one or more mature lions and a number of lioness with juveniles or cubs.

Indian Tiger (*Panthera tigris*)

It is the magnificent and best known animal of Indian wildlife. The population of tigers reduced from 40,000 at the turn of century to 1827 in 1972 due to hunting, habitat destruction by deforestation and taming of the rivers for human needs. It is described ad endangered in IUCN Red data book. Fit its conservation *Project Tiger* was started on April 1, 1973. At present, the project is operating in 23 tiger reserves located in the 14 States of the country.

Indian Rhino (*Rhinoceros unicornis*)

Several species of rhinoceros were surviving on the earth million years ago, and out of them only five of them are surviving. The common species are: Asian – *Rhinoceros sondaicus* (Javan rhinoceros), *Dicerorhinus sumatrensis* (Sumatran rhinoceros), *Rhinoceros unicornis* (Indian rhinoceros), African – *Ceratotherium simum* (white rhinoceros of Africa) *Diceros bicornis* (black or hook-lipped rhinoceros of Africa). All of them are threatened with extinction. Rhinos has its economic value. Its flesh and blood are considered highly acceptable food in Nepal. Urine is considered as antiseptic. However, rhinos are mostly killed for their horn which is believed to be a strong aphrodisiac and an antidote for poison.

The great Indian one-horned Rhion (*Rhinoceros unicornis*) was earlier extensively distributed in the plain of Indus river (Pakistan) and Ganges in northern India, however, at present they are confined to a few pockets of suitable habitat in the Brahamputra valley, and small sanctuaries of North Bengal and the Royal Chitwan National Park in Nepal. The distribution of Rhino population in various parts of protected areas of India is: Brahamputra Valley, Assam (Kaziranga N.P. = 1,200, Orang WS = 100, Manas WS = 80, Laokhowa WS with Burachapori and Kochmora Area = 20, Pobitora WS = 70, Sonai Rupai

WS = 10, Deosur, Kukrakata, Pani, Dihing, Kurua and other scattered Areas = 50, and in North Bengal (Jaldapara WS = 20, Gorumara WS = 10). The total available species are 1560. The number is reducing due to destruction of the natural habitat and wanton killing that eliminated the species from most parts of its former range. The surviving population (than 2,000) is scattered and is on the verge of extinction. These species have been listed as endangered in Schedule I (the Entry 30) of the Wildlife (Protection) Act, 1972 and in Appendix I of the CITES.

Indian Elephant (*Elephas maximus*)

They are widely distributed in the Himalayan Terai in northern India and in Karnataka, Kerala and Tamilnadu is southern India. They live in dense tropical and subtropical forests near water. In the country, elephants have been domesticated and trained for hunting, transportations, processions, traveling, circuses and several heavy works.

Though the population of Indian Elephant is increasing in past decade (about 8 to 10 per cent). In India wild elephant population is about 18,000 to 20,000. They need protection due to habitat destruction by the local people for firewood, grazing land, forest produce, encroachments and poorly planned development activities. Efforts have been made and Project Elephant was launched recently by the Government of India which will be executed in 11 States of India. It has been notified as endangered species in Schedule I (the Entry 12-B) of the Wildlife (Protection) Act of 1972 and also in Appendix I of the CITES.

Golden Langur (*Presbytis geei*)

The golden langur, is endemic to north-east India. The species was discovered in 1955-56. It is confined to a small area of reserve forest between the Manas and Sankosh river along the foot of Bhutan Himalayas. On the north its range further extends into the central Bhutan region. The surviving population of the species comprises around 1,000 individuals, living in herbs of 7 to 15. The species is threatened mainly due to destruction of habitat. Golden Langur are distributed in various parts of India. Data of various sanctuaries reveal that they cover total 2,18,229 ha of land as: Ripu = 60,529, Kachugaon = 21,446, Chirang = 59,254, Manas = 77,000. The body coat of golden langur looks uniform deep cream in dull light.

The species is endangered due to indiscriminate felling of the trees in the forests of North Assam and north-eastern States has caused the monkeys homeless and subsequently perished in large numbers. Golden langur bas been included in Schedule I (the Entry 10) of the Wildlife (Protection) Act, 1972 and also in Appendix I of the CITES.

Pigmy Hog (*Sus salvanius*)

Pigmy hog is distributed along the Himalayan foot hills from Assam to the terai areas of Uttar Pradesh. The pigmy hog is about 25 cm in height. They live in small herd to 5 to 25 individuals. They are shy and nocturnal. The habitat consists mainly of grasslands with interspersed patches of trees in the moist deciduous forests. However, it has disappeared from most parts of its earlier range as a result of habitat destruction for human settlement and agriculture development. At present, the pigmy hogs are restricted to a few pockets along Assam's border with Bhutan and Arunachal Pradesh. The only areas where viable population of Pigmy hog is found are Manas and Barnadi wildlife sanctuaries in Assam. The total surviving population of Pigmy hog in the aforementioned two sanctuaries would be around 500 individuals. Destruction of grasslands by converting them to agricultural fields in the terai region coupled with plantation of exotic species are the main causes of disappearance of the species. They have now been included in the first IUCN/WWF 1984 list as one of the twelve most endangered animal species. It is also included as endangered species in Schedule I (the Entry 29) of Wildlife (Protection) Act, 1972 and in Appendix I of the CITES. The species was thought to be extinct until its rediscovery in 1952.

Breeding efforts have been made to save the species in the field. World's smallest pig was set up at Basishta under a Pigmy Hog Conservation Programme in 1995. At the Centre, the population of the nearly extinct species has increased by 666 per cent in just 18 months, *i.e.* 43 pigmy hogs bred in capacity from the original stock of 6 captured from the Manas National Park. The research and breeding programme at the Centre was begun in 1966.

Hispid Hare (*Caprolagus hispidus*)

The hispid hare shares the same habitat as that of the pigmy hog. The species has disappeared from most parts of its earlier range of distribution as a result of destruction of its natural habitat. It has already been listed in IUCN Red data book. It is an endangered species and has been included in Schedule I (the Entry 11) of the Wildlife (Protection) Act, 1972 and in Appendix I of the CITES. The surviving population of the species is known to exist in Manas and Borandi wildlife sanctuaries and some other suitable habitats in the region. Only 600 individuals of the hispid are available.

Brow-Antlered Deer (*Cervus eldi*)

The brow-antlered deer or dancing deer of Manipur is locally called *Sangai*. Brow-antlered Deer is the endangered species and is perhaps the rarest and most localized mammal sub-species in the world. In Manipur, the species is confined to a small area in Keibul Lamjao National Park. Until 1950, the species was extinct, however, after declaration of Keibul Lamjao sanctuary in 1966 and later as National park (1977) the species could be conserve. The present surviving population of the species in the wild has been reported to be 76 as per census (April 5,1990). About 29 males, 35 females and 12 fawns were reported. About 100 individuals are now available in 14 zoos of India. It has been included in the list of endangered species (Schedule I, the Entry 3 of the Wildlife Protection Act. 1972.

Wild Buffalo (*Bubalus bubalis*)

The wild buffalo (commonly known as *Van Bhainsa*), is riverain and grassland species. The animal lives in small herbs in the swampy grasslands. They were once associated with the large rivers and their tributaries in the Gangetic plains, the north-east, and the eastern peninsular India, extending from the riverain grasslands of Rohilkand terai to Assam in the east and Godvari in the sough-east. It is now extinct in the terai of Uttar Pradesh, Bihar and West Bengal, and has become very rare in Orissa and Madhya Pradesh. The only stronghold of the species at present is the Brahmputra valley in Assam. The wild buffalo is not much different in general appearance from the domesticated one, except for the former it is heavier and more robust in looking. The height of a bull at the shoulder level is around 170 cm, weighing 900 kg. The colour, like the domestic one, is slaty black. They have two types of horns (i) covered upwards in a semi-circle and the tips remain separated by a small gap; and (ii) spread outwards horizontally, slightly curving near the tips. The species has been drastically reduced in numbers, therefore, they have been included in the list of endangered species [Schedule I (the Entry 41) of the Wildlife (Protection) Act, 1972[

The surviving population of the species in the area is about 3000 and out of which the major population (about 1000) is found in Manas and Kaziranga National parks. The Kaziranga NP is the most suited location for conservation of this species. The major reason for its disappearance is the non-availability and shrinkage of riverain and grassland habitats. There is no natural enemy of the species except tiger. Incidence of poaching is rare, though some local inhabitants relish its meat.

Indian Crocodiles

There are 22 species of crocodiles in the World. In India, three types of crocodiles are available: the freshwater crocodile or marsh crocodile or mugger (*Crocodylus palustris*), saltwater or estuarine crocodile (*Crocodylus porosus*) and gharial (*Gavialis gangeticus*). In India, Orissa State is the home for all the three species of Crocodiles found in India. The commonest of all the three species is the broad snouted mugger or marsh crocodile, which inhabits all kind of the fresh water habitats. In South India, muggers are found even in tidal influenced saline water. The salt-water crocodile in India is confined to its highly adopted mangrove habitats found in Sunderbans in West Bengal, in Bhitarkanika in Orissa, and Andaman & Nicobar Islands in the Bay of Bengal. The gharial, with a long and slender jaw, once found in the Ganges, Indus and Brahmaputra and in the Mahanadi river system, now it survives in the Chambal river in Madhya Pradesh/Uttar Pradesh/Rajasthan. These species were once abundant in all the major rivers and even ponds, however, they are now threatened animals, therefore, they have been listed in Schedule I, Pt. II (the Entry 1-D and 2) of the Wildlife (Protection) Act of 1972). The decline in population is due to uncontrolled and all season hunting for skin, flesh and sport. Loss of habitat due to construction of dams, diversion of rivers and human interference are some other factors. Efforts have been made to save these species. The Government of India has launched the 'Crocodile Breeding Project' in 1975.

White-Winged Wood Duck (*Cairina scutalata*)

They are the resident bird of north-east India. They are also distributed in Burma, Thailand, Indonesia, and through Malaysia to Sumatra and Java. In India, the species are found in Buri Dihing, Upper Dihing, Joypur, Doom Dooma, Dangari, Saikhowa and Dibru reserve forests in Assam and adjoining forests of Arunachal Pradesh. The species has become drastically reduced due to hunting, collection of eggs and destruction of habitat as a result of large scale clearance for cultivation of tea and for oil exploration. For maintaining the viable population of the species, Dibru and Saikhowa reserve forests with some other adjoining areas have been declared as a sanctuary in 1986. White-winged Wood Duck is listed as endangered species, and has been included in Schedule I, Pt. III (the Entry 18) of the Wildlife (Protection) Act, 1972.

Hornbills

Hornbills belong to Family-Bucerotidae. Hornbills are large birds with broad curved bills. They nest in suitable trees. Deforestation poses serious problem to their survival because of scarcity of suitable nesting trees. They occur in India. The common available hornbills in India are: grey hornbill (*Tochus birostris)* Malabar grey honrbill (*Tochus griseus)*, White-throated brown hornbill (*Ptilolaemus tickelli)*, Rufous-necked hornbill (*Aceros nipalensis)*, Wrethed hornbill (*Rhyticeros unduletus)*, Narcondam hornbill (*Rhyticeros undulates narcondarni)*, Giant hornbill (*Buceros bicornis)*, Indian pied hornbill (*Anthracoceros malabaricus)*, Malabar pied hornbill (*Anthracoceros coronatus).* The area of their distribution are North India in semi-open forests, Western Ghats, evergreen forests; 300-1500 m altitude, deciduous evergreen forests of Sikkim, Arunachal Pradesh, Manipur and Mizoram, evergreen forests along Himalayan foothills sough of Brahmaputra, Narcondam Island of Andaman group, Narcondam Island of Andaman group, heavy forests of Terai upto 2,000 m altitude, Western Ghats, Terai and lower foot hill forests and Plains to 300 m altitude forests of South India. Tribals kill them for the alleged medicinal value of their flesh and bones. Hornbills (*Ptiloaemus tickelli austeni*, *Aceros nipalensis*, *Rhyticeros undulates-ticehursti)* are included as endangered in Schedule I, Pt III (the Engry 4-C) of Wildlife (Protection) Act of 1972.

The Great Indian Bustard (*Choriotis or Ardeotis nigriceps*)

The Great Indian bustard (popularly known as *Godawan)* belongs to Family-Otididae. It is one of the largest flying birds in the world. The cock is polygamous. The hen lays one (rarely two) egg per clutch in a shallow depression at the base of a bush. It is a great friend of farmers as it feeds on locust, mice, grasshoppers, beetles, centipeds, small snakes and lizards. Sometimes, it raids field and eats grains and tender shoots of crop plants. The Great Indian bustard is one of the rare species of the birds that wear majestic look. The bird is larger in size, four feet tall with a long white neck and legs. It is a very heavy bird, probably the heaviest Indian bird to be able to fly. It can weigh 20 kg and is sandy-brown and white bird with a black head. Its wings span in almost two and half metres. Earlier it was abundant in the zones of India, as far as south of the Malabar coast and Sri Lanka, is now rare and restricted mainly to the deserts of Rajasthan. The males is larger than female. It is found singly or in pairs or threes in semi-arid regions of Gujarat and Rajasthan; lives in scattered droves of 20 to 30. It is estimated 1,000 Great Indian Bustards in the world and 75 per cent of them are found in Rajasthan (Thar desert, specially in Jaisalmer, Jodhpur and Bikaner. In Rajasthan, large areas of Desert National Park have been fenced so that bustard may not be disturbed during breeding season (July-October). To save the bird in Rajasthan, 'Save Godawan Campaign' has been launched in the desert district of Jaisalmer by the Bombay Natural History Society with assistance from the Salim Ali Centre for Ornithology and Natural History, and WWF. In Madhya Pradesh, the bird is mainly found in Karera sanctuary (202 km^2) in Shivpuri district.

The destructive human activities (hunting) has threatens the species. Its population has declined due to habitat description and therefore, it is considered as endangered. It has been included in IUCN Red data book and in Schedule I, Pt III (the Entry 3) of the Wildlife (Protection) Act, 1972. This is clearly evident from the growth pattern of the population of the species in Desert National Park, Jaisalmer.

Bengal Florican (*Houbaropsis bengalensis*)

It belongs to the group of bustards and floricans (Family Otididae) of the old world. Its habitat is characterised by *Phyragmites-Saccharum-Imperata* type of grassland. They are found in the terai grasslands of Nepal, Uttar Pradesh, West Bengal and the Assam valley. Its population has declined sharply in recent years because of destruction of grassland habitat. In the north-east India, the species can still be seen in the grassland habitats scattered between the Sankosh river in the west and upto the Dihing river in the east. In the protected areas of India, it is found in Dudhwa N.P. (UP), Jaldapara (WB), and Manas, Kaziranga, Orang and Pabitora (Assam). A few individuals may be surviving in Barandi and Sonai Rupai sanctuaries. The surviving population of the birds in the protected areas could be 200-300. It has become extinct in Bangladesh but survives in Nepal. As an endangered species, it is included in Schedule I, Pt. III (the Entry 1-C) of the Wildlife (Protection) Act, 1972. The Bengal florican, has been notified by the IUCN as being one of the 12 most endangered species of the world.

THREATENDED SPECIES

The species which are liable to become extinct if proper measures are not taken to provide them protection, food and proper habitat so as to realize their full biotic potential. Red Data book contains full information about threatened plant and animal species. This book has pink pages for critically endangered species and as soon as species recovers, it is deleted from pink pages and entered on a green page.

Based on history of distribution, decline in number of individuals, nature of habitat and the potential value of species, IUCN has classified the plant and animal species into four groups:

Endangered (E) Species

These species are represented by small number of individuals and they are in danger of immenent extinction because of unfavourable environmental or human factors. *e.g.*, Lion Tailed macague, Asiatic wild Ass.

Vulnerable (V) or Depleted Species

These are the species having sufficient number of individuals but the organism is threatened with depletion due to some factor and in near future they may represent the category of endangered species if unfavorable conditions in environment continue to operate For example - Addax nasomaculatus, a member of Antelope family, was common from Egypt to Mauritiava. Now it has become extinct from Egypt, Libya, Algeria and Sudan and found in Mauritiana where it is hunted by nomads for dried meat.

Rare (R) Species

The species has small world population that are not at present endangered or vulnerable, but are at risk. Such species are usually localised within restricted geographical areas or habitats or are thinly scattered over a more extensive range. *e.g.*, clouded Leopard (Neotelis nebulosa), Hawaiian Monk Seal (Monachus schauinslandi) Great Indian Busterd.

Indeterminate (I) Species

Those species are in danger of extinction but the reason of extinction is not known. *e.g.*, Three. Banded Armadillo of Brazil, Short Eared Rabbit of Snmataci, Maxican Prairie dog.

RED DATA BOOK

IUCN was formed the Survival Service commission, which sought to supply upto date information about every species of wildlife in danger of extinction. The Red Data Book provides information about endangered species. According to an estimate, in last about 2,000 years the world has lost about 160 species of mammals and 88 species of birds. by way of extinction. In India 134 plant species have been declared. threatened as against to mammals, 22 reptiles and amphibians and 41 birds.

Endangered species of mammals, amphibians, reptiles and birds

Mammals

1. Andaman wild pig (*Sus scrofa* & *S. amanensis*)
2. Bharal (*Ovis nahura*)
3. Binturong (*Arctictis binturong*)
4. Bison or gaur or mithun (*Bos gaurus*)
5. Black buck (*Antelope cervicapra*)
6. Blue whale (*Balaenoptera musculus*)
7. Brown-antlered deer or Thamin (*Cervus eldt*)
8. Capped langur (*Presbytis pileatus*)
9. Caracal (*Felis caracal*)
10. Cetecean species
11. Cheetah (*Acinonyx jubatus*)
12. Chinese pangolin (*Manis pentadactyla*)
13. Chinkara or Indian gazelle (*Gazella gazella bennetti*)
14. Chital (*Axis axis*)
15. Clouded leopard (*Neofelis nebulosa*)
16. Crab-eating macaque (*Macaca irus umbrosa*)
17. Desert cat (*Felis libyca*)
18. Dugong (*Dugong dugong*)
19. Fishing cat (*Felis viverrina*)
20. Flying squirrels (all species of genera *Petaurista*, *Eupetaurus. Belomys*, *Hylopetes*)
21. Four-horned antelope (*Tetraceros quadricornis*)
22. Gangetic dolphin (*Platanista gangetica*)
23. Glant squirrels (*Ratufa macroura. R. indica. R. blcolor*)
24. Golden cat (*Felis temmincki*)

25. Golden langur (*Presbytis geei*)
26. Gorals (*Nemorhaedus goral, N. hodgsoni*)
27. Himalayan black bear (*Selenarctos thibetanus*)
28. Himalayan brown bear (*Ursus arctos*)
29. Himalayan crestless porcupine (*Hystrix hodgsoni*)
30. Himalayan ibex (*Capra ibex*)
31. Himalayan tahr (*Hemitragus jemlahicus*)
32. Hispid hare (*Caprolagus hispidus*)
33. Hog badger (*Arctonyx collaris*)
34. Hoolock or gibbon (*Hylobates hoolock*)
35. Hump-backed whale (*Megaptera nevaeangliae*)
36. Hyaena (*Hyaena hyaena*)
37. Indian elephant (*Elephas maximus*)
38. Indian lion (*Panthera leo persica*)
39. Indian wild ass (*Equus hemionus khur*)
40. Indian wolf (*Canis lupus pallipes*)
41. Kashmir stag or hangul (*Cervus elephus langul*)
42. Leaf monkey (*Presbytis melalophos*)
43. Leopard cat (*Felis bengalensis*)
44. Leopard or panther (*Panthera pardus*)
45. Lesser or red panda (*Wilurus fulgens*)
46. Lion-tailed macaque (*Macaca silenus*)
47. Loris (*Loris tardigradus*)
48. Lynx (*Felix lynx isabellinus*)
49. Malabar civet (*Viverra megaspila*)
50. Malay or sun bear (*Helarctos malayanus*)
51. Marbled cat (*Felis mormorate*)
52. Markhor (*Capra falconeri*)
53. Mouse deer (*Tragulus meminna*)
54. Musk deer (*Moschus moschiferus*)
55. Nilgai (*Boselaphus tragocamelus*)
56. Nilgiri langur (*Presbytis johni*)
57. Nilgiri thar (*llemitragus hylocrius*)
58. Otters (*Lutra lutra. L. perspicilata. Aonyx cinerea*)
59. Ovis ammon or nyan (*Ovis ammon hodgsoni*)
60. Pallasts cat (*Felis manul*)
61. Pangolin (*Manis crassicaudata*)
62. Pig-tailed macaque (*Macaca memestrina*)

63. Pygmy hog (*Sus sulvanius*)
64. Ratel (*Mellivora capensis*)
65. Red fox (*Vulpes vulpes*)
66. Rhinoceros (*Rhinoceros unicornis*)
67. Rusty-spotted cat (*Fellis rubiginosa*)
68. Sambar (*Cervus unicolor*)
69. Serow (*Capricornis sumatraensis*)
70. Sloth bear (*Melursus ursinus*)
71. Sloth bear (*Melursus ursinus*)
72. Slow loris (*Nycticebus coucang*)
73. Small travancora flying squirrel (*Pteromys fuscocapillus*)
74. Snow leopard (*Panthera uncia*)
75. Spotted linsang (*Prionodan pardicolor*)
76. Swamp deer or gond (*Cervus duvauceli*, all species)
77. Takin or mishmitakin (*Budorcas taxicolor*)
78. Tibetan antelope or Chiru (*Panthelopes hodgesoni*)
79. Tibetan gazelle (*Procapra picticaudata*)
80. Tibetan wild ass (*Equus hemionus kiang*)
81. Tiger (*Panthera tigris*)
82. Urial or shapu (*Ovis vignei*)
83. Wild buffalo (*Bubalus bubalis*)
84. Wild dog or dhole (*Cuon alpinus*)
85. Wild yak (*Bos grunniens*)

Amphibians and Reptiles

1. Agra monitor lizard (*Varanus griseus*)
2. Atlantic ridley turtle or Kemp's ridley turtle (*Lepidochelys kempii*)
3. Barred, oval or yellow monitor lizard (*Varanus flavescens*)
4. Estuarine crocodile (*Crocodylus porosus*) Salt water
5. Crocodile (*Crocodylus palustris*)
6. Gharial (*Gavialis gangeticus*)
7. Ganges soft-shelled turtle (*Trionyx gangeticus*)
8. Green sea turtle (*Chelonia mydas*)
9. Hawksbill turtle (*Eretmochelys imbricata inlscata*)
10. Himalayan newt or salamander (*Tryletotriton verrucosus*)
11. Indian egg-eating snake (*Elachistodon westermanni*)
12. Indian soft-shelled turtle (*Lissemys punctata punctata*)
13. Indian tent turtle (*Kachuga tecta tecta*)

14. Large Bengal minitor lizard (*Varanus bengalesis*)
15. Leathery turtle (*Dermochelys coriacea*)
16. Loggerhead turtle (*Caretta caretta*)
17. Olive-Back loggerhead turtle (*Lepidochelys oivacea*)
18. Tortoise (genera of families of *Testudinidae, Trionvchidae*)
19. Viviparous toads (*Nectophyrynoides* spp.)
20. Water lizard (*Varanus salvator*)

Birds

1. Andaman teal (*Anas gibberifrons albogularis*)
2. Bazas (*Aviceda jeordoni* and *A. leuphotes*)
3. Bengal florican (*Eupodotis bengalensis*)
4. Black necked crane (*Grus nigricollis*)
5. Blood pheasants (*Ithaginis cruentus tibetanus, Ithaginis cruentus kuseri*)
6. Brown headed gull (*Larus brunnicephalus*)
7. Cheer pheasant (*Catreus wallichii*)
8. Comb duck (*Sarkidiornis melanotos*)
9. Forest spotted owlet (*Athene blewitti*)
10. Great Indian bustard (*Choriotis nigriceps*)
11. Great Indian hornbill (*Buceros bicornis*)
12. Hooded crane (*Grus monacha*)
13. Hornbills (*Ptilolaemus tickelli austeni, Aceros nipalensis. Rhyticeros undulatus ticehursti*)
14. Houbara bustard (*Chlamydotis undulata*)
15. Humes bar-backed pheasant (*Syrmaticus humiae*)
16. Indian pied hornbill (*Anthracoceros malabaricus*)
17. Jerdon: courser (*Cursorius bitorquatus*)
18. Lammergeier (*Gypaetus barbatus*)
19. Large falcons (*Falco peregrinus, F. biarmicus* and *F. Chicquera*)
20. Large whistling teal (*Dendrocygna bicolor*)
21. Monal pheasants (*Lophophorus impejanus*)
22. Mountain quail (*Ophrysia superciliosa*)
23. Narcondom hornbill (*Rhyticeros undulatus narcondami*)
24. Nicobar megapode (*Megapodius freycinet*)
25. Nicobar pigeon (*Caloenas nicobarica pelewensis*)
26. Peacock pheasant (*Polyplectron bicalcaratum*)
27. Peafowl (*Pavo cristatus*)

28. Pinkheaded duck (*Rhodonessa caryophyllacea*)
29. Sclater's monal (*Lophophorus sclateri*)
30. Siberian white crane (*Grus leucogeranus*)
31. Spurfowl (*Gallaperdix* spp.)
32. Tibetan snow-cock (*Tetraogallus tibetanus*)
33. Tragopan pheasants (*Tragopan melanocephalus, T. blythii, T. satyra, T. temminckii*)
34. White bellied sea eagle (*Haliaeetus leucogaster*)
35. White-eared pheasant (*Crossoptilon crossoptilon*)
36. White spoonbill (*Platalea leucorodia*)
37. White-winged wood duck (*Cairina scutulata*)

WILDLIFE CONSERVATION

Conservation is practical embracing preservation, maintenance, sustainable utilization, restoration and enhancement of the natural environment. It takes into consideration of following objectives: (1) Maintenance of the ecological equilibrium between biotic and abiotic components of the ecosystem. (2) Preservation of the total gene pools of the different species at the global level. (3) Ensuring the optimum utilization of the present animal and plant species.

Wildlife of India

Girlion

Cheetah

Tiger

Wild Bear

Indian Elephant

Rhino

Wildlife of India

Pig

Zebra

Dog

Indian Wildass

Camel

Monkey

Wildlife of India

Rabbit

Wildpig

Fresh Water Crocodile

Lizard

Gharial

Owl

Eagle

Peacock

Conservation methodologies, to be meaningful can take the following two forms-

- *In situ* perservation
- *Ex situ* preservation

In situ Conservation

This type of conservation includes conservation of plant and animals in their native ecosystem or in man made ecosystem where they naturally occur. This type of conservation is applied only to wild flora and fauna and not to the domesticated animals and plants, because conservation is achieved by protection of population in nature. It mainly aims at preservation of lend races with wild relatives in which genetic diversity exists and/or in which the weedy/wild forms present hybrids with related cultivers. In-Situ conservation includes a system of protected areas of different categaries *e.g.*, National park, Sancturies, Biosphere Reserves, cultural landscapes, National monumentet The In-situ conservation of habitats has received high priority in the world conservation strategy programones launced since 1980. Institutional arrangements, especially in countries of the developing world, have been emphasised.

National Park

IUCN defined national park as a relatively large area **(a)** where one or several ecosystems are not materially altered by human exploitation and occupation, where plant and animal species, geomorphological sites and habitats are of special scientific, educative and recreative interest or which contain a natural landscape of great beauty and **(b)** where the highest competent authority of the country has taken steps to prevent or eliminate as soon as possible exploitation or occupation in the whole area and to enforce effectively the respect of ecological, geomorphological or aesthetic features which have led to its establishment and **(c)** where visitors are allowed to enter, under special conditions, for inspirational, cultural and recreative purposes.

Sanctuary

A wildlife Sanctuary, similar to national park, is dedicated to protect the wildlife, but it considers the conservation of species only and also the boundary of it is not limited by state legislation. Further, in the sanctuary, killing hunting or capturing of any species of birds and mammals is prohibited except by or under the control of highest authority in the department responsible for management of the sanctuary. Private ownership may be allowed to continue in a sanctuary, and forestry and other usages permitted to the extent that they do not adversely affect wildlife.

Biosphere Reserves

Biosphere Reserves is undisturbed natural area, is dedicated to conservation of biological diversity and genetic integerity of plants, animals and microorganism in their totality as well as scientific study. A protected area that can be declared as a biosphere, should satisfy the following essential criteria:

- Should provide a network of protected terrestrial and coastal environments which form a coherent system on a world scale.
- Should occur in each of the 193 biogeographical provinces of the world distinguished in the classification of Udvardy (1975), so as to exhibit the maximum genetic diversity.
- Should show a complete range of the different types of human intereference, from ecosystems untouched to those which have been degraded by humans.
- Structure and size should ensure the efficient conservation of the desired ecosystems.
- Should have sufficient resources available for ecological education, training and research to be carried on in respect to conservation of nature.
- If possible, should have geographical continuity with other types of protected areas.
- Should have adequate long-term legal protection.

Comparison of National Parks, Sanctuaries and Biosphere Reserves

TABLE 14.2: A comparison of National Parks, Wildlife Sanctuaries and Biosphere Reserves

National Park	Sanctuary	Biosphere Reserve
Attention is not given on biotic community as a whole, *i.e.* conservation being hitched to habitat for particular wild animal species like tiger, lion, rhino, etc.	Attention on biotic community not given; conservation being species oriented	Attention is focused on biotic community as a whole ecosystem oriented.
The approach is not based on scientific principles	Not based on scientific principles	Based on sound scientific on scientific principles
The size ranges from0.04 to 3162 sq. km; the usual size being between 100 and 500 sq. km. (in about 39%) and between 500 and 1000 sq. km. (in about 16%)	Size ranges from 0.61 to 7818 sq. km; usual size being between 100 and 500 sq. km. (in about 39%), between between 500 and 1000 sq. km. (in about 24%)	Size well over 5670 sq. km.
100 and 500 sq. km. (in about 39%), between between 500 and 1000 sq. km. (in about 24%)		
Boundries circumscribed by state legislation.	Limits are not sacrosant.	Boundaries circumscribed by state legislation.
No biotic interference except in buffer zone.	Limited biotic interference.	No biotic interference, except in buffer zone.
Tourism is not only permissible, but often encouraged	Permissible	Normally not permissible.
Research and scientific management lacking.	Lacking	Carried on
Due attention to gene pool conservation of economic	Lacking	Due attention being given to

National Park	Sanctuary	Biosphere Reserve
species, particularly of plants, has not been given.		conservation of plants as well as animal species.

In recent time approximately 4.2% of the total geographical area of the country is being used for extensive in-situ conservation habitats and ecosystem. A Protected area network of 8 Biosphere Reserves, 85 National Parks, 448 Wildlife Sancturies has been created which are useful in restoreing viable population and large mammals Table 14.3 gives the state wise details of protected areas and Table 14.4 provides the list of important National parks Wildlife Sancturies in India whereas, Table 14.5 provides the list of Biosphere Reserves.

TABLE 14.3: Wildlife Sanctuaries and National Parks

State and Union Territory	Total Number	Sanctuaries Area (Sq. Km.)	Total Number	National Park Area (Sq. Km.)
Andaman and Nicobar Islands	94	372.15	8	900.77
Andhra pradesh	21	11837.54	4	372.23
Arunachal Pradesh	09	6177.45	2	2468.23
Assam	08	990.58	2	930.00
Bihar	19	3881.75	2	567.32
Goa	04	355.78	1	107.00
Gujarat	21	16970.16	4	479.67
Haryana	10	342.65	1	1.43
Himachal Pradesh	30	40702.87	2	1295.00
Jammu & Kashmir	15	10157.67	4	3900.07
Karnataka	20	4238.21	5	2471.98
Kerala	12	2143.36	3	536.52
Madhya Pradesh	32	10567.05	1	6485.72
Maharastra	25	13995.49	5	958.45

State and Union Territory	Total Number	Sanctuaries Area (Sq. Km.)	Total Number	National Park Area (Sq. Km.)
Manipur	01	184.85	2	81.00
Meghalays	03	34.21	2	267.48
Mizorum	03	560.00	2	250.00
Nagaland	03	24.41	1	202.02
Orissa	18	6214.96	2	1212.70
Punjab	06	249.82	0	
Rajasthan	22	5662.87	4	3856.53
Sikim	04	92.10	1	850.00
Tamil Nadu	17	2671.03	5	401.63
Tripura	04	603.62	0	
Uttar Pradesh	29	8107.52	7	5429.83
West Bengal	15	1055.55	5	1695.65
Daman and Diu	01	2.18		
Delhi	01	13.20		
Chandigarh	01	25.42		

TABLE 14.4: National Parks and some important wildlife sanctuaries in India with indications of some of the more important animals

National parks/ Sanctuaries	Area	Fauna
Andhra Pradesh		
Pakhal Wildlife Sanctuary Warangal	54400 h	Tiger, panther, hyaena, fox, jungle cat, chawsingha, etc.
Pocharam Wildlife Sanctuary, Medak	2950 h	Horned games, aquatic, birds, including spot bill
Kawal Wildlife Sanctuary, Adilabad	89,096 h	Horned game and carnivores.
Kolleru Pelicanary, West Godavari	67,340 h	Pelicans.
Namidapha Wildlife Sanctuary, Tirap	807.82 sq km	Tiger, leopard, snow leopard, clouded leopard, several species of ca s, elephant, gaur, Jakin, swamp deer, hog deer, sloth bear, Himalayan black bear, slow loris,

National parks/ Sanctuaries	Area	Fauna
		hoolock, Malabar squirrel, etc.
Assam		
Kaziranga National Park, Kaziranga	430 sq km	Great Indian one-horned rhinoceros, Wild buffalo, gaur, swamp deer, hog deer, sambar, elephant, tiger, leopard cat, wild boar, langur, pelican, florican, patridge, python, etc.
Manas Wildlife Sanctuary, Kamrup	580 sq km	Some as in Kaziranga, also golden langur, pigmy hog, water monitor; bird life is rich and interesting.
Sonai-Rupa Wildlife Sanctuary, Kamrup	195 sq km	One-horned rhinoceros, elephant, wild buffalo, wild boar, sambar, swamp deer, barking deer, tiger, leopard, wild dog, sloth bear, hornbill, imperial pigeon.
Bihar		
Hazaribagh National Sanctuary Hazaribagh	184 sq km	Tiger, leopard, sloth bear, wild dog, hyaena, sambar, harking deer, chital, chawsingha, neelghai, civet cat, wild boar, etc.
Betla National Park, Palamau	345 sq km	Tiger, leopard, jungle cat, chital, guar, elephant, sambar, wild boar, langur, rhesus, etc.
Ganauli Sanctuary, Bettiah	132 sq km	Leopard, wild boar, sloth bear, chital langur, rhesus, etc.
Goa		
Mollen Wildlife Sanctuary, Goa	240 sq km	Panther, gaur, sambar, barking deer, mouse deer, malabar squirrel, flying squirrel, ant eater, porcupine, slender loris, grey jungle fowl and number of other birds, python, king cobra, etc.
Cotgao Wildlife Sanctuary, Goa	105 sq km	Panther, gaur, sambar, barking deer, mouse deer, malabar squirrel, flying squirrel, ant eater, porcupine, slender loris, grey jungle fowl and number of other birds, python, king cobra, etc
Gujarat		
Gir National Park, Junagarh	140.40 sq km	Indian lion, panther, hyaena, sambar, chital, neelgai, chawsingha, chinkara,

National parks/ Sanctuaries	Area	Fauna
		wild boar, langur, crocodile.
Gir Wildlife Sanctuary, Junagarh	1412.13 sq km	same as above.
Velavadar National Park, Bhavnagar	17.83 sq km	Black-buck, wolf, etc.
Wild Ass Sanctuary in Little Rann of Kutch, Surendra Nagar	4840.83 sq km	Wild ass, neelgai, wolf, chinkara.
Nal Sarovar Bird Sanctuary, Ahmedabad	115 sq km	Water birds.
Haryana		
Sultanpur Lake Bird Sanctuary, Gurgaon	28.87 sq km	Most of the birds are migratory.
Himachal Pradesh		
Sechu-tun-Nallah Sanctuary, Chamba	414.40 sq km	Goral, serow, ibex, Himalayan Tahr, musk deer, Himalayan brown bear,
Gamgul-Siya-Behli Sanctuary, Chamba	900.75 sq km	Himalayan black bear, Snow fox, martin, weasal, monal, tragopan,
Kugti Sanctuary, Chamba	11828.70 hectares	snow cock, koklash, kalij, chakor.
Daranghati Sanctuary, Kinnaur	16740 hectares	Same as above.
Nargu and Winch Camo Sanctuary, Mandi	27837.60 hectares	Same as above.
Gobindsagar, Dilaspur	10034 h	Water birds.
Jammu & Kashmir		
Dachigam Wildlife Sanctuary, Srinagar	55 sq km	Hangul, serow, musk deer, Himalayan black bear, brown bear, pine martin, other avian fauna.
Karnataka		
Bandipur National Park, Mysore	874.20 sq km	Elephant, gaur, sambar, chital, barking deer, chawsingha, wild boar, tiger, leopard, sloth bear, jungle cat, langur, wild dog, Bird life quite rich.

National parks/ Sanctuaries	Area	Fauna
Nagarhole National Park, Coorg	571.55 sq km	Same as Bandipur.
Ranganthitto Bird Sanctuary. Mysore	26.70 sq km	Open bill, stork, white ibis, little egret, cattle egret, darter, cormorants, river tern, spoon bill, crocodile.
Kerala		
Periyar Wildlife Sanctuary	777 sq km	Elephant, tiger, leopard, sloth bear, wild dog, gaur, neelgai, sambar, barking deer, wild boar.
Wynad Wildlife Sanctuary	344 sq km	Similar as Periyar.
Neyyar Wildlife Sanctuary	128 sq km	Elephant, sambar, chital, neelgai, wild boar.
Madhya Pradesh		
Kanha National Park	446.60 sq km	Tiger, leopard, gaur, swamp, deer, of hard ground, sambar, chital, black-buck, etc.
Shivpuri national Park	155 55 sq km	Tiger, leopard, neelgai, chawsingha, sambar, chital, etc.
Bandhavgarh National Park	267.75 sq km	Tiger, leopard, gaur, sambar, chital, barking deer, chinkara, wild boar, neelgai, sloth bear.
Maharshtra		
Tadoda National Park	116.55 sq km	Tiger, panther, sloth bear, gaur, sambar, chital, neelgai, chinkara.
Dhakna-Kolkaz Wildlife Sanctuary (now under Project Tiger)	381.58 sq km	Tiger, panther, gaur, sambar, barking deer, chawsingha, sloth bear, wild boar and chital confined to flat tracts, Bird life rich.
Yawal Wildlife Sanctuary	177.52 (sq km)	As in Dhakna Kolkar and also jungle cat, bonnet macaque, langur, neelgai, wild dog etc.
Karnala Bird Sanctuary	4.48 sq km	140 species of birds seen during October to April: other wildlife are panther, chawsingha and common langur.
Manipur		
Keibul Wildlife	25 sq km	Brown-antered deer and also some water

National parks/ Sanctuaries	Area	Fauna
Sanctuary		birds.
Meghalaya		
Balpakram (Proposed) Sanctuary	221 sq km	Elephant, gaur, wild boar, sambar chital etc.
Mizoram		
Dampa Wildlife	180 sq km	Tiger, leopard, elephant, gaur, sambar, barking deer, wild boar, wild dog, Himalayan black bear, leopard cat, etc.
Nagaland		
Intangki Wildlife Sanctuary	202.02 sq km	Tiger, panther, clouded leopard, elephant, gaur, barking deer, etc.
Orissa		
Simplipal National Park (Proposed)		Elephant, sambar, barking deer, leopard, tiger, etc.
Khalasuni Wildlife	115 sq km	Tiger, leopard, sloth bear, elephant, gaur, neelgai, sambar, barking deer, chital,
Punjab		
Abohar Wildlife Sanctuary	228 sq km	Black buck and several species of birds.
Rajasthan		
Tiger Project Rathambar	392 sq km	Tiger, leopard, jungle cat, sloth bear, neelgai, sambar, chital, wild boar, etc.
Sariska Wildlife Sanctuary	195 sq km	Tiger, leopard, hyaena, jungle cat, sambar, neelgai, chawsingha, etc.
Ghana Bird Sanctuary	29 sq km	About 300 migratory and resident birds. Also black buck, wild boar, sambar, chital, etc.
Sikkim		
Kanchenjunga National Park	800 sq km	Musk deer, goral, bharal, Himayalan black bear, show leopard, Tibetan wolf.
Tamil Nadu		
Mudumalai Wildlife Sanctuary	321 sq km	Tiger, leopard, elephant, gaur, sambar, chital, sloth bear, wild dog.
Vedanthangal water	30 sq km	Several species of water birds.

National parks/ Sanctuaries	Area	Fauna
Bird Sanctuary		
Uttar Pradesh		
Corbett National Park	525 sq km	Tiger, leopard, sloth bear,, elephant sambar chital, hog deer, barking deer, chawshingha, wild boar, crocodile, rich bird life.
Dudwa National Park	500 sq km	Tiger, leopard, sloth bear, swamp deer, sambar, chital, hog deer, barking deer, neelgai.
West Bengal		
Sunderban Tiger Reserve	2585 sq km	Tiger, sambar, chital, wild boar, several species of birds and crocodiles.
Jaldapara Wildlife Sanctuary	115.53 sq km	Rhino, elephant, tiger, leopard, wild boar, gaur, sambar, barking deer, hog dear.
Senchal Wildlife Sanctuary	38.88 sq km	Serow, Himalayan black bear, goral, etc.

TABLE 14.5: List of Biosphere Reserves

Name of Bio-sphere Reserve	State/union territory	Area in sq. km.	Data of Set-up
Nanda Devi	Uttar Pradesh	2,236.74	18.01.1988
Nokrek	Meghalaya	80.00	01.09.1988
Nokrek Manas	Assam	600.00	14.03.1989
Sunderbans	West Bengal	9,636.00	29.03.1989
Gulf of Mannar	Tamil Nadu	10,500.00	18.02.1989
Nilgiri	Karnataka, Kerala & Tamil Nadu	5,520.00	01.08.1986
Great Nicobar	Andaman & Nicobar Islands	885.00	06.01.1989
Similipal	Orissa	2,750.00	21.06.1994

Desert Biosphere Reserve yet to be established.

PROJECTS TO CONSERVE WILD LIFE

Programmes have also been launched for scientific management and use of fragile ecosystems specific programmes for management and conservation of wetlands, mangroves and coral reef systems are also being implemented. Six internationally important wetlands of India have been declared "Ramsarsites" under Ramsar convention and eleven wetland have been identified for intensive conservation and management. The Tura range in Garo Hills of Meghalaya is a gene santuary for preserving the rich native diversity of wild citrus and *Musa* species. Sancturies for Rhododendrons and Orchids have been established in Sikkim.

Large Mammal species targeted projects based on the perception of threat to them have been implemented.

Save the Barasingha Campaign

In 1969 the Government of Madhya Pradesh launched the Save the Barasingha Campaign. The Barasingha (Cervs duvauceli) was once plentiful in central, northern and eastern India. In 1970 only 66 were left in and around Kanha. The action plan, to save the animal species from extinction, included the following activities:

- Regeneration of the grasslands
- Reclamation of the habitat
- Removal of human population from the area
- Construction of enclosure
- Taking up of anti-poaching measures.

There is increase in Barasingha population from 66 in 1970 to 574 in 1988 due to above activities.

Gir Lion Project

In 1972, a five year plan was proposed by the Government of Gujarat to protect this magnificent feline species in the Gir Sanctuary. It has an area of about 1412 km^2. It is now declared as a national park and the ecological balance of the habitat is properly protected. The lion population has increased from 177 in 1968 to 180 in 1984.

Project Tiger

The population of Tiger (*Panthera tigris*) reduced from 40,000 at the turn of the century to 1827 in 1972. In 1, April 1973, Project Tiger was launched by Government of India, which resulted in increase in tiger population in country.

Crocodile Breeding Project

Crocodile Breeding and Management Project was launched by Government of India in 1975 for all the three endangered crocodile species:

- The freshwater crocodile (Crocodylus palustris).
- Saltwater crocodile (Crocodylus porosus).
- The rare gharial (Gavialis gangeticus).

Operation Rhino

Number of Indian rhino or one horned Rhinoceros (R. unicaris) are last due to hunting and flood. To protect the Indian species, centrally sponsored rehabilitation programme was undertaken in Dudhwa National Park.

Project Elephant

The population of Indian elephant *Elephas maximus* is threatended due to poaching for ivory and habitat destruction. An ambitious programme "Project Elephant" was launched by Ministry of Environment and forest for restoring the lost and degraded habitat of elephant, which will focus on solving the problems of humans and elephants competing to share the same habitat.

All these programmes, though focused on single species, have a wider impact as they conserve habitats and variety of other species in those habitats.

ORGANIZATIONS FOR WILD LIFE CONSERVATION

Indian Board for Wildlife (IBWL)

It is first constituted in 1952 as the advisory body under the name Central Board for Wildlife which is later renamed as Indian Board for

Wildlife. It is mainly responsible for wildlife conservation with the assistance of the central and state governments. It works in close co-operation of WWF. The functions of the IBWL, among others are:

- To devise ways and means for the preservation and control of wildlife through coordinated legislative and practical measures;
- To sponsor the setting up of national parks, wildlife sanctuaries and zoological gardens;
- To promote public interest in wildlife and the need for its preservation in harmony with natural and human environments;
- To advise the Government on policy in respect of export of plants and animals; and
- To prevent cruelty to birds and beasts caught alive with or without injury.

World Wildlife Fund-India (WWF-India)

It was established in India in 1969 at the time of XII General Assembly of the IUCN, held at Delhi. It was founded as a branch of WWF-International formed in 1961 with its headquarters at Glands, Switzerland.

ACTS FOR WILDLIFE PROTECTION

It emphasis on conservation of ecosystem and support to the management of the country is protected areas network. To prevent wildlife depletion, several Acts have been made from time to time, by State as well as Central Government, The important ones are:

- Madras Wildlife Act, 1873
- All-India Elephant Preservation Act, 1879
- The Wild Birds and Animals Protection Act, 1912
- Bengal Rhiniceros Preservation Act, 1932
- Assam Rhimoceros Preservation Act, 1954
- All-India Wildlife Protection Act, 1972, amended in 1983, 1986 and 1991.

TABLE 14.6: Important faunal diversity of Gujarat.

SN	Animal Name	Ecosystem	Habitat Type		Status	Remarks
			Terrain	Distribution		
CARNIVORE						
1.	*Panthera leo persica (Asiatic Lion)*	Forest	Flat to gently sloping	Open thorn scrub, Open dry deciduous (Gir-Girnar)	R	Last surviving polulation in World
2.	*Panthera tigris (Tiger)*	Forest (dense)	-do-	Moist deciduous Bamboo breaks (Dangs)	E	Only few
3.	*Panthera pardus (Panther)*	Forest,	Flat, hilly & non-forest ravines	Dry deciduous thorn scrub, moist deciduous, Bamboo breaks Hilly Savanah (All over Gujarat)	C	Common all over state
4.	*Felis caracal (Caracal)*	Desert	Flat to gently sloping	Desert thorn scrub (Kachchh)	R & E	Sighting very rare
5.	*Felis chaus (Jungle Cat)*	Forest Grassland	-do-	Dry deciduous Moist Deciduous Grassland, Bamboo breaks (All Forests of Gujarat)	C	Restricted to forest & ravines
6.	*Felis libyca (Desert Cat)*	Forest (open) Grassland desert	Flat	Dry deciduous desert grassland, desert thorn scrub, Grassland and Hilly savannah	R	Not common

SN	Animal Name	Ecosystem	Habitat Type		Status	Remarks
			Terrain	Distribution		
7.	*Felis rubiginosa (Rusty-spotted Cat)*	Forest (dense)	Flat to gentle sloping	Moist deciduous, Dry deciduous (mixed), Bamboo breaks	R	Sighting rare
8.	*Felis bengalensis (Leopard Cat) (dense)*	Forest	-do-	Moist deciduous, bamboo breaks	R	-do-
9.	*Mellivora capensis (Ratel)*	-do-	Flat	Dry deciduous, Moist deciduous	R	-do-
10.	*Vivericula indica (Small Indian Civet)*	Forest	-do-	Dry deciduous, Moist deciduous Thorn scrub	C	Sighting rare
11.	*Paradocurus niger (Palm civet)*	Forest	Flat to gentle sloping	Moist deciduous, Bamboo (Moist)	R	-
12.	*Hyaena hyaena*	Forest	Hilly to flat	Dry deciduous, Moist Deciduous, Dry Teak, Thorn scrub. (All over Gujarat)	C	Fairly common
13.	*Canis lupus (Wolf)*	Grassland	Flat	Grasslands & open Dry deciduous scrub	Very rare	Occassional (not common)
14.	*Canis aureus (Jackal)*	Open Forests Grasslands	Flat to gentle sloping	Dry deciduous, Moist deciduous Dry teak, Grasslands (All over Gujarat)	Very Common	Common

SN	Animal Name	Ecosystem	Habitat Type		Status	Remarks
			Terrain	Distribution		
15.	*Cuon alpinus (Wild Dog)*	Forest	Flat	Moist deciduous, Dry deciduous	R & E	Sighting doubtful
16.	*Vulpus bengalensis (Fox)*	Forest, Grassland	-do-	Dry deciduous, Thom scrub, Teak (Gir & few other forests)	Not common	Not very often
HERBIVORES						
17.	*Axis axis (Chital)*	Forest	Flat to gentle	Dry deciduous, Moist deciduous Riverine dry teak, Thorn scrub, Bamboo breaks, (Gir & Girnar and Rajpipla)	C	Common in Gir only
18.	*Cervus unicolor (Sambar)*	Forest (dense)	Hilly, sloping & flat	Dry deciduous mixed, Moist deciduous, Riverine moist, Bamboo breaks (Gir, Girnar & (Rajpipla)	-do-	-do-
19.	*Muntiacus muntjak (Barking deer)*	-do-	Hilly	Moist deciduous mixed Moist Bamboo breaks	Fairly Common	Only in School-paneshwar PA & Dangs
20.	*Tetracerus quadricornis (Four-horned antelope)*	-do-	-do-	Dry deciduous Moist deciduous Hilly Savannah Moist bamboo breaks (Gir. Girnar and Rajpipla)	C	Common in Forests

SN	Animal Name	Ecosystem	Habitat Type		Status	Remarks
			Terrain	Distribution		
21.	*Gazella gazella bonnetti (Chinkara)*	Open Forests, Dry grassland	Hilly to undulating	Desert grassland, Hilly Open Thorn Hilly Open thorn Scrub, (Eastern Gir, Kachchh)	R	Common in Grasslands only
22.	*Boselaphus tragocamelus (Bluebull)*	Forests, Grassland,	Hilly, sloping& flat	Dry deciduous, Open scrub, Thorn scrub, (All over Gujarat)	Very common	Not found in South Gujarat
23.	*Antilope cervicapra (Blackbuck)*	Grasslands	Flat	Grasslands Velavadar, parts of Saurashtra	C	In Saurashtra &N. Gujarat
OMNIVORES						
24.	*Melursus ursinus (Solth bear)*	Forest	Hilly	Dry deciduous, Moist deciduous mixed (Shoolpaneshwar, Ratanmahal Jessore)	Not common	Found where choice flowering fruiting trees & shrubs found
25.	*Sus scrof a (Wild pig)*	-do-	Flat to gentle slope	Dry deciduous, Moist deciduous Sugar cam & groundnut fields	C	Their movement depends upon agricultural crops
26.	*Presbytis entellus (Common langur)*	Forest non-forest habitations	Flat	Dry deciduous mixed, Dry deciduous teak,	C	Forms useful symbiotic link with ungulates in forests
27.	*Macaca mulatta*	Forest	Flat to hilly	Moist deciduous, Riverine	Not	Under pressure

SN	Animal Name	Ecosystem	Habitat Type		Status	Remarks
			Terrain	Distribution		
	(Rhesus macaque)	(dense)		village and city environs (All over Gujarat) (Shoolpaneshwar & Dangs)	common	
28.	*Varanus varanus (Monitor lizard)*	Forest Non-forest	Flat	Dry deciduous, Moist deciduous	Very common	-
29.	*Uromastrix hardwikii (Spiny-tailed lizard)*	Desert Grassland	Flat	Open thorn scrub Desert grassland, wasteland	R	Only in Surendra Nagar district
30.	*Crocodilus palustris (Marsh crocodile)*	Aquatic	Flat	Lake, Rivers, Nallahs (Gir, Narmada river Girnar, Ajwa lake and Saurashtra reservoirs)	C	-
31.	*Lutra lutra (Common otter)*	Aquatic	Flat	Rivers (Narmada) downstream)	R	Under pressure, rarely seen
32.	*Ratufa indica dealbata (Dangs giant squirrel)*	Forest	Hilly, Undulating & Flat (Streams)	Moist deciduous, mixed, Moist bamboo breaks	R/E	Sighting rare found in area with less human pressure
33.	*Petaurista petaurista philippensis (Giant flying squirrel)*	-do-	Undulating to flat, near streams	Moist deciduous mixed	R/E	-do-

SN	Animal Name	Ecosystem	Habitat Type		Status	Remarks
			Terrain	Distribution		
34.	*Herpestes edwardsi (Common Mongoose)*	Forest Non-forest Wastelands	Flat	Thorn scrub, Dry deciduous, Moist deciduous (Gir, Girnar, Rajpipla)	C	Any type of scrubby and forest habitat
35.	*Herpestes auropunctatus (small Indian mongoose)*	Forest	Flat	Dry deciduous, Thorn scrub (Gir, Girnar)	Not common	Forest areas
36.	*Herpestes smithi (Ruddy mongoose)*	-do-	-do-	Dry deciduous, Thron scrub (Gir, Girnar)	Not common	Forest areas
37.	*Hystrix indica (Porcupine)*	-do-	-do-	Dry deciduous Thorn scrub (All forests of Gujarat)	C	In forest areas only
38.	*Manis crassicaudata (Pangolin)*	Forest Grassland	-do-	Dry deciduous, Dry Grasslands (Gir, Saurashtra, North Gujarat)	Not common	Over grazed open areas
39.	*Python molurus (Python)*	Forest	-do-	Dry deciduous, Moist deciduous, Riverine (Dangs, Rajpipla, Gir, Girnar)	-do-	Dense forest areas
40.	*Lepus nigricollis (Indian hare)*	Grassland Forest Non-forest	Flat gentle sloping	All land habitats (All Gujarat)	C	Open areas
41.	*Geochelon spp. (Star tortoise)*	Forest,	Flat	Dry deciduous Riverine	R/E	Presently found in Gir, Girnar &

SN	Animal Name	Ecosystem	Habitat Type		Status	Remarks
			Terrain	Distribution		
						Grasslands of Saurashtra
AVIFAUNA						
42.	*Great Indian Bustard*	M	Desert grassland	Desert thorn scrub, Desert grasslands	R	Kachchh & Saurashtra
43.	*Houbara Bustard*	M	Desert grassland	-do-	R	- do -
44.	*Lesser Florican*	M	Grassland	Grasslands Savannah	R	- do - Panchmahals
45.	*Lesser Flamingo*	M	Coastal (Marine) wetland	Coastal mangrove, intertidal waters, lakes,	C	- do - along coast
46.	*Great Flamingo*	M	- do -	- do -	C	- do -
47.	*Grey Hornbill*	R	Forest	Moist decidous mixed, Dry deciduous mixed	R/E	Areas with tall trees
48.	*Hodgson's Frogmouth*	R	Forest	Moist deciduous mixed Moist Bamboo breaks	- do -	Hilly Bamboo areas
49.	*Streaked spider hunter*	R	Forest	Moist deciduous mixed Moist Bamboo breaks	R	- do -
50.	*Emerled Dove*	R	Forest	Moist deciduous Teak Moist deciduous mixed	R/E	Dense wooded areas

SN	Animal Name	Ecosystem	Habitat Type		Status	Remarks
			Terrain	Distribution		
51.	*Alexendrine Parakeet*	R	Forest	Moist deciduous	- do -	Shoolpaneshwar
52.	*Demoiselle Crane*	M	Wetland Agri-fields	Lake banks Agri-fields	C	Saurashtra
53.	*Common Crane*	M	- do -	- do -		Occassional More than a million visit Gujarat.
54.	*King Vulture*	R	Forest	Dry deciduous, Riverine	R	- do -
55.	*Peregrine Falcon*	R	Forest	R		Saurashtra Gir
56.	*Imperial Eagle*	R	Forest	Dry deciduous, Moist deciduous Riverine		Gir, Rajpipla
57.	*Crested Serpent Eagle*	R	Forest	- do -		- do -
58.	*Crested Hawk Eagle*	R	Forest	- do -		- do -
59.	*Marsh and other Harriers*	M	Grassland Forest	Grassland, Dry deciduous		Velavadar, Gir
61.	*Grey Jungle Fowl*	R	Forest	Moist deciduous		Shoolpaneshwar
62.	*Marbled Teal*	M	Wetland Marine	Wetlands,		Jamnagar coast

SN	Animal Name	Ecosystem	Habitat Type		Status	Remarks
			Terrain	Distribution		
63.	*Indian Pitta*	M	Forest	Dry deciduous, Moist deciduous, Riverine		Gir, Girnar, Velavadar

(r = rare, e = endangered, c = common)

TABLE 14.7: List of marine animals with their zones.

S.No.	MARINE ANIMAL	ZONE	STATUS	REMARKS
MARINE FAUNA				
1.	*Delphinus delphis* (Dolphin)	Deep sea and intertidal zone	Rare & endangered	
2.	*Balanoptera sp.* (Whale)	Deep sea	Rare	
3.	*Dugong dugon* (Dugong)	Deep sea	Rare & endangered	
4.	*Chelonia mydas* (Green Sea Turtle)	Deep sea and intertidal zons Marine island beaches	Rare	Nesting in Gulf of Kachchh and Junagadh, Bhavnagar coast and
5.	*Lepidochelys olivacea* (Olive Ridley's Turtle)	Deep sea and intertidal zons Marine island beaches	Rare and endangered	- do -
6.	*Dermochelys coriacea*	Deep sea and intertidal zons Marine island beaches	Rare and endangered	Only seen near Bhaidar island in Gulf of Kachchh
7.	*Ikedosoma pirotanensis*	Coral reefs near lagoons	Rare and	Mostly found in Porroitis corals. Rare

S.No.	MARINE ANIMAL	ZONE	STATUS	REMARKS
	(Bonnelia)		endangered	in world
8.	*Ikedosoma pirotanensis* (Bonnelia)	Coral reefs near islands	Rare and endangered	Endemic
9.	*Placenta placenta* (Pearl Oyster)	Gulf of Kachchh near Pirotan Island	Rare and endangered	Mostly destroyed due dredging by cement company
10.	*Pinctada fucata* (Window pan Oyster)	Gulf of Kachchh	Rare and endangered	Commercially exploitable / Fisheries Deptt

Several non-government organizations in the country are engaged in specific areas of target species in-situ conservation measures through external or Natural assistance or through a combination of assistance from both. *e.g.*, In-situ conservation of medical plants by Foundation of Revitalization of Local Health-Tradition (FRLHT) in the southern state of country.

Gaps between Provisions and Practices

Vast variety of plant and animal species occurs in nature. Attention is given to only few species out of spectrum of species existing in ecosystem. Selective exploitation of species (which are economically important and are of other direct use values) for several years does reflect in the imbalance of ecosystem and less production.

This selective management by man has resulted in cultivation of some selected species and gradual elemination of presently less important ones and resulting in loss of biodiversity.

The current protected area network is unevenly distributed over states and biogeographic areas. Some of biodiversity such areas are not protected. Many National parks and Santuries are yet to complete legal procedures prescribed under the Wildlife (Protection) Act 1972 and in several areas, issues relating to settlements of right yet to be resolved, consequently, there are gaps in information on several biological and managerial Parameters.

Protected Areas of Gujarat

Gir Lion National Park and Sanctuary

Location: Junagadh and Amereli district/ ***Area:*** Sanctuary/ 1153.42 sq.kms/ National park 258.71 sq.kms./ Total: 1412.13 sq.km.

The last abode of Asiatic Lions (*Panthera leo persica*) in the entire world. The habitat represents the best example of the dry deciduous forests in the country. It has got the highest concentration of the two largest predators in the country *i.e.* Asiatic lions (304) and panthers (230). Other wild animals include cheetal, sambar, chowsingha, chinkara, wildboar, nilgai, ratel, rusty-spotted cat, pangolin, crocodile, etc. It is one of the best managed national Park and Sanctuary in the country.

Marine National Park and Sanctuary

Location: Sea coast in Jamnagar District/ ***Area:*** Sanctuary/458 sq.km./ National Park: 163 sq.km. National Park area is included in Marine Sanctuary area.

It is the first Marine National Park and Sanctuary in the country with rich marine floral and faunal diversity. There are more than 40 species of Corals and 70 species of Sponges. Bonnelia, which is recorded only at three placed in the world, is found here. Three of the world's six marine turtles (leather back, green and Oliver Ridley's turtle) are found here. Besides, large marine mammals like whales, dolphins and dugongs are also seen in the Gulf of Kachchh. Other marine life Includes sea horse, sea anemone, star fish, crabs, coral fishes, sea hare, octopus, squid, sea shells etc. According to late Dr. Salim Ali, the country's best aquatic and marine bird concentration and one of the best mangrove forests are found here.

Velavadar Blackbuck National Park

Location: Bhavnagar District/ ***Area:*** 34.08 sq.km.

A grassland of very high ecological value in the saline Bhal region has almost flat terrain. It falls in the low rainfall region of the semi-arid Saurashtra. It has the largest concentration of blackbucks along with the only predators of this area, *i.e.*, wolf. With effective improvement of grassland status in the park, the area now has perhaps the largest concentration of lesser floricans (above 42) during breeding season.

Vansda National Park

Location: Valsad District/ ***Area:*** 23.99 sq.km.

This contains moist deciduous forest which falls in the Western Ghats, and contains wildlife such as panther, cheetal, sambar, wildboar, barking deer, racket tailed drongo and orioles etc. Although, the habitat is well suited for wild animals, the animal population is very low.

Nal Sarovar Bird Sanctuary

Location: Surendranagar District/ ***Area:*** 120.82 sq.km.

The largest natural wetland habitat in the state which attracts large number of winter migrants such as ducks, geese, storks, spoonbills, flamingoes, plovers, coots, cormorants and pelicans etc. A heaven for ornithologists, naturalists and bird watchers.

Khijadia Bird Sanctuary

Location: Jamanagar District/ ***Area:*** 6.05 sq.km.

Being situated close to the sea coast, this sanctuary attracts marine as well as fresh water birds. Although small in area, it is probably richer in bird diversity than Bharatpur. The unique location and typical terrain of the area ensures the availability of both fresh as well as sea water in the same area. This sanctuary attracts migratory birds such as flamingoes, pelicans, cranes, plovers, spoonbills, arctic terns, gulls, skimmers, grebes etc.

Thol Bird Sanctuary

Location: Mehsana District/ ***Area:*** 6.99 sq.km.

This bird sanctuary attracts a large population of ducks, such as shovellers, brahminyduck, pintail, teals, widgeon, cranes and other migratory birds.

Porbandar Bird Sanctuary

Location: Junagadh district/ ***Area:*** 0.09 sq.km.

Located in the middle of the coastal city of Porbandar which also happens to be the birth place of Mahatma Gandhi. The most peculiar feature of this city which falls in the semiarid drought prone Saurashtra is the terrain of the whole city which is saucer shaped. Due to this, even during low rainfall years, sufficient water is available for birds. This small lake attracts large concentrations of flamingoes, cranes, egrets, stilt, etc.

Gaga Great Indian Bustard Sanctuary

Location: Jamnagar district/ ***Area:*** 3.33 sq.km.

A typical grassland habitat which has great Indian bustard besides other birds like pipits, larks, coursers etc.

Kachchh Bustard Sanctuary

Location: Kachchh District / ***Area:*** 2.03 sq.km.

In this Desert thorn scrub and grassland habitat, good concentration of great Indian bustard is reported.

Wild Ass Sanctuary

Location: Surendranagar and Kachchh District/ ***Area:*** 4,953.70 sq.km.

One of the largest sanctuaries in the country, represents true desert habitat. It is inhabited by Asiatic wild asses (*Equas hemionus khur*), one of the seven sub-species found in the world. More than 2,000 wild asses roam over this vast arid habitat alongwith nilgai, blackbuck etc. This sanctuary also has some rare birds like great Indian bustard, houbara bustard, lesser floricans, cranes, pelicans, spoonbills etc. It is a unique ecosystem, spread over a large tract of saline land.

Ratanmahal Sloth Bear Sanctuary

Location: Panchmahal District/ ***Area:*** 55.65 sq.km.

It is famous for sloth bears, having typical hilly, deciduous vegetation rich in floral biodiversity. The sanctuary falls in the tribal area of the state and it has richest biological diversity in the whole district.

Jessore Sloth Bear Sanctuary

Location: Banaskantha District/ ***Area:*** 180.66 sq. km.

This is also a sloth bear sanctuary with dry deciduous scrub type of forests. Besides sloth bear, nilgai, wildboar and panther are other major species found here.

Jamughoda Wildlife Sanctuary

Location: Panchmals District/ ***Area:*** 130.38 sq. km.

This area is known for its floral diversity and has panthers, wildboars etc. It is believed that till few decades back, the whole district had the same type of floral and faunal diversity.

Purna Wildlife Sanctuary

Location: Dangs District/ ***Area:*** 160.84 sq. km.

This sanctuary has a typical tiger habitat with moist deciduous forests and is rich in floral and avifaunal diversity. This sanctuary is characterised by typical western ghat vegetation and it also represents the best forests of Western Ghats which falls in the Gujarat state. It is one of the most important gene pool of floral resources and a unique ecosystem of the state.

Narayan Sarovar Chinkara Sanctuary

Location: Kachchh District/ ***Area:*** 765.79 sq.km.

This sanctuary has desert thorn scrub and grassland habitat with excellent concentration of Chinkaras and occasional Bustards. Recently, the area of this sanctuary has been reduced.

Shoolpaneshwar Wildlife Sanctuary

Location: Bharuch district/ ***Area:*** 607.70 sq.km.

Falling in the catchment area of Karjan and Narmada rivers, Shoolpaneshwar has excellent floral and faunal diversity. Animals include sloth bear, sambhar, wildboar, rusty spotted cat, toddy cat, leopard cat, panther, giant flying squirrels, barking deer, chowsingha and a variety of birds like sun-birds, parakeets, birds of prey, grey hornbill, woodpeckers, etc.

Barda Sanctuary

Location: Junagadh and Jamnagar districts/ ***Area:*** 192.31 sq.km.

The habitat is hilly and dry deciduous, located in arid regions of Saurashtra. The rainfall is very low, scanty and erratic, often leading to droughts. The biotic pressure on this sanctuary is very high. The forest is degraded but during the past few years, a concerted effort has been made to conserve and improve the ecosystem. This area has been envisaged as an alternative home of Asiatic lions. The moisture conservation efforts and improved habitat protection has given excellent results. This scrub forest is very rich in floral diversity. Animals reported are sambhar, nilgai, wildboar, panthers etc. This area falls in the Greater Gir Ecosystem along with Girnar, coastal forests and grasslands.

Rampara Wildlife Sanctuary

Location: Rajkot District/ ***Area:*** 15.01 sq.km.

A small sanctuary with grassland habitat, is mainly inhabited by nigai besides wildboar, wolf, chinkara, hyaena etc. The terrain is Suacer shaped and scarcity of water is quite common.

Kachchh Desert Wildlife Sanctuary

Location: Kachchh District/ ***Area:*** 7506.22 sq.kms.

Typical desert habitat with desert flora and fauna such as bustards, nilgai, caracal, chinkara etc.

Paniya Sanctuary

Location: Amreli district/ ***Area:*** 39.63 sq.km.

It is a part of Gir forests with the same kind of habitat and wildlife as in Gir. In this sanctuary blackbuck, nilgai, Asiatic lions, panthers etc are reported.

Balaram-Ambaji Wildlife Sanctuary

Location: Banaskantha District/ ***Area:*** 542.08 sq.km.

Typical dry deciduous habitat with animals such as nilgai, chowsingha, panther, sloth bear etc. are seen in the area. The area is rich in floral diversity.

Hingolgadh Nature Education Sanctuary

Location: Rajkot District/ ***Area:*** 6.54 sq.km.

This Sanctuary is famous as a Nature Education Centre with excellent open deciduous type of vegetation. It is a major centre for imparting nature education. The area is characterized by the presence of fauna such as chinkara, reptiles and birds, etc in semi-arid, drought prone region.

WILD LIFE OF MANAGED AND PROTECTED FORESTS OF NORTH-EAST INDIA

The North-East India is one of the mega biodiversity centres in the Indian sub-continent. It is also one of the 10 distinct biogeographic zones of the country (SAARC, 1992). Its ecosystems vary from tropical wet evergreen, moist deciduous, sub-alpine, alpine forests, and grasslands to numerous freshwater lakes, rivers, swamps and marshy wetlands. These diverse ecosystems are the home of equally diverse range of flora and fauna.

Located in the north-east of the Indian sub-continent, criss-crossed by Himalayan ranges flanking the Brahmaputa and Surma valleys, the constituent units of the region, *i.e.* Aruncahal Pradesh, Assam, Manipur, Meghalaya, Mizoram, Nagaland and Tripura offer a complex-variety of habitats and ecosystems. The rich forests have greatly suffered due to biotic interference and land exploitation such as shifting cultivation on the hills and rice cultivation in the valleys. This has drastically affected the distribution and abundance of the faunal wealth of the region which, however, still retains numerous unique and rare/endangered species of great scientific and economic value (Ghosh & Tiwari, 1984).

Faunal Wealth of North-East India

The faunal resources of North-East India has been described earlier by Ghosh & Tiwari (1984). Their description mainly includes vertebrate Phyla Mammalia, Aves, Reptilia, Amphibia, Pisces and some groups of invertebrates, notably butterflies and beetles. Since then, many more species were described from North-East India, particularly the invertebrate groups belonging to Rotifera, Annelida, Crustacea, Cladocera, Myriapoda, Odonata, Orthoptera, Phasmida, Dermaptera, Dictyoptera, Isoptera, Mallophaga, Hemiptera, Diptera, Trematoda, Nematoda and soil arthropods, notably Acari and Collembola. Many of the species recorded from the region were new to science. Some of the recently described new species from North-East India, whose para-types are in the holdings of Eastern Regional Station, Zoological Survey of India, Shillong include at least 94 new species belonging to different groups.

It is important to note that these animals are crucial for decomposition and nutrient cycling, and hence for efficient forest productivity. These figures only serve to emphasise the fact that degradation results in disturbance of the complex web of life and a resultant destructive chain reaction sets in, effecting not only the smaller diminutive forms of life, but also the well being of the whole system (Alfred, 1990). The end result is not only depriving the capacity of the forest and its inhabitants to recoup but also losing a rich reservoir for biodiversity, much before they could be known to science.

TABLE 14.8: Some Fauna restricted to North-East India

Group		Species
Mammals	**Primates**	*Nycticebus coucang* Bodd. (Slow loris)
		Presbytis geei Khajuria (Golden langur)
		Presbytis phayrei Blyth (Phayre's leaf monkey)
		Presbytis pileatus Blyth (Capped langur)
		Hylobates hoolock Harl. (Hoolock gibbon)
		Macaca nemestrina Blyth (Pig-tailed macaque)
		Macaca arctoides Blyth (Stump-tailed macaque)
	Carnivora	*Arctonyx collaris* F. Cuv. (Hog badger)
	Artiodactyla	Cervus eldi eldi (Brow antlered or Thamin deer)
Aves	**Falliformes** (pheasants)	*Tragopan blythis* (Jerdon) (Blyth's tragopan)
		Lophophorus scalateri Jerdon (Sclater's monal pheasant)
		Crossoptilon crossoptilon Elwes (Elwe's eared pheasant)
		Syrmaticus humiae humiae (Hume's bar-backed pheasant)
Reptilia	**Lizard**	
	Lacertidae (Lacertids)	*Takydromus sexllineatus khasiensis* (Blgr.)
	Tortoises	Emydidae (Freshwater tortoises)
		Geoemyda mouhati Gray (Assam Freshwater tortoise)
		Cyclemis dentata (Gray)
		Khachuga sylhetenisis (Jerdon) (Assam

Group		Species
		sawback turtle)
	Testudinidae (Land tortoises)	*Indotestudo elongata* (Blyth)
		Indotestudo emys (Schlegel & Muller) (Assam tortoise)
	Ranidae	*Rana assamensis* Sclater
		Rana garoensis Boul.
		Rana danieli Pillar
		Rana mawphlangensis Pillai
		Micrixalus borealis Annandale
	Rhacophoridae	*Philautus shillongensis* Pillai & Chanda
		Philautus garo Boul.
		Philautus cherrapunjiae
Amphibia	**Microhylidae**	*Microhyla berdmorei* Blyth
	Bufonidae	*Bufoides meghalayana*
		Pedostibes kempi (Boul.)
	Hylidae	*Hyla annectens* (Jerdon)
	Cyprinidae	*Barilius tileo* (Hamilton)
		Danio meghalayensis Sen
		Danio deyi Sen
		Garra nagaensis Hora
		Garra rupecula
		Puntius shalynius
	Psilorhynchidae	*Psilorhynchus homaloptera*
	Cobitidae	*Lepidocephalus annandalei*
		Mesonoemacheilus reticulofasciatus
	Pillaiidae	*Pillaia indica*
		Garo khajuriai
Pisces	**Sisoridae**	*Glyptothorax striatus*
		Glyptothorax shawi

C. eldi eldi is endemic to N.E. (Manipur); *P. geei* is also distributed over Bhutan; all the other mammals are also found in Southeast Asia.

WILDLIFE OF INDIAN ARID ECOSYSTEM

More than one-third of the world's land surface is arid or semi-arid. A little over half of this area or more than 2300 million hectares lies in the developing countries. This area exceeds by nearly 50 per cent all the arable and permanent croplands in both developed and developing countries. In India, nearly 41.4 per cent of the country's total land mass of 3.28 million sq km falls in the category of arid (11.8%) and semi-arid (29.6%) zones. High agricultural risks, resulting from scarcity and/or variability of rainfall, and various attendant edaphic factors characterize these pockets of infertile lands. However, despite the inherent drawbacks of these areas, the human and livestock population of the world's arid and semi arid-zones increased by 75 per cent and 79 per cent, respectively during the 25 years from 1949 to 1974 (FAO, 1982). In Rajasthan desert, corresponding rise in livestock population is 129 per cent (Goat: 194.3%, sheep: 138.5%, Cattle: 47.9%, Buffalo: 163.4%, Camel: 169.3%, Horse and Donkey: 32.8%). However, no such figures are readily available for wild life. Although 80,000 black bucks were present in India in 1947 which dropped to 8000 in 1964. It is the enforcement of Wild Life Protection Act in 1971 which has preserved the wild life. Because of this as high as 2,300 heads of black bucks are recorded from a sanctuary in Thalchapar area in Rajasthan desert in 1987. Interestingly, black buck population may rise to 3000 to 4000 in a favourable habitat. Among wild mammals, rodents out number all other mammals, not only at species level but in total number also. About 20 species of rodents inhabit Rajasthan desert. These rodents not only damage field crops and ravage general vegetative cover, but also cause severe damage to rangelands, afforestation, plantation and are responsible for soil erosion problems. Among 4 gerbil species, desert gerbil (*Meriones hurrianae*) alone make 450-15,000 burrows/ha and thus dig out 61,500 kg soil/km^2/24 hrs from cropped areas and 1,61,000 kg soil/ km^2/24 hrs from uncultivated areas. This dig out soil is blown away by strong winds, which adds to desertification process. This has naturally resulted in increasing encroachments on the available grazing areas and almost irreversible deterioration of the land, besides causing frequent conflicts between the pastoralists and the cultivators for the reason that the fodder deficit is over 40 to 50 per cent.

TABLE 14.9: Livestock population status in arid districts* of Rajasthan.
(Geographical arid area 2,08,521 sq. km.)

Animal type	Census years				Population (000)		
	1956	1966	1972	% change (1966-1972)	1983	1988	% change (1983-1988)
Cattle	3921	4689 D	3482	- 25.7	4570 D	3386	-25.9
Buffalo	722	1055 R	1109	+5.1	1760 R	1759	-0.06
Sheep	4750	5541 O	5160	-6.9	8773 O	6485	-26.1
Goat	3495	4256 U	5814	+36.6	7447 U	5562	-25.3
Horses & Ponies	18	16 G H	10	-37.5	09 G H	09	--
Donkeys	82	91 T	76	-16.5	125 T	100	-20.0
Camels	362	555	625	+12.6	639	568	-11.1
Pigs	4	6 *	10	+66.6	27 *	34	25.9
Total	13403	16209	16286	+0.5	23349	18202	-22.0
% of Rajasthan State	41.3	43.3	41.9		47.0	44.5	
Total Rajasthan State	32427	37476	38876	+ 3.7	49650	40917	-17.6

TABLE 14.10: Some ecological and ethological characteristics of the wildlife in the Thar desert

Characteristics	Black buck	Chinkara	Blue bull
Habitat	Plains, flat scrub lands, saline flats with 1-2 water holes, gravelly wastelands, hard pans	Salt range, sand dunes, sandy plains, gravelly patches.	Hills, gravelly plains, piedmont plains with bushes, loamy soils with double cropping patterns.
Herd behaviour	Gregarious	Less gregarious	Does are gregarious
Herd size	80-120	Not fixed	3-35 numbers
Movement route	Fixed tracks	Not fixed	Not fixed
Jump	1-20 m. high	---	Over 2mt. high
Hearing	Moderate	Highly developed	Moderate
Sight	Keen	---	Good
Olfaction	Fair	---	Good
Feeding habits	Mainly grazer	Mainly browser	Browser & grazer
Feeding rhythm	Morning till noon, evening, seldom in nights	Early hours and late afternoon, full day in winters	Very early morning and late evenings
Breeding	Year round mainly Feb. & March	Non-seasonal	Nov. to February
Gestation period	170-180 days	150-170 days	240-250 days
Litter size	One	One to two	Twins common

Selected Bibliography

Cannon, W.B. 1923. Bodily changes in pain, hungerr fear and rage. Boston: Branford.

Carpenter R. 1965. The howlers of Barro Colorado is land. In: Primate Behaviour.

Darling, F.F. 1937. Study of red deer. Oxford, Clarendon press.

Darwin, C. 1898. The Expression of Emotions in man and animals, London, John, New York, Appleton and Co.

Emllen. J.J. 1952. Social behaviour in nesting Cliff Swallows. Condor, 54: 177-99

Huxley, J.S. 1914. The Courtship habits of the great crested grebe. Proc. Zool. Soc. London. 1914 (2), 441-562.

Jenning, H.S. 1906. Behaviour of the lower organisms, New York, Columbia, University Press.

Lashley, K.S. 1950. In search of the engram. Symp. Soc. Exp. Biol., 4:454-82

Lehrmann, D.S. 1964. The reproductive behaviour of ring dove. Scientific American, 211 (Nov): 48-54 offprint 488

Lorenz, K.Z. 1950. The Comparative method in studying innate behaviour patterns. Symp. Soc. exp. Biol., 4: 221-68.

Lorenz, K.Z. 1969. Innate bases of learning. In: On the Biology of Learning. K. Pribram (Ed) Harcourt Brace Jovanovich, New York.

Mathews, G.V.T. 1968. Bird migration. Cambridge University Press, New York.

Papi, F. 1969. Orientation by night: The Moon. Cold Spring Harbour Symp. Quant. Biol., 25: 475-80 (291)

Pavlov, I.P. 1927. Conditioned reflexes. Oxford Unviversity Press, London, Humphrey Milford

Skinner, B.F. 1938. The behaviour of organisms. New York: Appleton-Century-Corfts

Thorpe, W.H. 1961. Bird Song. Cambridge University Perss. Cambridge

Thorpe, W.H. 1963. Learning and instirct in animals, 2ed. London, Methurn

Tinbergen, N. 1951. The Study of instirct. Oxford; Clarendun Press.

Tinbergen, N. 1953. The Herring Gull's World. Collins, London.

Tinbergen, N. 1959. Comparative Studies of behaviour of gulls. Behaviour, 15: 1-70

Walsh, E.G. 1964. Physiology of Nervus system 2ed. Longmans, Green, London.

Glossary

Action potential. An abrupt change in the charge differential across the membrane of a nerve cell caused by a change in the permeability of the membrane to sodium ions; the nerve impulse.

Activational effect. The capacity of key hormones to cause certain behavioural responses to occur by activating proximate mechanisms underlying these behaviours.

Adaptation. A characteristic that conders higher inclusive fitness to individuals than any other existing alternative exhibited by other individuals within the population; a trait that has spread or will spread through the population as a result of natural selection or indirect selection,

Adaptationist. A behavioural biologist who uses the assumption that traits are adaptive to generate testable hypotheses on the fitness consequences of a particular trait.

Aggression. General term applying to behaviour aimed at hurting other, or threat of action by one individual that reduces the freedom or genetic fitness of another. Aggression functions as a motive, often in response to insults, threats or frustrations.

Agonistic behaviour. General term when specific kind of aggression involved is not known.

Allele. A form of a gene; different alleles typically code for distinctive variants of the same enzyme.

Allomimetic behaviour. When members of a group perform various behaviours together, for example, food gathering, singing, bathing and social courtship.

Altruism. Helpful behaviour that raises the recipient's direct fitness while lowering the donor's direct fitness.

Ambivalent behaviour. Behaviour which consists of two different, often incomplete reactions occuring simultaneously.

Amygdala. A structure of prosencephalon connected with hypothalamus and concerned in emotion.

Avoidance learning. Learning to avoid a noxious stimulus by responding to a warning signal.

Behaviour. Any observable action of person or animal, in response to stimulus.

Behavioural ecology. The study of the adaptive value of behavioural attributes of individuals in solving environmental abstacles to reproduction.

Behaviourural changes. During increased stimulus intensity a sudden transition from one behavioural state to another may occur.

Biological drive. A motive triggered by a homeostasis of the body.

Broca's area. The postion of the frontal lobe of the cerebrum controlling the patterned movements.

Brood parasite. An animal that exploits the parental care of individuals other than its parents.

Care-giving behaviour. Behaviour of guarding and protecting of young. Mutual nibbling and licking, also called allogrooming. Submissive gestures and infantile behaviour often elicit epimeletic behaviour which serves to divert aggression.

Central pattern generator. A group of cell in the central nervous systems that can produce the particular pattern of signals needed to cause a fully functional behavioural pattern.

Change in motivation. When a behaviour pattern takes on a different or additional function in the course of evolution, the underlying drive must be changed, the new behaviour is released from its original motivation and develops its own motivating mechanisms.

Chemotaxis. An orientational reaction in free moving animals by a chemical stimulus.

Circadian rhythm. A 24 hour rhythm or day or night rhythm in the behaviour and other physiological body function. In many cases it represents an endogenous rhythm present in the organism itself.

Classical conditioning. A form of learning in which an automatic, or unconditioned, response (such as salivation upon detedction of food stimuli) comes to be performed in reaction to a stimulus other than the one that normally elicits the behaviour (such as the sound of a bell or the shining of a light.)

Cleaner fish imitator. The Sabertoothed blenny, Aspidontus taeniatus has copied the form, coloration and locomotory behaviour of the true cleaner fish, Labroides dimidiatus, and profits from the mimicry by biting small piece out of the skin, the fins and the gills of the fish expected to be cleaned.

Coefficient of relatedness. A measure of genes shares as a result of having a common ancestor; the probabilityu that an allele present in one individual will be present in a relative; the proportion of the toral genotype of one individual present in the other, as a result of shared ancestry.

Communication. Signal transmission and information exchange as a prerequisite of social behaviour. The cooperative transfer of information from a signaler to a receiver.

Comparative method. A procedure for testing hypotheses on the adaptive value of a trait using disciplined comparisons among species.

Conditioned reflex. A response produced by a conditioned stimulus after learning.

Conditioned stimulus. The stimulus which is originally in effective but which after pairing with in conditioned stimulus evokes the conditioned response (CR)

Conditioning. A term used for learning by classical conditioning or operant conditioning.

Conflict behaviour. The actiona that result when two different motivational systems are activated simultaneously within an individual.

Conspecific. A member of the same species.

Convergent evolution. The independent acquisition over time of similar characteristics in two or more unrelated species as a result of natural selection stemming from shared environmental pressures.

Cooperation. A mutually helpful action.

Courtship behaviour. Behaviour patterns and signals, that attract the sex partner, that reduce shyness and that synchronize the partners with each other permitting mating and conception.

Critica period. A phase in an animal's life when certain experiences are particularly likely to have a potent developmental effect,

Critical period. The period of time in which an organism is ready for the acquistion of certain responses. Imprinting in birds can be observed in this period.

Dance language. A general term for the mode of communication among bees with regard to the distance and direction of a food source.

Depressive behaviour. Characterized by crying, and restless activities.

Developmetal homeostasis. The capacity of developmental mechanisms within individuals to keep the course of development guided toward an adaptive end poing despite potentially disruptive effects of mutant of mutant genes and suboptimal environmental conditions.

Dilution effect. Safety in numbers; the decreased probability of being taken by a predator that stemes from being a member of a large group of prey as opposed to a small group.

Diploid. Having two copies of each gene in one'genotype.

Display behaviour. The behaviour which may impress or intimidate the partner or rival and which is frequently directed at a rival or rival in the presence of the mate.

Display. A stereotyped action used as a communication signal by individuals.

Divergent evolution. The evolution by natural selection of differences among closely related species that live in different environments.

Dominance behaviour. Demonstration of superiority in maintaining the dominant position within a social group. The removel of an-animal by a previosly lower ranking group member is called change of leadership.

Dominance hierarchy. A social ranking within a group in which some individuals give way to others. Often conceding useful resources to others without a fight.

Drive-or motive. A term implying an impetus to behaviour.

Echolocation. Bats produce ultra-sonic emissions during flight that are used to locate by means of the echoobstacles and prey. Certain moths are capable of detecting these sounds which then release escape manoeuvres. Echolocation also occurs in whales and dolphins.

Egg rolling. Fixed action pattern observed in ground breeding birds by means of which eggs that have rolled outside the nest are retrieved.

Entrainment. The effect of environmental changes on the mechanisms controlling circadian (or circannual) rhythms, leading to the synchronixation of the activity pattern of an individual with local conditions.

Ethology. The study of the proximate mechanisms and adaptive value of animal behaviour.

Exploratory drive. A drive to explore.

Explosive breeding assemblage. The formation of large groups of reproducing individuals in species that breed on only a few days each year.

Female defen polygyny. The polygynous males directly defend their mates from other males.

Fitness benefit. That aspect of a trait that tends to raise the inclusive fitness of individuals.

Fitness cost. That aspect of a trait that tends to decrease the inclusive fitness of indivivuals.

Fitness. A measure of the genes contributed to the next generation by an individual, often stated in terms of the number of surviving offspring produced by the individual. **Direct Fitness.** The genes contributed by an individual via personal reproduction in the bodies of surviving offspring. **Indirect Fitness.** The genes contributed by an individual indirectly by helping non-descendant kin, in effect creating relatives that would not have existed without the help of the individual. **Inclusive Fitness.** The sum of an individual's direct and indirect fitness.

Fixed action pattern. An innate, highly stereotyped response that is triggered by a welldifined, simple stimulus; once the pattern is activated, the response is performed in its entirety.

Forced copulation. Rape, in which a male in seminates a female against her will and with the consequence that her fitness is reduced on average.

Free-running cycle. The clycle of activity of an individual that is expressed in a constant environment.

Game theory. An optimality approach to the study of the adaptive value of traits that focuses on the effects of the activities of other individuals of the same species in determining the fitness payoffs for the attributes of interest.

Ganglion. A dense cluster of many neurons in the central nervous system.

Genetic mosaic. An individual whose tissues are a mix of different genotypes.

Genotype. The genetic constitution of an individual; may refer to the alleles of one gene possessed by the individual or to its complete set of genes.

Good genes hypothesis. The argument that mate choice advance direct fitness because it enhances the survival chances of offspring of choosy individuals by providing them iwht genes that promote viability.

Habituation. A form of learning in which individuals stop responding to stimuli that carry no reinforcing consequences for the individuals that are exposed to them.

Haploid. Having only one copy of each gene in one's genotype; for example, the sperm and eggs of sexually reprocucting diploid organisms are typically haploid.

Heritability. The proportion of the total vari-ance in the phenotypes in a population that arises because of genetic variance among individuals, or Vg divided by Vg + Ve, where Vg = phenotypic variance cauxed by genetic differences among individuals and Ve = phenotypic variance among individuals that is environmentally induced.

Home range. An area that an animal occupies but does not defend, in contrast of a territory, which is defended.

Homeostasis. The tendency of the body to maintain a balance among internal physiological conditions.

Honest signaling. Providing signals to others that accurately convey information about the signaler's fighting ability or quality as a potential mate.

Hunger. A drive stemming from a physiological need for food.

Hyperphagia. Over eating, often as a result of lesions made in hypothalamus.

Hypothalamus. A region in the prosencephalon which contains centres for the regulation of sleep, body temperature, sex, thirst, hunger and emotion.

Imprinting. A form of learning in which individuals exposed to certain key stimuli, usually during an early stage of behavioural development, form an association with the object and may later show sexual behaviour toward similar objects.

Inbreeding depressing. The tendency of inbred organisms to have lower fitness than noninbred members of their species.

Innate releasing mechanism (irm). The IRM is a releasing mechanism which the species has acquired by phylogenetic adaptation to a certain environmental situations.

Innate. Refers to behaviour not learned, acquired during ontogeny, present at the birth but not functional, appear only in the course of ontogenetic development.

Instinct. A behaviour pattern that reliably develops in individuals that receiv adequate nutrition and that is expressed in functional form on its first performance. Tinbergen regarded instinct as a hierarchically organized nervous mechanism which reacts to priming, releasing and directing stimuli of either endogenous or exogenous character.

Instinctive behaviour. A behaviour sequence involving innate pathways of C.N.S. This is initiated by an IRM.

Interneuron. A nerve cell located in the central nervous systems (CNS) that relays messages either from receptor neurons to other CNS cells (a sensory interneuron) or from cells in the CNS to neurons commanding muscle cells (a motor interneuron).

Kin discrimination. The selection treatment of members of the same species in a manner linked to the degree of genetic relatedness between the interacting individuals.

Kinesis. Refer to an orientation behaviour which depends on the stimulus intensity but not on the direction from which the stimulus is perceived.

Learning. A durable and usually adaptive change in a animal's behaviour traceable to a speicific experience in the individual's life.

Lek polygyny. The polygynous males use displays to attract several females to them as small, resourceless display sites.

Lek. A traditional display site where males gather to defend small territories that lack resources useful to females, which nevertheless visit the site to mate.

Lesion. Any damage in a tissue due to injury, electrical stimulation or by any other means.

Limbic system. A series of related structure in the brain connected with motivation and emotion. The septal area, hypothalamus, amygdala and cingulate gyrus are important limbic system structures.

Lunar periodicity. In many marine animals living in the tidal zone reproduction cycles are limited to the periods of spring tide and coincide with moon phases.

Maze. A device used in animal learning experiments that has blind alleys and a correct path.

Modes of communication. It includes tactile, chemical, optical and acoustical stimuli. Among tactile stimuli we include such epimeletic stimuli as grooming, among chemical stimuli belongs to pheromones and scent signals. Optical signals include certain movement patterns as well as mimics and certain colors.

Monogamy. A mating system in which one male mates with just one female in a breeding season.

Mutualism. A mutually beneficial relationship or action.

Negative reinforcement. The reinforcement is a stimulus that strengthens a response when it follows a response, negative means that reinforcement occurs when the learner escapes from a noxious stimulus.

Neuron. A nerve cell.

Neurotransmitter. A chemical that is released by one neuron and affects the probability that the next cell in the network will fire.

Nondescendant kin. Relative than offspring.

Nuptial gift. A food item transferred by a make to a female just prior to or during copulation.

Operant conditioning. A kind of learning, allied with trial-and error learning, in which an action (or operant) that is rewarded becomes more frequently performed.

Operant conditioning. Learning to make a particular response.

Operational sex ratio (osr). The ratio of receptive males to receptive females in a population at any one period; a measure of the intensity of competition among males for mates.

Optimality theory. The theory that the attributes of organisms are optimal (*i.e.*, offer the best ratio of fitness benefits to fitness costs); a theory used to generate hypotheses about the adaptive value of characteristics, as in optimal foraging theory, which analyzes alternative foraging decisions in terms of their fitness payoffs.

Organizational effect. The effect of certain hormones in shaping the development of the proximate mechanisms that underlie a behavioural ability.

Orientation. The perception of one's position in space. Primary orientation control the body posture whereas secondary orientation control the response to a stimulus from the environment.

Parental investment. The risks taken by a parent and the time and energy it invests in an existing offspring that reduce its chances of producing additional offspring in the future.

Phenotype matching. A proximate mechanism of kin discrimination in which an individual's behaviour toward another is based on how similar they are in appearance, odor, or some other phenotypic trait.

Phenotype. Any measurable aspect of an organism; an attribute or trait of an individual that arises because of a developmenta interaction between heredity and the environment.

Pheromone. A volatile chemical released by one individual to communicate with another.

Photoperiod. The number of hours of light in 24 hours.

Phylogeny. A genealogy that reflects the evolutionary relationships among a number of species, genera, or other clusters of organisms.

Pleiotropy. The capacity of one gene to have multiple effects on the development of an individual.

Ploygyny. A mating system in which one male mates with several females during a breeding season.

Polyandry. A mating system in which one female mates with several males during a breeding season.

Polygeny. The capacity of several genes to influence the delopment of a trait.

Proximate cause. An immediate, underlying cause, one related to the operation of the internal machinery of an individual or thing.

Reasoning. Thinking in which an animals attempts to solve a problem.

Receptive field. That portionof a receptor surface that is monitored by a higher-order nerve cell.

Reciprocity. A synonym for reciprocal altruism; a helpful action that will be repaid in the future by the recipient.

Reflex. An involuntary unlearned response of an organism to a stimulus in which the response proceeds in a clearly prescribed fashion.

Reinforcement. In classical conditioning the presentation of un-conditioned stimulus (UCS) immediately following the conditioned stimulus (CS).

Releaser. A sign stimulus given by one individual as a social signal to another.

Reproductive success. The number of surviving offspring produced by an individual; direct fitness.

Resource defense polygyny. The polygynous males monopolize resources that receptive females use.

Reticular formation. A net work of cell bodies and fibers extending through medulla, mesencephalon, hypothalamus and thalamus, forming a sensory pathway to the cerebral cortex.

Satellite male. A male that waits by a dominant rival to intercept females attracted to the advertisements of the rival.

Scramble competition polygyny. The polygyny males are nonterritorial and seek scattered receptive females.

Search image. A hypothetical mental picture of a prey item used by a predator to search specifically for a cryptic, common, edible prey.

Selection. The differential capacity of individuals to transmit copies of their genes to the next generation. **Artificial Selection.** A process that is identical with natural selection except that humans control the reproductive success of alternative types within the selected population. **Cumulative Selection.** The accumulation of many small changes in a population over time that occurs because of repeated bouts of natural selection. Many small changes can add up to great evolutionary change. **Frequency-Dependent Selection.** A form of natural selection in which the fitness of an individual is dependent upon the frequency of its phenotype in a population with two or more discrete phenotypic alternatives. **Group Selection.** The process that occurs when groups differ in their collective attributes and the differences are correlated with differences in group survival. **Indirect Selection.** The process that occurs when individuals differ in their effects on the survival of nondescendant kin, creating differences in the indirect fitness of the individuals interacting with this category of kin. **Kin Selection.** The process that occurs when individuals differ in ways that affect their parental care or helping behaviour, and thus the survival of their own offspring or the survival of nondescendant kin. **Natural Selection ("Direct Selection").** The process that occurs when individuals differ in their traits and the differences are correlated with differences in reproductive success. Natural selection can produce evolutionary change when these differences are inherited. **Runaway Selection.** A form of sexual selection that occurs when female mating preferences for certain male attributes create a positive feedback loop favoring males with these attributes and females that prefer them. **Sexual Selection.** A form of natural selection that occurs when individuals vary in their ability to comete with others for mates (the competition for mates component of sexual selection) or in their attractiveness to members of the opposite sex (the mate choice component of sexual selection). As with natural selection, when the variation among individuals is correlated with genetic differences, sexual selection leads to genetic changes in the population over time.

Selfish herd. A group of individualsm each one of which uses the others as living shields against predators.

Sensory exploitation. In communication, when a signaler is able to tap into the preexisting biases of the sensory system of the receiver with the consequence that its message has more impact than its otherwise would.

Sexual dimorphism. A difference in appearance between the males and the females of a species.

Sign stimulus. The effective component of an action or object that triggers a fixed action pattern in an animal.

Skinner box. It is a simple box with a device at one end which if operated, will produce reinforcement.

Sociobiology. A discipline that uses evolutionary theory as the foundation for the study of social behaviour.

Sperm competition. Competition among the sperm of two or more males for egg fertilization.

Stimulus filtering. The capacity of nerve cell and neural networks not to respond to some stimuli.

Strategy. A genetically distinctive set of rules for behaviour exhibited by individuals. **Conditional Strategy.** A set of rules that enables individuals to exhibit different different tactics under different environmental conditions; the capacity to by behaviourally flexible. **Evolutionarily Stable Strategy (ess).** That set of rules for behaviour that when adopted by a certain proportion of the population cannot be replaced by any alternative strategy.

Submissive behaviour. Behaviour of subordination in order to prevent attack.

Supernormal stimulus. A sign stimulus that is more effective in eliciting a response than naturally occurring actions or objects would be.

Synapse. The point of near contact between one nerve cell and another.
Tactic. One of the options that may be exercised by an animal whose behaviour is guided by a conditional strategy.
Taxis. Orientating reaction in freely moving organisms.
Territory. An area that an animal defends against intruders.
Ultimate cause. The evolutionary, historical basis for why something is the way it is.
Unconditioned stimulus. A stimulus which elicits a response.
Unconditioned. Response. The response elicited by the unconditioned stimulus.
Urine marking. Behaviour pattern among mammals in which the path and boundaries of the territory are marked with urine.
Waggle dance. Means of communication in bees.